From Fear to
Fulfillment

Also by C. Elliott Haverlack

Unbundle It

From Fear to Fulfillment

A FIGHT *for* FAITH, FAMILY *and* FREEDOM

C. ELLIOTT HAVERLACK

O'LEARY
PUBLISHING
The Influencer's Press

NAPLES, FL

Published in the United States by
O'Leary Publishing
www.olearypublishing.com

ISBN (print): 978-1-952491-32-0
ISBN (ebook): 978-1-952491-33-7
Library of Congress Control Number: 2021914931

Editing by Heather Davis Desrocher
Line Editing by Boris Boland
Proofreading by Kat Langenheim
Book Design by Jessica Angerstein

Printed in the United States of America

For my grandchildren –
Sophia, Lorelei, Tristan, Everett and Wesley –
and those yet to be born.
You are the future; I love you.

Contents

Book I The Moral Compass

Book II The Blockbuster

Book III The Commentary

Preface

Wordsmithing

★　　★　　★　　★　　★　　★

L INGUISTS ESTIMATE THAT THERE have been over one million words or word variants in the 1400-year history of the English language. It is estimated that about 170,000 are in use as of today. Words fall out of the general lexicon and new ones emerge on a continuing basis; about 1,000 new words make the scene each year.

Many words are extraordinarily powerful; yet others seem rather mundane. I have always been fascinated with the four-letter variety. In an odd sense, I seem quite comfortable with employing them with great regularity. Is it because I find it comforting that their rather simplistic structure somehow hides my ineptitude at spelling? While that sentiment is indeed true, I find that in their use there is rarely any ambiguity.

The term "four-letter word" often elicits a rather ominous or vulgar reaction, but it is not that variety of "four-letter word" that I am referring to. Rather, I am referencing everyday words – the ones we teach our children. Two of my favorites are "love" and "free." Jesus taught that we must love all our brothers and sisters. No easy task to be sure, but a mandate from the Creator nonetheless.

"Free" is a rather interesting word, as it has been hijacked over time. Being free and living in a free country are two of the greatest blessings one can have bestowed upon them by others. Yet, we hear a loud drumbeat that everything from healthcare to college should be free.

It is a true paradox – nothing is actually "free," not even the blessing of being free. There is a stanza from a song that I love:

Freedom Isn't Free,
You've Got to Pay the Price
You've Got to Sacrifice
For Your Liberty.

As our leaders foolishly assure the populace that they have a human right for a panoply of free things, the more danger that the blessing of being free is in jeopardy. It is downright terrifying when one can envision the eventual demise of the very freedoms we enjoy. Simply stated, I love being free. Yet, we live in rather precarious times, and a significant percentage of the population is smothered through fear.

"Fear" is an extraordinarily powerful four-letter word. It crushes dreams and stifles opportunities. The first 23 years of my life were largely driven by fear. It gripped me and suffocated my very existence. I was blessed to have great parents who loved me. While we struggled economically for most of my youth, my parents provided for me a safe and nurturing environment. So why the fear?

I was a rather awkward child, and as such, was the recipient of significant bullying throughout my youth. That appears to be a likely source of my preoccupation with fear. There seemed to be a beating or an embarrassment around every corner.

Most who knew me never quite realized that fear consumed me, as I adopted a rather eloquent charade. In 1964 at age 6, I recall being terrified as my mother announced that we would be watching Gilligan's Island (the TV show) before bedtime. In my preschool mind, I had deduced that it was Devil's Island, and the thought of it literally froze me with fear.

The obsession with fear followed me into high school and college. I convinced myself that I was never quite good enough, strong enough, or smart enough. While I have an enormity of happy memories, all were shrouded in an aura of uneasiness.

On my 23rd birthday, God removed fear from my psyche, and in its place instilled confidence and courage. No one would describe me as being brave; rather, I am driven by the courage of my convictions, and have come to believe that through God everything is possible. In fact, I am convinced that God wants all His children to live lives overflowing with abundance and fulfillment. Before one can reap the benefits of abundance, they must address their fears.

Living a full life – the one God intended – requires discipline and planning, but is generally quite attainable. Tragically, without identifying and coming to terms with our fears, it is a nearly impossible task.

In my first book, *Unbundle It*, I stuck to professional topics and kept it secular. Likely stemming from an unidentified fear, for most of my career, I felt compelled to keep my religious life and my work life separate. While I conducted myself in a fashion that followed my values I never overtly spoke of my faith unless directly asked and only in private settings. In my first book, I referred to the events in my life as secular epiphanies. But faith has always been a huge part of who I am, and even influenced my professional life greatly. I do not believe there was anything secular about the experiences in my life. As I reflect, I see God's hand all over the entirety of my experiences. And so in this, my second book, I am more open about who I am and what I believe.

It has been said that a pessimist sees the glass as half empty and that an optimist sees it as half full. I believe that there are countless glasses, yet undiscovered, that are awaiting our fulfillment – we simply need to look. Simply stated, those vessels abound and are all within our reach. Let us go discover them together.

Fulfillment is within the grasp of each of us; it is ours for the taking, and it is free. While fulfillment means something a bit different to each of us, the inner peace we discover will fill us with abundant joy. The first step is releasing ourselves from fear. This book takes you on my journey, *From Fear to Fulfillment*, and each of the words within this volume were chosen to help illustrate how absolutely amazing the journey can be. In time, you will share your story through deed, speech, or within the pages of a book. The words you employ will be self-selected to achieve your mission.

What about those 800,000 words that have been lost to history? What happened? How did they just disappear? Did someone wake up one day and decide, "This word will be lost to anonymity," or did they disappear over time? Was some skullduggery afoot, or is their demise all part of a greater plan?

When I think about the future, I often wonder what words that are currently employed with great regularity will go the way of many of their predecessors. It is a rather interesting topic that often leads to contemplation over those words' ultimate rediscovery. Will archivists from some future era "excavate" them for some vital research? What can be learned from their use? What can be learned from their downfall? Can volumes of words simply become extinct?

Is it possible that words can be akin to the dinosaurs that once inhabited the planet? Can some be relegated to extinction, only to be unearthed millions of years later and metamorphosed into a cultural phenomenon?

So fervent is my infatuation with words – and dinosaurs – that I often imagine myself as a dinosaur seated at the typewriter as I write. In fact, I originally envisioned the title of this book to be *When the Dinosaurs Roamed: Life Lessons on Faith, Family and Freedom from Recent History*. My publisher, who is normally extraordinarily poised, could not mask her aversion. In classic nudging fashion, we took a baby step to *From Fear to Fulfillment: A Dinosaur's Tale*. And then one day, just as the real dinosaurs disappeared 65 million years ago, my dinosaur reference vanished, never to return. In its place is the best of both titles. As you dig through the pages of this book, you will find vestiges of my dinosaur metaphor throughout.

Enjoy excavating my mind a bit. Consider your investment in reading this as an exploration into **the art of the possible**. Our mutual reward is your realization that there is a life available to you that far exceeds your wildest expectations. When your well-being soars, I am blessed through your self-discovery; and our country and the world benefit from you having enriched yourself. The future is within your grasp. Take the first step with me.

A Note to the Reader

★ ★ ★ ★ ★ ★

After reading this book, you will have a deep understanding of my love of God, country and family. They are the triad that has made my journey so full. My hope for all who read this is that they enjoy a full relationship with God; and if this book helps strengthen that relationship, so much the better.

My personal views acknowledged, one of the things that makes the United States of America the greatest entity in all of history is the brilliance of the founders. The fact that every American is welcome and free to worship as he or she sees fit – or even to choose not to worship at all – is an important element of the foundation that makes this country so extraordinary.

As a Christian, I am called to invite you to know God and His Son, Jesus. Your decision, however, should be yours alone, and it should be respected. I feel incredibly blessed to live in a country that affords everyone the freedom to choose, without fear of reprisal.

Introduction

It's Messy

"The world is a mess."

"People have gone mad."

"Division and hatred have become the norm."

"Historically, every great society has crumbled."

I regularly reflect upon these statements. In my 64th year, I find myself mired in a seemingly constant state of contemplation. Questions haunt me regarding the quality of life of the generations who will follow. Among those questions: How did we get so screwed up? Why is there so much anger? Why do those who seek power appear to bask in the imaginary divisions they themselves create? What kind of world will we leave as our legacy?

My mind wanders to my ancestors and the legacy they left for future generations. In a rather odd reality, each of us has descended from a 200,000 year lineage. Many of us are aware of notable characters hidden within the branches of our family trees, yet others know very little of their heritage, and still others become adoptive members implanted into a family history. Whether biologically connected or societally connected, the ways of our ancestors and others within our orbit mold us into the beings we become.

So it is true for the future generations. Those who we raise will be greatly impacted by us having been part of their life journey. Whether you have decided to become a parent or not, the influence you bestow upon the future generations molds the future of our family, our country, and our world. It is an awesome responsibility; one each of us should consider with great care.

Even some of the most influential families only know a tiny fragment of the entirety of their genealogy. The Lurie family of Israel can trace its roots to King David around 1000 BC, and if we include the Biblical genealogy, there are another 14 generations before him. That time span only represents about two percent of the entirety of the family's history. What is your story? What role does your family play in it? How will you impact those yet to come?

My family remembrances start here. This is my story, but it holds elements common to any family. My grandmother was not a significant part of my daily life, but her influence has been a cornerstone of it. She resided in her beloved Canada, a country from where my mother had fled after her "quasi-arranged" marriage collapsed. That happened in an era when Canadian society judged that such a circumstance was fatal to one's station in life.

When I reflect upon my memories of my grandmother, I am immediately transformed to a time and place starkly different from my current environment. She was the stereotypical English Lady – refined and dignified. She dressed impeccably and her demeanor mirrored her wardrobe. Stoic and seemingly unflappable, each of her actions appeared choreographed, and every word was uttered with purpose. Her vocabulary was vast, yet she had a great economy with words. Ostensibly emotionless, I do not believe I ever heard her laugh, and smiles were scarce.

She had been born into great wealth and significant status. She was the daughter of an Anglican priest and a debutante. Both of her parents' lineages had been documented for centuries and were full of noteworthy members. The family's self-portrayal includes descriptors such as sanctimonious and stodgy. She married an Anglican priest, cementing her upbringing. My grandfather served in both world wars as a chaplain. He had earned significant recognition for valor because, while under enemy fire, he regularly attended to the injured and dying. In place of a gun, he was equipped with a chalice and plate, which were protected by a flag adorned with a red cross.

I often wonder if my grandmother reacted when she received the telegram that he had been shot and wounded. As there were limitations on communication from the theater of war at that time, details were limited to a few short words in the communique. As she was attending to four young children at the time, it must have been quite disquieting to receive such news.

My recollections of my grandmother are few, yet vital. She was driven through a strong faith in God, an intense duty to country, and a strong devotion to family. She passed those three essential fundamentals onto me. I am unable to recall a day in my lifetime that those imperatives have not directed my moral compass. Bible verse recitations and Canadian and English history were commonplace topics of discussion. Reflecting upon one specific verse now seems quite curious. It is from Proverbs 23:31: "Look not thou upon the wine when it is red, when it giveth his colour in the cup, when it moveth itself aright."

I learned the words to *Maple Leaf Forever*. Written by Andrew Muir in 1867, upon the formal creation of the Dominion of Canada, its lyrics include, "The thistle, shamrock, rose entwine the maple leaf forever." In 1964, when parliament adopted a new flag for her homeland, my grandmother lamented, "We've cast out the cross in favor of an article of foliage."

The best descriptors of my feelings about my maternal grandmother would be respect, reverence, and honor. In a rather stark incongruity, my specific reminiscences seem to contradict my sentiments – an interesting paradox.

My sharpest recollection is of an incident that I would describe as an unforced error on the part of my mother. Both my brother and I are Eagle Scouts, a moniker and dedication that my mother proudly trumpeted. Not just your garden-variety Eagle Scouts – my brother was most likely the youngest ever to earn the award, as he fulfilled the requirements at age 12. I followed, earning the status at 13.

My mother demanded that I don my uniform and present myself to my grandmother. Begrudgingly, I complied, and when I entered her abode, my grandmother's glare was most disparaging. She then uttered, "How lovely; I believe I see a fleur-de-lis. Please remove this uniform immediately." I recall her adding something about how the French could ruin a good piece of beef, somehow justifying her disdain. My grandmother loathed the French, and even though Scouting had been created by Lord Robert Baden-Powell, an English general, the Scouting symbol looked quite similar to an emblem that my grandmother found objectionable.

Another poignant recollection is of her apartment walls, which were adorned with pictures of her grandchildren. I was saddened when she advised me that my picture was missing, as I had not accomplished anything. She added that until I gained post-collegiate employment, a picture of me would not earn a place in her dwelling.

Tragically, she died the day after I started my first "real" job, and I recall asking my mother if she had been told that I had secured a management position. My mother assured me that she had been advised and was "most pleased." As I reflect upon that exchange, I assume it was likely a myth created to avert my disappointment.

Her funeral was an affair that reflected her life – scripted, refined, and elegant, with her ten grandchildren flanking her polished wooden casket. I remember thinking that the casket must have cost a small fortune, considering that it was only to be placed in a hole in the ground forever. She was laid to rest at the end of an emotionless and exhausting series of services in the family cemetery plot, surrounded by headstones bearing the names of many of her cherished ancestors. *Exactly as she would have wanted it*, I thought, as I made the six-hour drive home afterward.

Her brother, my great uncle John, was the male version of my grandmother. However, his haberdashery was not nearly as interesting, as he wore mostly black suits. While he was certainly not an avuncular character, he was quite kind. He was a doctor who had run a large psychiatric hospital, and was an accomplished writer. His writings and those of his father remain in print today, and continue to be distributed throughout the faith community.

He delighted in hosting me at dinners and he always left a gratuity for the server that was overly generous. The tip was always inserted within a two-page pamphlet that included an invitation to know God. The money was placed in such a fashion that it could not be seen unless the recipient opened my uncle's message. I often wondered how many servers left the tract unopened and cast his token of gratitude into the rubbish.

My love for my uncle was similar to what I felt for my grandmother. So strong was my reverence for him that I named my son after him. In a very odd parallel, my uncle died very shortly after my son's birth. In sort of a redundant Pavlovian episode, I asked my mother if my uncle had known that my son, Zane, the Old English version of John, had been born and named in his honor. As with her reply four years earlier, she affirmed he had. *How interesting*, I think, as I pen these words.

His funeral was a much less ostentatious affair, but was also unemotional. His casket was placed near the remains of his beloved sister. In an odd twist of dark serendipity, an unwitting attendant bent down, grabbed a handful of dirt, and sprinkled it onto the casket in the shape of a cross. My mother immediately approached the casket and stoically wiped the dirt from its surface. She returned to my side and loudly stated, "Uncle would have been most displeased." Immediately, she broke down sobbing – a display of emotion that was not welcomed by the others in attendance. *These people are quite harsh*, I recall thinking. *How dreadful*, l thought, channeling their parlance.

As so it was with the passing of my mother, her brother, and her sisters. As time went on, I did witness some softening of the emotionless rituals throughout the proceedings. When visible displays of emotion manifested during my uncle's funeral, my mother's older sister stated, "Thank God, your mother is not here to witness this." She added, "And you know what I mean." Tragically, I knew exactly what she meant.

This same sister, an octogenarian, upon the passing of her husband, approached the altar at the conclusion of the service. Facing the large gathering of congregants, she spoke with poise and grace. "Thank you all for attending this service. Don would have been most pleased."

As I helped to carry my uncle's casket to the hearse waiting at the base of the cathedral stairs, I suddenly became overcome with terror. What if we dropped my uncle's casket as we descended the steep stone steps? Uncle Don's lifeless body careening across Bloor Street would have been unacceptable by any standard. He certainly would not have been "pleased."

My father's family could not have been more different than my mother's. He and his seven siblings were children of a coal miner who had emigrated to the United States from his homeland of Slovakia. Interestingly, my grandfather and two of his brothers arrived on different vessels and in different years. Each was processed through Ellis Island and each was assigned a different last name. None of the names matched the original, but they were variants of the same surname.

I recall my father's siblings as being generous and approachable. An apt descriptor would be "salt-of-the-earth people." Each lived their version of the American dream and seemed to enjoy every minute. Laughter and lighthearted banter echoed throughout the venues of family gatherings. My father's sisters were steeped in Slavic tradition and I delighted in learning their rituals. They, in turn, appeared to love teaching them. At age nine or ten, I recall being placed on a bus from Pittsburgh to Cleveland to spend a week preparing for our annual Easter celebration. It was an indelible experience that I recall often.

By today's standards, I suppose that generation of my father's family would be considered lower-middle class. None attended college, and most did not graduate from high school. They toiled long hours, and many worked the evening or midnight shifts to provide for their families. They found a way to fund college for all but three of the 22 members of my generation.

Funerals involving my father's family were emotion-fests. They were so starkly different from the rituals I attended in Canada with my mother's family that one might find it difficult to believe that both were consecrating similar events. Sobs of anguish and open caskets were the norm, and were followed by the actual lowering of the deceased's coffin into the prepared ground. I remember them as exhausting and draining.

In comparing the two families from whence I came, I find glaring contrasts between my father's family (left) and my mothers's family (right):

Squirrel stew – Beef Bourguignon

Melmac – Sterling silver

Plain old folks – Lords and ladies

Corn kernel bingos in dusty fire halls – Lavish banquets in splendid gilded ballrooms

Playing cards – Dance cards

Motel 6 – The Four Seasons

The contrast I find most interesting is that on my father's side I am third generation with a fabricated surname – while my mother's side boasts 600 years of lineage that flows with the blood of at least six noteworthy families from England and Scotland. But when it came to the things that matter, both families were eerily aligned. While they traveled disparate paths, they were each grounded in a deeply held belief system. Strong faith in God, an intense duty to country, and a strong devotion to family were universal. Though some were made of gold and others of steel, all their moral compass settings were unified in navigating lives of purpose.

As of last year, all the members of my parents' generation have gone to be with God. The generation that preceded them is mostly a distant memory. In a whisper, none will remain who knew them, were led by them, or were loved by them. Gone the way of the dinosaurs – and with them, their customs, idiosyncrasies, and peculiarities. And yet, these dinosaurs, my Dinosaurs, blessed me with the greatest gifts imaginable. A strong faith in God, an intense duty to country, and a strong devotion to family have been hard coded into my psyche.

As I evaluate the evolving societal priorities, I am quite cognizant that I, too, am going the way of the Dinosaurs. Soon I will draw my last breath, and in a historical instant none will remain who knew me. This Dinosaur prays that his obligation to future generations will be fulfilled as admirably as his Dinosaurs fulfilled their obligations. What follows are short messages on faith, family, and freedom. These musings have been penned over a time frame that spans three decades. I love to write commentary on subjects that embody the phrase, **"Things that matter."**

Where one travels and what one achieves pale in comparison to how one conducts himself or herself. Living a life that aligns with a properly calibrated moral compass is paramount. Not unlike the physical waymakers that have guided explorers for centuries, this virtual navigation system charts our actions throughout our lives and must be fine-tuned regularly.

I share my story and my experiences to inspire you, the reader. This book is meant to serve as an incubator for action. I want to enable engagement that leads to fulfillment, a fulfillment that manifests into a life of abundance – one more amazing than is reasonably imaginable.

This book is carefully crafted into three parts. Book I does multiple things simultaneously. It details a model approach to achieving fulfillment, opines on the importance that a higher being plays in that realization, and celebrates the singularity of our great land. It is a powerful triad.

Book II explores how the imperatives outlined in Book I have played out for me through the sharing of vignettes from my life. It also points out that it is **the stuff** we do between those first and last steps that defines us and leaves our legacy. Book III challenges you, the reader, to open your mind and consider new paths that may lead to fresh thinking on important societal issues.

I cannot say it nearly as eloquently as our 40th president, so let me conclude this Introduction with his wise words:

> *May each of you have the heart to conceive, the understanding to direct, and the hand to execute works that will make the world a little better for your having been here. May all of you as Americans never forget your heroic origins, never fail to seek divine guidance, and never lose your natural, God-given optimism.*

> **– RONALD REAGAN,** August 17, 1992

THE MORAL COMPASS

Introduction to

Book I

★   ★   ★   ★   ★   ★

B
OOK I INCLUDES A comprehensive discussion of the current strife within our society. An epic battle for the hearts and minds of our citizens rages on, and both faith and family are under attack. While Book I includes my views on the sources of the strife our country is currently enduring, and includes some very uncomfortable subject matter, it closes with solutions and a message of hope and unity.

The fight for faith, family and freedom has never been more dire. This is a battle worthy of your consideration, but as with all such engagements, preparation is vital if we are to be successful. As flight attendants remind us before every flight, we must affix our oxygen mask before assisting others. Similarly, we must ensure we are healthy and equipped with the proper tools, because only then can we assist others and help guide them to fulfillment.

The proper construction and calibration of a life-guiding moral compass is key to living a life of fulfillment and to taking effective action to better our world. Maybe you are not acquainted with such a vital tool, or maybe your moral compass needs to be recalibrated. Without such a waymaker, you will likely carreen into despair – and usually when you are most vulnerable. My proven moral compass includes strong beliefs in love of God, love of country, and love of family.

This moral compass is a delicate tool, and is constantly under siege both internally and externally. We've all been there. We knew the proper course to take, but chose another. The ideal route was just too hard, or the alternate one was too appealing. The sick feeling of regret that keeps us up at night is there to offer us a constant reminder.

Outside influences can lead us off course and result in potentially painful consequences. These influencers can be friends, family members, and even marketing professionals.

Consider smoking. Most, if not all of us, are aware that smoking is an unhealthy habit that often comes with deadly consequences. But the "cool people" smoke. After convincing ourselves that we must join them, and after taking a revolting first few puffs, an addiction is born. The health and financial ramifications are stark. Precious time and resources that could be used to enrich our lives are wasted in valiant yet unsuccessful attempts to quit. Addiction comes in many forms, and is always a deterrent to our moral compass.

In Book I, I share my views on how I believe we should conduct our life's journey to achieve fulfillment and abundance. Life is an amazing gift from God, and we are provided all the tools necessary to live an abundant life. Abundance in this sense is not a reference to wealth or earthly possessions. Rather, it is defined as living one's life to the fullest degree as God intends. Each individual's story to be written is based on gifts and blessings from God.

For example, if one is blessed with elite athleticism, it would be a tragedy for that person to not develop that skill, because his or her talent could enhance society. That development could include the accumulation of material wealth that could be deployed to enrich oneself and others. It could also include mentorship, stewardship, and benevolence.

Understanding where one's talents reside is a key element that leads to satisfaction. The earlier in the life journey that one can define those blessings, the more apt they are to live full lives. Often, parents attempt to live vicariously through their children, and so they push them beyond a sense of reasonability. The psychological damage that can ensue from mismanaged expectations may remain throughout life.

I chose athleticism as my metaphor because it appears to be one of the largest paradoxes of the day. Only an elite few will ever earn their livelihoods in sport, yet tens of millions compete. Within that group there is an unhealthy percentage who believe they will join the ranks of Michael Jordan. Long-term elite talent can rarely be discerned early in development. Sadly, the motivations of parents who believe their 6-year-old is the next John Elway may be to the detriment of their child's wellbeing.

I am a significant believer in youth sports, and urged both of my children to participate. Learning the importance of physical fitness as part of a healthy lifestyle at an early age equips our children with beneficial, lifelong skills. The earlier that healthy disciplines are instilled within our children's routines, the more likely that those routines will become lifelong habits that provide them with the opportunity to enjoy lives of abundance.

Every church has a cherub who inspires the congregants with an angelic voice, and while few will ever earn fame or fortune from that blessing, they can and do gain fulfillment through the delight of others. The angelic voice might touch one congregant struggling with insurmountable pain and lift them out of agony.

Determining one's talents – and more importantly, deciding how these talents will be used through one's life journey – will fuel contentment. Such aptitudes are the building blocks that formulate our most basic ethical roadmap and serve as the calibration for our moral compass. Goals may change and circumstances may dictate differing routes, but the moral compass must remain unaltered.

Most of the thoughts and ideas within Book I are mine, but the underlying impetus is the work of the Dinosaurs who nurtured me. Contained herein are the building blocks that will enable you to traverse *From Fear to Fulfillment*. Think of each tidbit as a waymaker for your life and legacy.

Chapter 1

The Incredible Journey to Fulfillment

★ ★ ★ ★ ★ ★

I F YOU ARE READING this, you are blessed. Not because you will receive any such godsend within these pages, but because you are alive and you have the power to achieve fulfillment and enjoy eternal life. Regardless of your age, it is not too late.

Jesus Christ died for our sins, and if we choose to follow him, our sins will be forgiven. As Paul wrote in Corinthians, when our earthly tent is destroyed, there is a building from God eternal in the heavens. This reality is further unpacked in the pages that follow.

With God's armor offering indelible protection, we can traverse the excursions of life without fear. Fear is likely the strongest limiter in our lives. Fear crushes dreams, erodes opportunity, and introduces rationalization for living a life of complacency. Complacency provides a tacit permission to follow a life path that is far less fulfilling than one we are capable of traversing. Such a path would be a tragedy and an insult to God, whose blessings breathe vast lungfuls of limitless possibilities into each of our existences.

The Fear Factor

Overcoming fear is no easy task, and is an ongoing struggle that must be kept in check on a continuing basis. Fear hides in the shadows of our mind, threatening to inject its poison through every challenge. As we navigate our lives, we find that fear evolves. The monster under our bed as a young child morphs into not being accepted by teenage friends or embarrassing oneself in front of classmates. As we advance into adulthood, such fears seem to subside; they become laughable in our memories. Adult fears manifest themselves as a multitude of self-contrived, fulfillment-crushing barriers. Sadly, we convince ourselves that these adult fears are genuine and vital to our well-being. The truth is that they are no different than the juvenile anxieties we have since come to mock.

Mastering one's fears is critical, and assistance might be required. Faith in God has been a strong facilitator for me, but you might also find that talking with a trusted friend or a professional will be helpful. In fact, finding a trusted confidant with whom you can share personal matters is an essential element of a well-grounded life plan. God uses us all, and the professionals sent our way may well be a blessing in human form.

It is essential that we do not confuse justifiable anxiety with debilitating fear. They are incredibly different. Fear keeps us from accomplishing our dreams and crushes optimism. However, exhibiting caution at appropriate times is not only wise, it may keep us from harm's way. Deciding to stay home when an ice storm is forecast is very different from being afraid to take a trip on a commercial airplane because you have convinced yourself that it will crash. Deciding not to confront a group of rioters is not the same as being afraid to voice your opinion in Bible study because you think the others are better Christians.

It is important to recognize that your fears may be very different from another person's fears. Most bullies are terrified. They convince themselves that they are not good enough to compete on an even playing field, so they employ abusive behaviors in an attempt to convince others in their orbit that they are superior. Sadly, many yield to that destructive tactic, which unwittingly fuels it. In the most damaging manifestations, those being bullied start to abuse another set of innocent victims, creating a destructive circle.

Humble Yet Courageous

Humility is often used as an excuse for not taking the bold action that could lead to fulfillment. Humility is a virtuous characteristic; but we must use the talents bestowed upon us by God in order to serve the greater good in spite of our desire to remain humble. Our contentment may hinge on our willingness to act in an audacious way.

One of the men whose life story has inspired me is Nelson Mandela. When I reflect on his life and the struggles he overcame, I find his writings motivating. One of my favorites:

There is no passion to be found in playing small –
In settling for a life less than you are capable of living.

Regularly performing a self-assessment to confirm that we are not taking ourselves too seriously is a critical element of a healthy life. We all have shortcomings, and recognizing them and lessening their impact is critical to achieving a healthy life.

Trust Me on This One

Another vital element that leads to a healthy life is learning about trust. By trust, I am not referring to believing that another will not steal from us; rather, I am referring to the understanding that others may see things very differently. We need to learn to trust the motivations of others with whom we disagree.

We will encounter people whose motivations are suspect – and upon such a discovery, we should limit their influence within our orbit. I urge all to assume positive intent until proven otherwise. That is a somewhat precarious position to take, as evil will most likely leave us battered and bruised from time to time. However, the overarching sense of well-being garnered from taking this approach provides benefits that far exceed the risks. When those bad actors dupe us, we simply move forward and learn from the experience. The benefits of learning how to trust will far outweigh the risks.

Now that we have addressed our fears, humility, and trust, we can commence the planning for the remainder of this most important journey – the journey to fulfillment in life. I find that the most critical error most people make is the failure to plan.

Planning the Path Less Traveled

Most of us would not consider setting out on even the simplest of excursions without knowing what the destination is, why we are embarking on the journey, and what path we will travel to arrive safely. Planning one's life should be an exhilarating process. Further, it is a lifelong task, as we will likely suffer setbacks and will also encounter opportunities that we could not foresee.

We must keep our eyes and ears open to successfully make the most of these unexpected encounters. Life planning is an iterative exercise. Some elements can be developed instinctively, while others require study and reflection. In the most basic sense, preferences can help develop one's life plan.

Orienteering for Life

Before we can create the roadmap of our lives, we must construct the compass that will guide us along our journey. Creating the compass requires prayerful reflection and a coach or mentor, likely one of your Dinosaurs, to optimize the exercise. Within the moral compass resides those values that are so vital to our code that they become synonymous and symbiotic with life itself. While values can be developed and shaped, the foundational moral code should remain unaltered.

For most, there are some obvious building blocks that should be hard-coded into our morality. Building blocks might include honesty and fidelity. For me, timeliness is one such value. Being on time is almost an obsession to me. I see it as extraordinarily disrespectful to be late. Further, I believe it connotes a lethargy that is indefensible. I see it as cutting into the core of everything I hold dear. For me, being late suggests I cannot be trusted to keep my word; therefore, lateness renders me dishonest.

As I have calibrated my compass over the years, I have come to comprehend that others do not share some of my values, and that some are not as consequential as I had once believed. For example, many see the stress of constantly being on time as overwhelming, and then rightfully ask me what other values I might have massaged or downright trampled to meet an arbitrary schedule. Maybe I violated traffic laws in order to be on time, or had conducted myself in a manner that violated my compass. To be candid, a sensitivity toward other people's feelings is a constant victim of my zeal to be punctual.

Recognition of this incongruity has not changed my passion for timeliness, but it has enabled me to be more understanding of the motivations of others. That, in turn, has led to a much more tolerant attitude on my part and enhanced my overall well-being. At the same time, chronic tardiness – which shows a wanton disregard for one's actions – is unacceptable.

As we are constructing and calibrating our compass, we must be cognizant that seemingly good character attributes may not be beneficial. For example: honesty, trustworthiness, and integrity are all great attributes; but, including all three at the expense of other more powerful and more encompassing character attributes like kindness or generosity represents a lost opportunity. It is difficult to be trustworthy without being honest, but it is extremely easy to be that way without being kind or generous.

Adding elements that do not enhance our character should be left out of the overall design. Further, incorporating values into our design plan just because they look good on paper is strongly discouraged. The overarching theme is that the plan should be crisp, meaningful, and easily accessible.

Write It Down

One important element of the moral compass exercise is that we keep notes. Your final product should be a one-page guide or "road map," encompassing your values and your goals. The guide serves as a regular reminder of why you conduct yourself in the manner you have chosen and of your destination or destinations. The words on the document should be something that you commit to memory, but the visual is an important reminder.

You might elect to post a note on your mirror or have the words become your screen saver. Notes that include goals and values can be liberating and empowering. Those notes are important, as they will serve as a vital reminder of why you chose the path you did. Temptation or other deleterious motivations will be waiting to nudge you off track, and the notes and your regular reflection will keep those impulses in check. Here is a sample of a Moral Compass.

My Moral Compass

VALUES

Inspiration– Engage in conduct that encourages others.

Education – Teach and be taught every day.

Timeliness – Respect for others means being on time.

Benevolence – Share freely without condition.

Honesty – Have impeccable integrity in all dealings.

Courage – Stand up for one's principles without exception.

GOALS

Win and keep on winning. Help as many people as possible with the fruits from those victories.

My body is a gift from God. Keep it nourished physically and spiritually.

Strive for a deeper relationship with God.

Champion the United States of America and fight for the founding principles that make her exceptional.

Care for my family members and guide them on their life journeys.

Learn something new every day.

A Coach and Those Falsely So Called

Selecting the right Dinosaur or set of Dinosaurs is vital. In fact, your preferred coach or mentor might not possess any of the attributes that would place them into the Dinosaur category. A blend of Dinosaur-like and other trusted advisors might result in the optimal outcome. Remember that advisors, like all humans, are fallible – and as such, even employing the most altruistic intentions might result in unproductive counsel. You should perform routine gut checks as you construct your moral compass, and if you experience a visceral reaction to any portion, reconsider it. Living the life that others wish for you is not the goal. Rather, the ultimate and desired outcome is to enjoy the blessings of enrichment that God has planned for you.

Before moving to an examination of how to develop our life journey, it is important to take a well-earned timeout to reflect upon the work that has been completed. Assuming you have completed the exercise, you have likely invested more energy than the vast majority of your peers. Bravo! You will look back upon this decision and relish it.

One of the pitfalls of making a life plan is relying on the belief that others have followed a similar track, or that everyone shares your values. They likely do not – and in some instances, they are so misaligned with what you believe, that it is unsafe or unwise to continue to associate with such people. It is not necessarily that they are evil people, but their value system is in opposition to yours. You will likely find such relationships to be tedious and destructive.

Communing with these individuals can be educational and lead to productive outcomes, but forging strong connections should be considered carefully. I had a 20-year friendship with a man whose company I thoroughly enjoy. He was intelligent, witty, and extremely empathetic. We formed a very close kinship; but during that time

I learned he was an atheist – and what was more troubling, he felt compelled to mock God publicly. I simply was unable to continue to be close to him as I found the behavior to be in conflict with my core principles. This person remains a great guy and a good friend. We see each other regularly and enjoy a glass of wine from time to time; but deep down I know that any deeper relationship is unwise. I do not intend to judge, and I do not recommend that you judge; rather, I implore you to ensure that you do not allow your value systems to be sullied.

Even more notable are the inconsistent value systems among cultures. Much like viewing a tree, we only see half of the complete being. For every branch and leaf that rises high, there are an equal number of roots burrowing deep into the soil. What we see is only half the story, and to foster mutually beneficial productive relationships, we must consider the entire body of work. The most eye-opening example I have found is the fact that, in many cultures, dogs are eaten. (If you happen to come from one of those cultures, you are probably thinking, *And your point is?*) Other examples could include the persecution and torture of gays, the use of child labor, slavery, and genocide. These realities do not regularly make the news, as they are uncomfortable topics and generally avoided. The fact that we choose not to talk about them does not deny their existence.

Paving the Way – Filling the Potholes

Walking the path that will lead us to fulfillment and abundance becomes a much more intuitive process once the intricacy of forming and calibrating our compass is complete. Most likely, through the process, you will enhance your self-awareness and begin to formulate ideas on what fulfillment means to you.

I have been blessed to mentor several wide-eyed and talented young people in my life. My first question to them is, "How do you define success?" The normal answer is, "I want to be rich." I typically probe as to their definition of "rich," and in turn, it usually is defined as having lots of money. I even had one 20-something define success as a private jet and a place in Telluride.

I always caution mentees on the pitfalls of lust, and urge them to reconsider their goals. There is no sin in owning a private jet, and I am certain that a place in Telluride could be enjoyable. Many people have both; however, having those goals as primary motivators for action feels quite lustful.

Lust of anything normally ends up with disappointment. Envy can easily consume our spirits, and our identity can become a slave to our desires. While I take no particular umbrage with money or wealth, it can be quite unhealthy if lusting for riches is the overarching motivator. I have been on both sides of the allure of money, and it is a great motivator. If used properly, it can be an extraordinarily powerful motivator. When it came to money, I always employed a few key principles. First, I never allowed myself to live beyond my means. Living within my means translated into very little debt and much less conflict within the family unit.

When a family is starting out, appropriate debt is quite helpful. As in the business world, a suitable amount of financial liability for a family can enable opportunities that otherwise would not be possible. For example, if a new job requires that I have a car, and I need to take a loan to afford the car, that feels fiscally responsible. However, when I convince myself that I must regularly have the newest or most expensive car, creating a mountain of debt that holds me hostage, it limits my ability to break through into the world of abundance. Large debt would use vast amounts of intellectual and emotional capital, rendering me too exhausted to pursue my dreams.

In 1989, I decided that I was finished with car payments. Though I owed a substantial amount on one car and a smaller amount on another, I put into motion a plan that would release me from the chains of indebtedness. I kept both cars for a decade, and as the payments ceased, I continued making "payments" – but instead, they were deposited safely in my bank account. It became a bit of a comedic exercise – most of the paint fell off of one vehicle, causing it to be known fondly as the "leprosymobile." The other car boasted a broken driver's seat that was remedied with a strategically-placed pillow. I raved to friends about my "lumbar support" seat! By 1994, I was out of the shackles of car debt and have remained free from that encumbrance since.

My second overarching principle was to never allow money to become my primary motivation. I was driven by winning. To me, winning is a force multiplier that leads to a cascading predisposition to win and win again. Along with winning came the fiscal rewards that were commensurate with the victories, but that was just scratching the surface. For me, the exhilaration of leaping the unscalable hurdle fueled a passion that created a strong desire for more achievement.

The shocked looks of bystanders who had elected to remove themselves from the game propelled me through the challenges. And it has been so exciting to witness the joy on the faces of others who chose to remain engaged when they climbed the unclimbable. Such achievement led observers to comment, "I guess they weren't smart enough to realize it was impossible."

Wisdom From a Hero

I was fortunate enough to enjoy a quiet breakfast with Jack Welch a few years ago. Jack Welch is known as the "CEO of the Twentieth Century" and you might imagine how shocked I was when he asked if he could join me. Unprepared and unnerved, I did the only thing I knew to do at the breakfast, and that was to be myself. He was arguably one of the premier businessmen of his era, and I found myself engaged in one of the most enjoyable conversations imaginable. I recall it as akin to a casual chat.

The conversation was both stimulating and fulfilling. Within seconds, I felt as if I was visiting with an old friend who genuinely was interested in where I had been and where I was going. Eventually we landed on the topic of winning. To paraphrase his comments, in his view, winning was essential – and only when you had already won could you then assist others. Essentially, he said, "If you don't win, you can't help a damn person." Quickly, the conversation switched to his love of a beer and a burger for lunch, and his disdain for having to attend lavish banquets.

Later that day, he took the stage to address the 120 business executives who had traveled from around the globe to hear him speak. He informed the attendees that he had just enjoyed a marvelous breakfast with me and encouraged them all to seek me out on a break. As you might imagine, I became quite the target. I have often wondered how disappointed those who were eager to meet me had been when they discovered how ordinary I am. Looking back, I have often wondered if Jack had been subtly attempting to educate the attendees on the virtues of humility – and that the seemingly ordinary can accomplish the extraordinary.

Sports and the Allure of Fame

I am a sports nut. Even though I would have been aptly described as an avid fan of many sports teams for most of my life, I watch very little sports today. I do, however, remain enthralled with the backstory of elite athletes and the unique journeys that led them to achieving excellence.

My favorite sports picture is that of Sarah Hughes sitting next to her trainer, learning she had won the gold medal in the 2000 Olympics for women's ice skating. The look on her face is the quintessential expression of unbridled joy. She had entered the finals in fifth position and the prospect of winning the gold was distant. She would have to skate a flawless routine and muster every element of skill she had within her, but even that would not be enough.

For Sarah to win, the competitor in first place would have to misstep as would the person in second place. Even more unlikely, they would have to finish in positions that would ensure that the first-place participant earned no more than third place in that evening's event. The impossible occurred; Sarah skated flawlessly, and she found herself atop the medal stand with her national anthem playing.

I have seen it thousands of times, I thought, as I wiped tears from my face – certainly not on the Olympic stage, but in every aspect of life. From the workplace to the classroom, and in countless venues across the globe, the impossible becomes possible – through a combination of talent, dedication, and a bit of "luck." Every Olympic medal is inscribed with the words, "Citius Altius Fortious," which is Latin for "Faster Higher Stronger." Imagine your life medal with those three words as the inscription.

Far too often, we recline on our couches of comfort and allow others to experience the thrill of achieving greatness. We doze through our opportunities, and tragically either fail to muster the energy required to reap the rewards or lack the curiosity to explore and discover them.

We find inspirational life stories packed with unimaginable success throughout the world of sports. Most of them appear to have built on similar foundations, including years of commitment, discipline, and extraordinary effort. While the vast majority of us are not blessed with the talents required to rise to the level of elite athletes, we certainly are easily capable of optimizing our talents. We can do that by employing a disciplined regimen similar to what athletes use. In doing so, we can experience fulfillment and enjoy a life of abundance. While there may not be any spotlights or front-page news, we have arguably the greatest tale ever told – our story. There are literally thousands of inspirational quotes to be found within the annals of sports. One of my favorites is from Kobe Bryant:

> *I want people to think of me as a talented overachiever.*
> *I was blessed with talent. But I worked as if I had none.*

Courage Counts

Courage is another essential attribute that facilitates a healthy life plan. It takes courage to endure the challenges that will most certainly try to block your path. Courageous people understand that failures are all part of the journey, and that learning from them is beneficial. Failures are rarely as significant as we lead ourselves to believe.

As professional baseball players know, when they stand at home plate, their objective is to get on base. If they fail to meet their goal two out of three times, but stick with it, they will likely wind up in Cooperstown. I believe that we suffer failures and hardships in part so that we can truly relish the thrill of the victories. John Wooden, the famed UCLA basketball coach and one of the greatest leaders in sports history, inspired millions through his teachings. When struggles abound, this quote by him motivates me:

Success is never final; failure is never fatal.
It's courage that counts.

A Commitment That Lasts a Lifetime

The actual construction of your life plan can take many forms. I usually commence with an exercise that takes me to the imaginary end of my life, and I survey the body of work that was my life. I ask myself what the overarching thematic elements of my life were. This can be an exhausting and sobering procedure, but incorporated within it are many insights and some clarity.

Next, I cascade into epochs of my life. I must grapple with those paradoxical enigmas that will challenge me. Two opportunities might indicate starkly different routes. Examples might be deciding on a new career path, or making a move to a place that is unfamiliar. Critical thinking dictates that I build a plan that will facilitate a successful outcome. As with building a house, we should not begin construction of the roof until the foundation is completed. In more complex construction, there may be years of planning and evaluation before the first shovel disturbs the soil.

Starting with our vision of the outcome we seek, we will create a road map that will most expediently take us home. Keep in mind that the journey will likely not be a direct one. To reap all the benefits found through abundant living, exploring every crack and evaluating each twist offers the most fulfillment.

Stormy Weather

When the head winds blow, threatening to force you off course, remember that your compass is there to help you remain true to your values. Through the centuries, the most skilled sailors have used the art of tacking to successfully traverse challenging winds and rocky seas. Each maneuver may appear to be pulling you further off course, but the ultimate destination is within reach – if you use your moral compass to guide you.

Before you set forth on your quests, a few reminders will serve you well. Your journey is not a fixed one; while your moral compass is sacrosanct, the actual journey should be fluid. Fear will likely attempt to insinuate itself into your psyche, and it will encourage greed as well. Fear and greed work as a tag team of evil, sowing discontent while paralyzing us. They need to be squelched immediately. Turning to God can facilitate their elimination; and a trusted companion – maybe one of your Dinosaurs – can help you regain your bearings.

When enduring the most tumultuous times, redouble your passion and find the resolve to push through to the other side. You are likely closer than you believe, and there is a new dawn breaking just over the next mountain.

Go Forth Joyously

Remember to smile, look people in the eye, use good posture, and take each step with purpose. Foster an insatiable and lifelong appetite for learning, and satisfy that hunger through both formal and informal avenues. Revel in the victories and reflect upon the failures – while discovering from each incident with equal vigor. Avoid the adoption of a perfection standard – and in its place instill a passion for discovery. Perfection generates an impenetrable line resulting in winners and losers. The art of discovery generates an aura of winners and learners. This creates "how fascinating!" moments upon which you will feast.

You are on a journey to abundance and fulfillment, and a key portion of that journey is serving as a living testimony for others to witness and follow. As your final days approach, you will avoid the debilitating feelings of regret; and a flood of well-being and a zest for the next chapter will ensue. I will close with the Howitt motto, the oldest and most storied of my ancestral lineages: "Be Just and Fear Not." I would add, "Have fun."

Chapter 2

The Case for Jesus

★　　★　　★　　★　　★　　★

W E LIVE IN INTERESTING times. Like previous generations, we find ourselves constantly grappling with a conflicting collection of opportunities and challenges. History is being rewritten. While other historical writings have fallen into anonymity, the Bible has stood for over 2,000 years as a guide to abundance. This era, like no other in the past 20 centuries, appears to be on a collision course with Biblical teachings. Interestingly, at its core, the Bible is a historical tome. It is fascinating that many in our current culture are quick to accept other historical writings as fact, but immediately discount the Bible as folly.

Biblical history and secular history have one thing in common. They are both historical records. As sure as Caesar reigned in Rome, Jesus walked the earth. Simply stated, if we believe one historical record, it is intellectually dishonest not to embrace the other. In fact, much of Biblical history has been challenged, and yet there is no genuine empirical evidence that it is not valid. Certainly, there are parts of the Bible that might be hard to contemplate. The creation story is one such section. Many have argued that the creation of the world in six days is an impossibility. I would argue that, in a metaphorical sense, six days could easily represent six billion years. Others would cite that humanity is incapable of comprehending God's way in its entirety. I suspect that both are valid theorems.

Four Elements That Fuel My Faith

Turning to Jesus and His ministry, we find plenty of secular historical evidence that He lived, preached, and was crucified. The question involves His resurrection. Did He truly rise from the dead, thus making Him indeed the Son of God?

There have been countless books, articles, and speeches written – pro and con. There is a veritable treasure trove of evidence that Jesus did indeed rise from the dead. For me, it has boiled down to four key elements.

The first is that the story itself is so unlikely that it seems implausible that one would choose such a series of events to fabricate a tale. Looking at the discovery of the empty tomb through a historical lens makes it seem almost impossible that it was contrived. Women held a very low status during that period. In fact, women were not counted in the population as part of regular census taking. One would think that if a group of men were concocting a tale to be repeated and then believed, it would not include two women discovering the empty tomb.

Paul's transformation on the road to Damascus is a strong testimony. Even the briefest study of Saul's early life (before he became Paul) would compel reasonable evaluators to conclude that he indeed encountered the risen Christ. Dual names were common in those days; but Saul's transition to Paul is significant, as it normally is viewed in conjunction with this transformation. Also, the fact that all the people who claimed to see the risen Christ affirmed their witness is powerful. Many suffered under torture and died, and not one recanted.

Finally, the element of faith fuels the most important determining confirmation. Faith is an interesting word that stimulates disparate responses. All of us rely on faith throughout our everyday lives. I cross the road having faith that the cars will abide by the traffic signal. We have zero control; we walk on faith. Moreover, almost everything that embodies astronomy is largely accepted as true, as we have faith in those scientists. Faith in God is no different. We are promised eternal life from the Creator, and he fills us with the Holy Spirit. Grace through faith is God's promise to us all.

I have always found it fascinating that many have no problem having faith that a car approaching a crosswalk will stop, but they struggle with faith when it comes to God's promise.

For it is by grace you have been saved, through faith –
and this is not from yourselves, it is the gift of God.
– EPHESIANS 2:8

Modern-Day Miracles Abound

Throughout the years, I have personally experienced several miraculous events for which there is no explanation other than the hand of God. Certainly, they can be written off to happenstance or good fortune, but when viewed through a faithful lens, the answer seems obvious. Explained differently, it feels like much more of a stretch that these events just occurred without the hand of God.

The first of my experiences happened when I was 12 years old. My Boy Scout troop decided to camp at the Youghiogheny River, a world-class whitewater rafting mecca. Three members of the troop – me included – decided to skip the actual rafting experience and remained at the campsite unsupervised. During our three-hour hiatus from the adults, we elected to explore. We found ourselves on the banks of a raging torrent. It was not the Yough, as the river was commonly known, but a powerful waterway that led into the larger river. As we surveyed the waterway, we began casting sticks into the water, and watched as they were beaten against the jagged rocks and ultimately succumbed to a waterfall downstream.

One careless step, and I found myself completely immersed in the thundering deluge. I immediately panicked and began to flail recklessly. Grabbing for any rock or overhanging limb I could find, I quickly discovered that they were too slippery to hold and that the current was too powerful to resist. Within seconds, I realized my life was to be cut short and that there was no possibility of another outcome. The question became how I would die. Was I to drown in the churning water or suffer blunt force trauma from being bounced off the rocks at the base of the waterfall? I found neither option particularly appealing.

It is quite interesting that during such a trauma, time seems to stand still just for an instant and a certain image becomes etched in your memory. Not unlike a snapshot from a Polaroid camera, I recall the shocked expression on the faces of my friends as they rushed along the bank of the river. I particularly recall both their mouths agape. It was the epitome of hopelessness and haplessness personified.

The entire episode lasted less than five minutes. It concluded as my limp body was taken up into an eddy that catapulted me to a swirling pocket adjacent to the rapids. After a brief pause, I was able to extract myself from the river. Within a minute or two, I was reunited with my terrified friends, who had continued to run down the banks.

The hand of God plucked me from the waters, as surely as a gardener collects a turnip from the soil. There is no other plausible explanation. In an odd twist of irony, I was unbruised and unimpacted. Five minutes of terror was supplanted by a sense of intense security. I have no other memories of that trip.

The Miracle Within a Miracle

Another miracle occurred near my 40th birthday. A work colleague of mine fathered a baby who was born with a hole in his spine. The prognosis was stark, and the anticipated surgery came with high risk. The best-case outcome would have been a successful surgery that would enable the child to walk, but the family was prepared for the child to be wheelchair-bound. The family was explicitly counseled that under no circumstance would the child ever be able to compete in sports at any level.

I had made it a policy to keep my faith life and my business life separate. My colleagues knew I was a regular church attendee, but I rarely – if ever – spoke about my faith in the workplace. This particular colleague was known to be agnostic and rather vocal in his opinion, although his wife was a woman of faith.

I mustered the courage to ask him to allow my church to pray for his son. He seemed a bit shocked, and even questioned why I would ask. I advised him that something had touched me, and that led me to ask him for permission. I did not share this with him, but for some reason my heart connected with my mind and I genuinely believed that a miracle would occur if he agreed to my request – but only if I asked.

That Sunday morning, our entire congregation held hands and we virtually lifted the infant up in prayer. As I recall, we did not pray that he would be cured, but rather that God would be with him and his family as they struggled during the coming weeks.

Later that week, my colleague entered my office and announced that the hole in his son's spine had miraculously healed and that no surgery was needed. I do not recall if he said anything else, but I was overcome with joy at the news.

Two Sundays later, my pastor informed me that the church had received a donation from my work colleague, along with a heartfelt note. The note read, in part: "I never believed much in God and I do not believe in miracles, but I believe you helped my child. I do not know how you did it, but thank you."

Knowing this colleague so well, I was not surprised by the donation, but his genuine outpouring in the note stunned me. He and I never spoke about the note, but I did thank him for the donation. We never discussed the matter again.

The years have distanced this colleague and me, but his wife is connected with me on social media. A few years ago, I saw pictures of the young man upon his graduation. Apparently, he had become quite an accomplished hockey player. I recall thanking God again for His providence.

Many of the other miracles I have experienced have not been so indelibly engraved into my memory, but were marvels just the same. I believe we, as a society, take ourselves too seriously. Each generation seems to think they are much smarter than the ones that preceded them. The apparent lack of miracles in today's age is only due to our unwillingness to see them; we think we are far too advanced to believe in them. Oddly, we appear to have become blinded by our own self-absorbed beliefs of supreme superiority.

No Easy Route

Many scoff at believers in Jesus through cruel jeering and taunting. It is best not to engage in response to such attacks. Just as it occurred with the Pharisees of Biblical days, people's taunts are normally intentional traps set to discredit your views. They are an attempt to rattle your faith. I have always found it fascinating that such elitists bring themselves off their self-absorbed pedestals and feel the need to point out the stupidity of followers of Jesus. They tend to cast Christians into one large receptacle – they suggest we all follow blindly, in lockstep, a nonexistent shepherd. Within the hallowed sanctuaries of their lives, they have a compulsion to ridicule and malign something they believe to be fictitious.

More amazingly, these self-appointed arbiters of truth rarely, if ever, utter disparaging remarks about any of the other world religions (except for Judaism). It feels a bit incongruous and smacks of hypocrisy, but it is quite fashionable to engage in such banter in select circles within the elite society.

These are the first individuals to mention scripture to bolster their cause. My favorite example of that occurs when the subject of illegal immigration comes up. They cite their belief that Mary and Joseph were immigrants, seeking a place for Jesus to be born. In a disingenuous and ignorant ruse, they suggest the Christians of today would refuse Jesus.

Since most – if not all – critics are not well steeped in the scriptures, they somehow seem to forget that nothing could be further from the Biblical text. Luke 2:1-6 sets the record straight. To summarize, the government required all people to return to their hometown for a census; that was the reason Mary and Joseph were traveling at the time of the birth. A government mandate compelled them to return to Bethlehem, the town of David. Government overreach is not anything new; in fact, that is why one of the founding principles of the United States of America was limited government.

Christianity is under attack, and it appears that the assaults will not subside any time soon. Jesus's resurrection changes everything, and following him as a Being of love and light is worthy of your strong consideration. Your reward is eternal life – no small fact. As a bonus, your life journey becomes more abundant and filled with joy. There is nothing quite like grace; and when you discover it is yours for the asking, the experience is overwhelming.

Chapter 3

The Greatest Society
Ever Known

★ ★ ★ ★ ★ ★

I T IS FAIR TO say that eternity is a difficult concept to comprehend. While acknowledging that there are different belief systems, the earth is estimated to be approximately 4,500,000,000 years old, give or take 100,000,000 years. Humans are estimated to have been in existence for 200,000 years. The United States has existed for less than 250 years as a sovereign nation. It is amazing to realize that mankind has only been on the Earth about 0.004 percent of the time the earth has existed, and that the United States has been an idea for only 0.001 percent of the time man has existed. Allow these numbers to marinate in the mind a bit.

If we consider the entirety of the earth's history, and envision it as the volume contained in the average backyard swimming pool, the USA would constitute just eight drops of water. Following that logic, the entire time it has taken for this great land to be founded and attain its current position could evaporate in a few seconds on a warm summer afternoon. From a geological perspective, we are rather insignificant.

We then must ask ourselves how this comparatively inconsequential entity has accomplished so much in so little time. The answer is rather clear. God has blessed us, and with this blessing comes great responsibility.

> *To whom much is given, much is expected.*
> **– THE BOOK OF LUKE**

We have an awesome responsibility.

Many of our Founding Fathers recognized the incredible influence God had on the creation of this great nation. The miracles surrounding the winter at Valley Forge alone are incomprehensible without believing that the hand of God guided the outcome. George Washington referred to it as "providence."

I believe that Biblical history and evolutionary history can coexist; and while none of us know when Christ will return, it is safe to presume that this Book may exist long into the future. Not that I believe it will become a book for the ages; rather, it might be handed down through my family. I am my family historian and I have writings, books, and other pieces of memorabilia from as far back as 500 years ago.

A Singular Status

As of this writing, the United States stands alone as the world superpower. It has achieved that singular status through an exceptionalism never previously witnessed in human history. Furthermore, the

United States has accomplished more in less time than any society ever. It has lifted a significant portion of the world to a status never previously achieved.

In all human history, there has never been an equivalent to the experiment known as the United States of America. No society has ever provided more opportunity for its citizens and immigrants alike. Moreover, the United States of America has done more for others in the world than any other people. Most astonishingly, it seeks almost nothing in return, other than fair treatment for the residents of those other nation-states, and a limit to aggression.

Many will argue to the contrary. However, while the USA has plenty of flaws and its past is pocked with abundant blemishes, those contrarians are simply misinformed. More concerning, such anarchists are so blinded by their jealousy they simply create divisive propaganda to erode the very core values that make the United States so unique. In a true paradox, the very liberties that make the USA so unique are the same freedoms that allow ideological poison to infect the population. The bodies of the men and women who died to preserve our blessings are trampled upon through radicals' deeds, speech, and disinformation.

The True Existential Threat

We are engaged in a desperate fight for the heart and soul of the country, and for protection of the founding principles that have created this unique phenomenon called the United States. It is a struggle worth our attention and immediate and sustained action. I am not suggesting armed conflict, but rather a conflict of thought, ensuring that history is not rewritten. Our youth must be educated on our system of government, and on why it is so singular and unequaled in all of history.

It is quite simplistic and cowardly to point to historical weaknesses and errors without including productive solutions. It is also important to perform an in-depth analysis of those events of the past and view them through the historical lens of the time. From our vantage point now, it is easy to recognize that many groups were treated unfairly throughout periods of our history. When one puts themselves into the historical time frame, it becomes a much more difficult exercise. The benefit of hindsight is that it enhances the vision, making solutions much clearer. It is intellectually dishonest to criticize and then vilify the intentions of those who were and are using the best information possible during the relevant time frame.

It is like criticizing a 19th century physician for using leeches to cure a patient. In the 1830s, the use of leeches in the practice of medicine was considered superior to the art of bloodletting that had been in existence for over 2,000 years. A doctor, educated in the finest medical school of that day, would not question the need to extract significant volumes of blood from the patient to provide the correct treatment; but rather, would consider which method to employ. Undoubtedly, many lives were unnecessarily cut short by using leeches; but most individuals recognize that those physicians were engaging in procedures that they believed were most beneficial to their patients. Their continued curiosity and resulting study led to advancements in medicine that have, in turn, added years to millions of lives. We do not besmirch the names of those doctors, nor do we remove their names from the sides of buildings. Instead, appropriately, we celebrate those pioneers and recognize that the world is a better place for having them as part of our history.

Besmirching History

At the same time, many feel compelled to sully the names of other historical figures who, in some cases, employed equally questionable tactics, but wanted to create a better world. By looking through a tainted and myopic lens, many use the current culture of shaming and intentional rewriting of history as a means to fuel discontentment of the broader population.

Andrew Jackson, the seventh president of the United States, is one such figure. He was a true American hero whose early life belied his unprecedented impact on the early history of our nation. His father died prior to his birth and before he reached age 15, he was an orphan. His two older brothers and his mother all died through activities involving the Revolutionary War. Andrew, a courier of the command of William Richardson Davie, was captured by the British and held as a prisoner of war. He endured all this tumult before today's average American is old enough to drive a car.

The orphan who would rise to be elected president led a note-worthy but somewhat checkered life. Not unlike many of his day, he was a slaveholder; and some of his treatment of his slaves is certainly questionable at best. That acknowledged, his accomplishments on behalf of the fledgling nation cannot be forgotten. He led the defense of New Orleans during the War of 1812, which many historians have cited as a miracle. Outmanned and outgunned, Jackson guided his men through a vicious attack. The unlikely victory made him one of the most notable heroes of his time.

However, there is the blemish of his status as a slave owner, and purportedly he was an unkind one. This status has sullied his legacy. A person who volunteered in the Revolutionary War as a child, who became an orphan in part due to his family's service in that war, who became a hero general in the War of 1812, and who ultimately ascended to the presidency is now the subject of intense scrutiny. So extreme is the criticism that the removal of his image on the $20 bill is under debate.

The legacy of Jackson is stained with another unfair character assassination. That is his doctrine surrounding native American treatment. Ironically, the same frauds who seek to divide our populace into competing factions would have you believe that Native Americans were one large harmonious nation who lived through peaceful means. Today, the federal government recognizes 574 distinct Indian nations. History is chock-full of bloody and vicious attacks between warring tribes. That part of history, along with a long and terrible litany of examples of harsh treatment of European settlers, is inconvenient – and therefore, it has been expunged. Also expunged is the treatment of captured slaves by the indigenous people. Simply stated, it was horrific.

While it might appear to the reader that I am taking sides regarding historical records, nothing could be further from the truth. My position is that attempting to paint a narrative that evil Europeans drove innocent peace-loving indigenous people from their homes is intellectually dishonest, overly simplistic, and a far too convenient misinterpretation of the actual historical record. The issue is far more complex than current conventional societal plutocrats would have you believe. Certainly, there are plenty of historical records that suggest that outrageous examples of inhumane treatment occurred, but all participants share responsibility for that checkered part of history.

Out of Many, One

"E Pluribus Unum" is Latin for "out of many, one" and served as our national motto from 1776 to 1956. It is considered the traditional motto to this day; it is found on the Great Seal of the United States, and is inscribed on all our currency. More than a motto, it embodies the historical significance of the very essence of the American ideal. Known as the "great melting pot," the United States offers refuge and opportunity for millions of immigrants seeking a better life. Historically, those immigrating to this land of unparalleled freedom sought fulfillment of a dream that was unobtainable in their homeland.

As part of becoming an American, candidates for citizenship are asked to pledge an Oath of Allegiance to the United States. Part of that oath includes a renouncement of allegiance to any other sovereignty. Throughout our history, people became Americans and left their foreign identities behind, but kept their traditions and religious beliefs. It truly was what distinguished America from any other place in the world.

There are plenty of examples throughout history where immigrants' views have been influenced by their ties to their birth nations, but traditionally when they swore the oath in the United States, they became Americans first and foremost. At the same time, there are also examples where immigrants were treated unfairly during times of political conflict between the United States and their countries of origin. In the most well-known example of mistreatment, America created internment camps for over 100,000 Americans of Japanese descent during World War II.

It is important to note that intense fear throughout the Americas seeded that improper action. Other countries, notably Canada, enacted similar draconian practices. As pointed out in an earlier chapter, fear manifests itself into unwise actions with drastic consequences. Historically speaking, the action taken by the United States government against Japanese-Americans serves as the most outrageous example of violations of civil rights of the 20th century. Interestingly, we do not hear much today about the use of internment camps during WWII, as it appears that it is not politically expedient to do so. While a black mark on the reputation of our country, the action was understandable when examined through the historical lens of the time.

So intense was the sense of patriotism among the immigrant families that millions sent their sons off to battle to defend the United States during WWII. In many cases, these immigrants had only been citizens for a relatively short period, yet their loyalty for their new country had been etched so deeply into their psyche that they made severe sacrifices without objection.

My grandfather and grandmother on my father's side were two such people. Barely surviving in their new land, many of their eight children were sent to the coal mines to sustain the family. When the call came to defend this great land, their three sons of fighting age eagerly enlisted to fight for freedom. One was refused enlistment due to severe myopia, but was later drafted as the vision standards were relaxed as more troops were needed.

All three served without receiving a blemish and were later reunited with their families, earning honorable discharges. As with most who served, the horrors of war impacted all three and they rarely – if ever – spoke of their service. After my father's death, I learned that one of the ships on which he had been transported had been bombed, and almost half of the occupants perished. Never a word was spoken about that horrific experience until long after his passing.

The amalgamation of cultures was unified in America as one great force for good. The American flag served as a beacon to the world, standing for freedom and liberty. During the last third of the 20th century, we began to see the destructive practice of identity politics. One can find examples of identity politics creeping into society throughout history, but it has manifested into an epidemic state in the latter part of the 20th century. The rhetoric and vitriol has only become more dangerous as we migrate into the third decade of the 21st century.

Urgency Required

The United States of my youth was one with a truly united people, except for a few anarchists. They assaulted the establishment from time to time, only to be rejected by the American people. Absolutely, there was intense political debate – and while viewpoints differed widely, it felt as if at their core, they were just on different paths attempting to achieve the same goal: a stronger and better America.

Children were taught to respect the flag, revere the police, and love their country. Instilled into most children was a strong sense of respect for authority and rule of law. Every morning, our youth stood while reciting the Pledge of Allegiance, followed by a moment of silence. God had already been unceremoniously extracted from our public schools, and the removal of the moment of silence followed shortly thereafter. Some found it intolerable that we ask for a moment of reflection each morning.

In less than 20 years, students would begin mocking this great land by refusing to stand for the pledge or the anthem. Feckless school administrators found it more convenient to ignore the dangerous and disrespectful actions, and a scourge ensued.

A slippery slope only slides in one direction, and it results in unproductive and uncontrollable consequences. Today, we endure an epidemic of outrageous behavior. Many have removed God from the pledge, and a second national anthem, that evidently speaks to one part of the population, has slipped into our routines with little objection.

If we have decided that the sacrifice of the brave men who died defending Fort McHenry during the War of 1812 are not worthy of our reverence, then so be it. Lobby Congress for a new anthem, and have it changed. As disgusting as I would find this eventuality, it is far more important that we maintain one anthem as a unifying and inspiring force that rallies the population. In my day, the family unit was strong, and parents reassured their children. Our political leaders delivered inspiring speeches, advising that citizens not ask what their country could do for them, but instead what they could do for our country. Tragically, "the shining city on a hill" has been buried in the deep snows of a dark winter.

Gun violence at schools was not a concern when I was a student. In fact, the parking lot of our school was packed with pickup trucks, most of which were adorned with gun racks that held rifles and shotguns to be employed during after-school hunts. There was also the rifle team; members could regularly be seen with guns on school grounds as they engaged in target practice. Nobody thought of using a gun to hurt someone. Certainly, criminals used weaponry, but that activity seemed as far away as the moon. The term "going postal" had yet to be created, but in 1986 everything changed.

In my schools, switchblades and brass knuckles were the implements of terror. While those weapons were rarely – if ever – seen, the mere rumor of a bully having one spread fear and panic. On the other hand, education was the key to safe gun usage. In fact, at age 13 as part of my Eagle Scout requirements, I led a hunter's safety course in the community where I lived.

It was a simpler life and a more collegial time. Sundays were family days; with only a very few essential service providers operating, most businesses were closed. Sunday drives and roadside picnics were commonplace. The change of the seasons caused millions to marvel as they admired the beauty of God's creation each October, when a palette of colors adorned the landscape. Then, with the leaves and grass replaced by a thick blanket of snow, the cold winters reminded us of the challenges we face in life. The spring would follow, and as the first crocuses pushed through the remaining snow, God's promise of eternal life was on full display. So it was repeated, year after year, in the world of my youth.

The 24/7 News Cycle

Most great achievements come with unintended consequences. Arguably, the most material development in my lifetime was the innovation of the internet and its accompanying technological advancements. Like nothing before, it has reshaped the world order. Communication races across the globe at nearly lightspeed. We can connect with people thousands of miles away and it is like they are in the next room. We can transmit electronic editions of books in seconds to faraway lands.

With the internet came the 24-hour news cycle, a nonstop bombardment of current events. Much of it is not properly vetted. The smartphone, which I am generously including as part of this new technology, has created millions of would-be reporters – all attempting to capture fantastical evidence. The new technology creates truly remarkable opportunities. A wave crashing into a cloud or an eagle dipping its wing tips onto the surface of the water are visuals that take our breaths away. Tragically, the technology has also contributed to a vulgar practice of videoing every prospective tragedy. An elderly woman is attacked by thugs, and vigilante journalists' instinctual reaction is to record the mayhem. What historically would have been a reaction to help or to call 911 has been supplanted with the zest to garner some fantastic footage.

A picture is worth 1,000 words, and possibly a video is worth 10,000, but we have learned that videos do not tell the whole story –

not even close. In fact, videos regularly depict what the videographer would have one believe. In January 2019, a group of teens waited outside the Lincoln Memorial in Washington, D.C. Among them was a youth named Nick Sandmann. Nick and many of his friends had purchased Make America Great Again hats and were wearing them proudly. That display was considered unacceptable by the professional protestors there, who took umbrage with the teens. Among them was longtime agitator Nathan Phillips. In an instant, videos surfaced, depicting a young man smiling sheepishly. The videos were shared by national media outlets; a twisted and false story emerged that the teen had mocked a Native American. While the initial videos showed very little, the fabricated backstory created a fervor.

The story line became, "Entitled Catholic school educated white teens harassed an indigenous Vietnam War veteran." Wheezing anchors insisted that the teens had mocked the proud indigenious patriot repeatedly, screaming, "Build the wall." Through tears, Mr. Phillips recounted the horrific experience. Then, in an outrageous act of politically correct cowardice, the Catholic diocese publicly admonished the youngster and his classmates, issuing a stunning apology. As judge, jury and executioner, the church leadership acted swiftly and deftly.

There was a bit of a problem – the story was a complete fabrication; but, like a hungry trout unable to resist the angler's fly, the media and the political class pounced, and they gobbled it up. In doing so, they defamed the youngster.

Two of the national media outlets that sensationalized and – with ill intent – propagated the myth have settled sealed lawsuits that are reported to be in the range of hundreds of millions of dollars. In my view, their hatred for all things Donald Trump caught them flat-footed and accordingly they paid the price.

As recently as August 2020, a now rich Nick Sandmann continues to have his reputation besmirched by partisan hacks. Amazingly, not one word was uttered by the media or our leadership throughout the entire episode about the fact that professional adult agitators harassed and demeaned a group of vulnerable minors whose crime was to wear some hats. What if the students had responded differently? Sadly, all of the elements of the story do not make it to the public square.

Hope Springs Eternal

Despite the current struggles, the United States remains the greatest country ever known. Contrary to the fabricated narrative of an untenable systematically racist entity, the United States stands as arguably the least racist country on the planet. There are millions of black and brown people begging to gain entrance. The unbelievable risks they face are in contrast to the dishonest description.

The battle rages on. The battle, mostly fought in cyberspace, is worth fighting. You are worthy of the effort, as are the generations to follow. God has us, but we need to act. With justice as our sword and righteousness as our shield, we will ultimately be victorious.

Chapter 4

Living in Unprecedented Times

★　★　★　★　★　★

URING THE TIME WHEN much of this tome was written, our country was mired in a dangerous and divisive debate. In fact, driven by the acrimony, I can see a distinctive impact on the tone and tenor of my writing. It appears that we have reached a dangerous tipping point. Ideologues from factions across the spectrum have fueled the inferno through discordant and intentionally dishonest rhetoric. The result has been an epidemic of protests that have led to perilous rioting. The hypocrisy is numbing, emotions are raw, and fear is rampant.

I have never been a fan of protest, even peaceful protest. I advocate for the rights of our citizens to engage in peaceful protest, but inherent risks render it extraordinarily dangerous. Since we do not know the motivations of others, there is a great probability that evil elements can infect an effort. For example, let us say that 95 percent of participants gather in support of an effort with altruistic intentions, but are shocked when a riot breaks out. The other 5 percent joined through more spurious motivations and with the intent of instilling chaos. As a result, lives are destroyed and the anger explodes across the country in an unavoidable chain reaction of outrage.

In 2020, the great pandemic crippled the world and the implications of the actions taken to address it will likely be felt for more than a generation. The psychological damage comes with a mountain of epic repercussions that will weaken our resolve and inflame the division. The situation remains fluid, and the future is uncertain in an almost unprecedented way.

The Unfathomability That Was 2020

The most talented author could not have envisioned the details of the horror story that was 2020. Ironically, the year embodying a numerical depiction of perfect vision left most blind with rage. The year started with an extraordinarily divisive impeachment of our president. In an expensive display of unproductive form over substance, our political class engaged in folly. The outcome was known before the first mouth opened.

While the country was caught up in that idiocy, an invisible and deadly enemy was already infecting our land. Our leaders assured us that there was nothing to fear from the virus and that our president was far more dangerous than any invisible foe from a foreign land. In a stunning display of insincerity after the impeachment debacle had concluded, we were immediately thrust into a lockdown; the virus threatened our very civilization.

While we still do not know the outcome, it appears that the scourge will likely kill less than 1 percent of the people it infects.

That is a stark and frightening statistic, to be sure; but the cost of the shutdown, in related deaths and life-altering despondency, appears to impact multiple times the numbers of people who suffered from the actual virus. In a true "red herring" fashion, as of this writing, there does not appear to be any correlation between approaches to fight the virus. Four of our most populated states adopted separate methodologies, with two opting for open approaches and the other two selecting more draconian lockdowns. The results appear to be statistically similar, and most statisticians would determine that the disparate approaches had no material impact on the results.

Examining the global situation and focusing on Europe, the statistics seem to paint a parallel picture. Germany, widely heralded as the model in combating the virus, has seen a significant resurgence and is currently suffering with one of the leading death rates. I do not point this out to criticize Germany in any way, but rather to demonstrate that the virus is not playing by any set of rules.

An Unconscionable Act Leads to Chaos

In May, the country was shocked as we saw images of George Floyd being kneeled upon by a police officer. For an instant, the country was unified. *This should never happen in the United States,* the vast majority screamed. But his tragic death was exploited by partisans intent on dividing the country. As is almost always the case, we did not initially have all the facts; but the outrage boiled over into protests that devolved into vicious riots. The protests adversely impacted the very citizens they were intended to support.

What might have been a unifying moment in history became bitterly divisive. Our political leaders doused the fire with dynamite; their intent seems dubious. So rancorous is the subject that one could be shunned for voicing some of the facts of the matter. Steadfast in my resolve, I will attempt to describe the facts as I have come to know them. I will restate that what happened to Mr. Floyd should never happen to any human – anywhere – ever. There is no excuse for the actions of the officer involved.

That noted, Mr. Floyd had lived a very checkered life, spending considerable time in prison. He was involved in a counterfeit money scheme. When the police engaged Mr. Floyd, he had a lethal dose of fentanyl in his system. He was extremely combative and deranged, but he did not appear to be a threat to the officers' lives, and so their reaction appears condemnable.

Throughout the entire episode, there is no evidence that what happened to Mr. Floyd had any remote connection to his race. Race as a factor in police behavior is a theme we see repeated again and again. As statistics prove out, there is no epidemic of police brutality that targets a specific race. I find it disappointing that we even feel the need to report statistics along racial lines; but sadly, it is now hard-coded into the philosophical framework of the country.

The Paradox of Profiling

Black men are statistically more likely to be killed by police than other segments of the populace, as they commit a higher percentage of the crime. That sentence could result in a scarlet letter of shame to be permanently hung around my neck – but it needs to be written and stated, or we will not be able to solve the problem. Further, I do not write with the intention of indicting Black men, or any other segment of the population.

While crime should not be justified, the statistic I mentioned has some extremely plausible underlying realities that make it understandable. If I am statistically more likely to feel a chronic sense of hopelessness due to generational poverty, I am more likely to become angry, and in turn, take action that would put me at odds with the law. At the same time, if one segment of the population commits more crime per capita, then it is not particularly surprising that it has statistically more negative interaction with the police.

When I was in college, I dressed rather shabbily, had long hair, regularly donned a bandana, and I enjoyed violating the traffic laws. The police stopped me regularly. Since I was taught to respect law enforcement, no life-altering negative consequences resulted. In fact, thinking back, I was 11 times more likely to be stopped by police in the four years from 1977 to 1981 than I have been in the past 30 years.

Similarly, as a 20-something, I had an interesting experience that shook me to the core. I was driving down East Ocean Boulevard in Long Beach when I was stopped by an officer. My crime was speed-ing. After the officer took my information, he returned and asked me to sign the violation. I politely declined. At that point, he removed his service weapon from the holster and directed me to get out of the car. I immediately complied with his first request and signed the paper. He never pointed the weapon at me, but I was frightened and felt his use of force was excessive. Maybe he was having a bad day, maybe he was a cop who liked to flaunt his authority, or maybe he thought I smirked the wrong way. Regardless, that event could have turned out far differently if I had chosen to remain defiant. Consider for a moment what might have happened if my parents had taught me that the police hate me and that I should fear them.

The numbers track similarly across all the segments of the popu-lation – those who commit the least number of crimes are less likely to be imprisoned. An unbiased assessor will quickly recognize that we do not have a broad racism problem with the police, although sig-nificant racism plagues our country. The issue is generational poverty that leads to hopelessness and manifests into anger. The impoverished, which constitute a higher percentage in the Black community, feel disenfranchised. Tragically, many are taught that they are the victims of an unfair system that targets them, and it is an impossible task to rise above it. We do not come out of the womb hating. Hate is taught, and our leaders have mastered the skills of instilling hate into our countrymen.

Poverty – the Inconvenient Reality

Interestingly, if we map poverty numbers with violent crime, the ratios create almost a perfect mirror image. Blacks are 2.7 times more likely to live in poverty than are whites. Hispanics are 1.7 times more likely to be impoverished. The 2019 crime statistics reveal that the ratio of violent crime comparing these three groups is almost identical to the poverty imbalance.

As I reflect on my life, police have pulled weapons on me on four different occasions. Except for the one I just described, they were all plausibly honest mistakes. I sincerely do not know the motivations of the officers involved. What if I had been taught to hate or fear the police? Would these stories have ended differently?

The Danger of Social Engineering

For my entire life, the government has been attempting to socially engineer racial equity. It has not worked for the past 60 years, and if we continue to do the same things over and over and expect a different result, we are crazy.

In the time of my youth, the country was indeed very racist. The statistics bear out that reality. Fortunately, no one told me I was supposed to hate or fear Black people. As such, one of my best friends was a Black kid. We were as close as two boys could be, and never noticed the whispers in the background. Somehow, he vanished from my life, and I have no recollection why. In reflecting upon the end of our friendship, I believe it occurred around the time of Dr. Martin Luther King Jr.'s assassination. Could it be that our parents' fear drove us apart? Maybe it was misappropriated anger. I will probably never know what transpired.

My mother worked the night shift in Pittsburgh, and I distinctly recall my father driving her to work during the riots of that era with my brother and me in tow. The flashing lights and what appeared to be a fiery backdrop are etched in my memory. So to say I was scared is an understatement. The first time I heard the N-word, it came from my uncle, and my father immediately rebuked him. This is not to deify my father's racial altruism – I believe he had some deeply-held biases, but he wanted to ensure that I did not become tainted.

A Mind Polluted

By the time I arrived in seventh grade, the government felt it was essential to bring Black students into our school. For me, the experiment was a disaster. The white students had been instructed that the Black students required understanding and care, and the resulting chaos wreaked havoc on the entire institution. Some of the Black students came to recognize that their actions would not result in consequences. Further, many came from economically challenged families, and in the world of junior high one-upmanship, they became bitter.

One of my starkest memories involves a new pair of shoes. After months of saving, I had finally been able to purchase a pair of Puma tennis shoes, replacing the ones with plastic soles that my mother had bought me. Within two weeks, they had been sliced up and thrown in a toilet by one of the Black students – with his friends cheering him on. So brazen was this group, they bragged to me that they had perpetrated the act. At the end of the school year, the same student, along with his friends, destroyed my yearbook in the woodshop with one of the power tools. As with previous bad deeds, there were no consequences, and the school's remedy was to give me a new book. The administration did not seem to recognize that the reason that yearbooks were so popular was because students wrote notes to each other in them.

With these experiences as an indelible element of my "education," a disturbing racial animus commenced growing within me, and I hated it. The students were not to blame. They were kids, doing the kinds of things kids do. When left to their own devices, all types of turmoil result. The blame falls squarely upon the political leaders of that time, who dreamt up the notion of forcing integration but failed to think through all the unintended consequences. Historically, there have been many programs that have been conceived by leaders who fail to contemplate the dire implications; this was but one. It was truly form over substance, and I have intensely disliked that sort of logic for my entire life.

The sting from the treatment that I received from the Black students softened over time; but I formulated some biases that remained with me for years. Tragically, I appeared unable to shake them.

A Horrific Wake-Up Call

When I moved to Mississippi in 1989, I experienced what appeared to me like outrageous racial injustice. I felt like I was in a completely different country, and it shocked me. Prior to seeing it with my own eyes, I would never have believed that humans could be treated so poorly. I found the treatment of many Black workers, by both Caucasians and Blacks in positions of authority, to be intolerable. I witnessed a lack of empathy for other humans that I had not thought was possible. Interestingly, no one – not even those who were the subject of the shabby treatment – appeared the least bit bothered by it.

I decided to buy lunch for my team, but I was still new in the area and had not found the grocery store. I ended up in a seedy place, and all they offered was bologna and American cheese. Equipped with four pounds of bologna and all the trimmings, I hosted the luncheon.

Afterward, one of the Black men remained behind – and with tears running down his face, he thanked me for treating him so well. It broke my heart; I was embarrassed to have arrived with such a spartan meal, while he was so deeply touched by the "generosity." I can still see his face today as I type.

A few weeks later, I was informed that one of the Black workers was ill and I questioned him about it. He was vomiting blood. After a rather lengthy exchange, he agreed to go to the hospital. I returned to my office; through the window, I saw him walking across the parking lot. It turned out that he had no car, so walking was his only option. I jumped in my car and asked him to get in so I could transport him. He was frightened and confused, and claimed it would not be right. Ultimately, I was able to urge him into the car and successfully dropped him at the hospital.

My short time living in the South was a true paradox, and I am grateful for it. I learned valuable lessons on life, the vast majority of which were positive. However, some lessons equipped me with a new and sobering perspective on the realities of prejudice. Since then, I have worked tirelessly to rectify – in some small way – some of the historical inequities. I seek to create opportunities for all I encounter, without regard to race. The results have been remarkable. Many of the finest and most successful men and women I have worked with have been Black, and for me their merit, not race, was the most important consideration.

Fabrication of the Unsolvable Myth

Today, many of our leaders and those in the media would have us believe that we live under a cloud of systemic racism. This is a dangerous and divisive lie that only serves to drive a poisonous wedge between the races. That belief convinces many Black youths that the deck is stacked against them and that there is no way to win. Imagine having that terrible myth drilled into your head repeatedly! It is no wonder that so many young Black men join gangs and commit crimes. Frankly, had I been brainwashed in such a fashion, I suspect that my life would have been far less rewarding. It is a tragic self-fulfilling prophecy.

Indoctrination of this fashion is just the beginning. We are now saddled with this fictitious notion of white privilege, and are urged to adopt a self-loathing because we were born a certain color. The notion of white privilege is, in many ways, the definition of racism. Our schools are considering embracing an educational platform that includes teaching our children that they need to feel guilty for having been born a certain color. I cannot imagine a more psychologically damaging practice. The fact that it is based on a complete fabrication renders it intolerable.

That noted, I recognize that the country is plagued by biases that may provide advantage to one classification of people over another. Race can be one of those biases, but so are height, weight, athleticism, attractiveness, and wealth, as well as a long list of other physical and mental attributes. There is little doubt that many in minority communities are born into suboptimal circumstances, and that finding a way to help lift them up with all the others who are disadvantaged is the preferred solution.

It's Poverty, Stupid

We have a significant and chronic generational poverty problem that has plagued this country for decades. Poverty knows no skin color, as it attacks the spirit without regard to race or creed. Focusing on helping to lift people out of poverty is the solution, and offering handouts only ensures that the situation will remain unaltered.

It is a statistical fact that poverty affects a larger percentage of the Black population than it does other groups, and I have no doubt that our history of slavery – and subsequent racial injustices – have done much to create the imbalance. That noted, the most recent government statistics that I could find reveal a very different part of the story. It is true that a Black person is more than twice as likely to be in poverty as their white counterpart. On an absolute basis, nearly 27 million white Americans are classified as living in poverty, which is nearly three times the total of Black Americans falling into the same category.

Introducing programs that offer a hand up for all who are born into dire circumstances would be a great start. If we adopted a color-blind approach, the program would be supported by the majority of the citizens. And, due to the realities I have described, statistics would suggest that more Blacks would be helped as a percentage of the population.

Another Month, Another Outrage

As the calendar pages were flipped, we were introduced to Jacob Blake. As with Mr. Floyd, Mr. Blake fell victim to a police shooting.

This shooting resulted in lifelong paralysis. As with Mr. Floyd, outrage ensued, cities were burned, and lives were ruined.

With circumstances that differed from the situation with Mr. Floyd, the police seemed far more justified in subduing Mr. Blake, as he wielded a knife and threatened the officers. Our media, intent on spreading a malicious narrative, lied and claimed that Mr. Blake had been unarmed. But Mr. Blake set the record straight, admitting he had been equipped with a knife. The realities of police work are often not pretty, and the graphic video of the incident is uncomfortable to watch.

Mr. Blake became a second face of the movement to vilify the police, and the man and woman who would later become president and vice president lauded him as a hero. Football teams emblazoned his name on uniforms and stadiums. I suppose one could say that the intentions were sincere, but as is often the reality, those who celebrated Mr. Blake did not think through the matter in its entirety. Moreover, the inherently dishonest media fanned the flames through misleading reporting. Many never heard that the police had engaged Mr. Blake as he was threatening an ex-girlfriend in violation of a restraining order. Mr. Blake had sexually assaulted the woman in the past, and she had called the police in a panic, as he was terrorizing her yet again.

While I am certain that I could discover the identity of this young woman, the media has rendered her an unimportant detail of the incident – so inconsequential that she is not even worthy of a name. I cannot imagine a crueler development than to have your abuser glorified while you exist in bullied anonymity. The thought of it sickens me.

Preparing for the Unthinkable

As Election Day 2020 neared, in cities across the country, business proprietors commenced boarding up their buildings. Massive riots were expected if Donald Trump were to be reelected. Yes, this is the tragedy of the times in which we live. Trump did not win, and the streets were filled with jubilant masses, completely ignoring the draconian social distancing mandates in effect at the time. The same people who could not be asked to vote in person for their safety were now engaging in much more perilous actions. In another example of the hypocrisy of our times, there was not a mention of that reality in the press.

The massive mail-in voting campaign cast a cloud of doubt over the validity of the election, with nearly 40 percent believing that there was massive fraud involved. I honestly do not know if there was widespread cheating, or if the outcome could have been affected if cheating could be proven. A fair and unbiased investigation is warranted. There are some outrageous claims that could be easily verified or debunked by a fair bipartisan board of review. In any case, whether you are happy or sad over the outcome of the election, I would think all Americans would want to know if our election was tainted.

Feeling disenfranchised and fueled by fiery rhetoric from President Trump, a large group of his supporters descended upon Washington, D.C. on January 6. Among the protestors were some agitators who were planning for violence. The Capitol was breached as some of the protesters transformed into rioters. The situation was so stark that most of the population was reviled by the scene.

Just as events had played out many times over the previous summer, a protest morphed into a dangerous riot. Just as before, a small percentage of those in attendance created the chaos and broke the law. Media reporting of the incident demonstrated a blatant, deceitful bias. The very people who had reported that the summer's protests had been mostly peaceful while fires raged behind them now painted a picture of mass anarchy – they claimed that all in attendance were somehow part of an insurrection.

The media lusted after any evidence to create an impression that the event was even more horrendous than it actually was. They breathlessly and errantly reported that one police officer was killed when a rioter threw a fire extinguisher at him. In an amazing display of reverse bias, the Capitol protesters were vilified while the police were celebrated. It was an amazing example of gross media malfeasance.

The Capitol riot was a national outrage and should be condemned by every American. That said, we learned of a number of tragedies that were the byproduct of the rancor. A woman, an unarmed rioter, was fatally shot by an officer. Evidently, three other people died because of unrelated health issues, but the media craftily included them in the death count. In a gross example of unbridled bias in journalism, it has been nearly impossible to find any information concerning the more than 20 people who lost their lives as part of the "mostly peaceful" protests of the summer of 2020, but the five who died who were connected to the Capitol riot were trumpeted throughout the media.

Two Tragedies, Two Responses

Let us compare and contrast the Floyd shooting to the one that took place on January 6 at the Capitol. In the Floyd case, an unarmed man was kneeled on by police and died shortly after. In the Capitol shooting, a woman who is rarely named – and was unarmed – was shot by police. In that case, there is no question as to the cause of her death.

In both cases, both victims were in the act of breaking the law. That is where the similarities end.

Mr. Floyd has been martyred, despite his history as a career criminal. The woman has been widely demonized, despite her history as a patriotic veteran who served many tours in combat. In the Floyd matter, all the police were immediately named and their reputations were ruined. Most remain in prison – and justifiably so. We have not heard much about the shooter in the other case, and to my knowledge, his name has not been released. I do not know enough about the specifics of the incident to form an opinion on the matter, but it seems rather suspect that – in a mob situation – the firing of a gun and the killing of a single person did much to impact the broader uprising.

I am a bit incredulous as to how so many can formulate opinions about the motivations of an officer in the conduct of his duties. "The officer who kneeled on Mr. Floyd did so because of Mr. Floyd's skin color and out of his intense hatred for Blacks" is the narrative we are spoon-fed, expected to digest, and then magically compelled to believe. At the same time, we are told that the officer who shot the woman in the Capitol had no choice and should be lauded for his actions.

For a moment, think about the Floyd situation. What sane person – officer or not – would elect to kneel on a person's neck in broad daylight and in front of a crowd, knowing that cameras were rolling? It appears implausible, if not impossible. A more likely scenario would suggest that the officer was triggered and lost control, possibly suffering from a temporary bout of insanity. In saying that, I am not proposing any such excuse, because there is none.

Since I am an advocate for law and order, I tend to have a personal bias that leans in favor of law enforcement. The apparent double standard employed by the press in these two instances feels far away from goodness. All summer, we had been told that the police are our enemy and must be either defunded or reprogrammed; then amazingly, less than a half a year later, police are extolled as heroes. I think the vast majority of law enforcement should be applauded for their service; but the inconsistent duplicity is troubling indeed.

Salem Has Nothing on This

As I write, our politicians are engaged in yet another impeachment proceeding, and soon will be attempting to try a civilian to determine if he should be thrown out of office. Despite being unconstitutional, it is an incredible waste of time and money. We have significantly more important issues to grapple with than the flagellation of a person who is no longer in office. Trump's rhetoric was inexcusable, but no harsher than the bombastic hate speech of other politicians. Once again, we see a dangerous double standard employed because of political biases.

The consequence of all this contentious ridiculousness is a bitterly divided country that probably harbors more racial animus than at any time in recent history. Tensions are at a breaking point and emotions are raw. Sadly, there appears to be no leader or set of leaders willing to provide some healing for our severely wounded populace. The years 2020-2021 could most aptly be described as an unfathomable sandwich, boasting impeachment crusts, and loaded with the vilest assortment of unpalatable ingredients imaginable. With such a revolting meal being forced down the throats of half the citizens, where we go from here is indeed in question.

Interestingly, the world learned a valuable lesson from the treatment of Germany after World War I. The harsh punishment of an entire group can foster the rise of the most unimaginable horror.

Sadly, it appears that many in this country have forgotten that essential lesson; they see no risk in desecrating a significant element of the populace.

Beyond the obvious, perhaps the more outrageous and damning prospects rise from the trampling of the Constitution. In the most overt attack on civil liberties ever in our country's history, we are silencing free speech – a cohort of powerful oligarchs have banded together to quash opposing views. Camouflaged by media who share their world view and protected by a political class that refuses to enact legislation to terminate the movement against freedom, these entities are shattering the very bedrock of our country.

Free speech is a key element in the foundation of our country that makes America like no other nation. If we allow it to be diluted, we will wash away any semblance of the land for which so many have fought and died.

Admitting One's Mistakes

During the time I wrote this book, we were all required to relive the George Floyd tragedy, as Derek Chauvin's trial was nationally broadcast. I became enthralled with the entire episode and I watched the vast majority of the trial. One unexpected outcome of this obsession was that I became educated, and realized that I had rushed to judgment on the case. I had been very wrong in my assumptions and conclusions. I was so disturbed by my folly that I considered rewriting a portion of the book to correct the record.

After reflection, I felt that it would be much more powerful to allow the book's content to remain unaltered; yet I felt compelled to set the record straight. The trial was a horrific affair and the videos that were displayed depicted an utter disregard for even an ounce of empathy. I found the initial contact between the police and Mr.

Floyd unconscionable and it left me wondering why they employed such hostile tactics. Mr. Floyd's crime did not warrant the treatment. There may be some additional information that will come to light, but the treatment seemed completely unwarranted.

While my initial beliefs proved to be true about Mr. Floyd having been combative, his resistance certainly did not rise to the level of the response given by the officers. What I had believed to have been a tragedy that ended in death was really more akin to a gross miscarriage of justice, devolving into criminal behavior on the part of the police. The chaos I had imagined simply did not exist; the demeanor of the police was more businesslike. Their poise during the majority of the episode left me questioning their judgment.

I still grapple with the reasoning behind the severity of the incident. It is quite easy to argue that it was an intentional act by bad cops aimed at the mistreatment of a person in their care. It seems likely that the environment and historical experience played some role.

As for the color of Mr. Floyd's skin and what role it played, we will likely never know what was in the hearts of the officers involved. It is hard to discern. To state that there is not a shred of evidence to race playing any role is incorrect, and I was wrong to have reached that conclusion.

Chapter 5

The Donald

★ ★ ★ ★ ★ ★

HAD NOT INTENDED TO include any section of the book on Donald Trump; but, the events that took place during the end of his presidency have rendered him such an enigma that it would be negligent not to discuss him. Never in my lifetime has a mere name been more polarizing. With most politicians, the public opinion takes on a reverse bell curve appearance. With this man, the bell has been tossed out the window and in its place there are two precipitous cliffs.

From the time he announced he would run for president, it was clear that he was going to shake up the status quo (almost as if Atlas had indeed shrugged like Ayn Rand had suggested in her famous book, *Atlas Shrugged*). In my mind there is no more apt visual as to the mystery that is Donald Trump.

When I first heard he was running, I scoffed at the idea. In my view, the fact that he was a crude and seemingly intense, self-centered individual made him unelectable. So strong was my disdain for this man that I had never watched an interview with him, nor had I ever seen a minute of his idiotic television show. As his campaign developed, I watched with a mix of horror and delight as he dismantled the other Republican candidates. His wit was quick and biting. It was clear he was operating from a different playbook. Over time, I grew to despise his garishness; yet his ideas seemed reasonable and, in many ways, revolutionary.

Trump's appeal grew with the public; they responded to him due to their disdain for Hillary Clinton and because they felt a genuine alignment with his "Make America Great Again" message. In a twist of irony, Trump brought a strong populist message to the Republican Party – and in doing so, changed the demographics. Each yin has a yang, and members of the traditional elite class fled the Republican Party with abandon. In doing so, they left their morality behind. One might argue that they did so for altruistic reasons, but the facts contradict that assertion.

A New Breed of Politician

Both John Kasich and Jeb Bush promised the American people that, no matter who the Republican presidential candidate would be in 2016, they would support him or her. Both signed a pledge to that effect. Both lied.

There are many deeply-held values that a Republican would have to completely ignore before actively supporting the opposing candidate. But the political class despised Trump. They shrieked about his lack of sophistication, racist views, and character flaws – traits that, in their view, rendered him unsuitable to serve. In reality, they realized that he could not be controlled, and that prospect terrorized them.

For most of my life, it has been evident that the media generally is biased, and that their biases would leak into their reporting. With the rise of Barack Obama, the floodgates opened, and once-cloaked prejudice was washed away in a torrent of pandering and fawning. Most reasonable minds would agree that the overwhelming media treatment during Obama's eight years in office was generous. With Trump, the media bias erupted at a rate of Biblical proportions. The media bias against Trump became so outrageous that it was almost laughable. With such overt and hate-filled cheerleading, the divisions widened, and emotions were frayed to the breaking point.

The Enemy of the People Emerges

The media transformed every molehill into a mountain, and described every mountain as built with the most vile and unthinkable evil intentions. To the casual observer, the media's presentation of Trump cast an aura of true immorality and wickedness over the man. This intentional manipulation of reporting became known as "fake news."

With half the country shell-shocked, Trump won the presidency. So unprepared was the media for his unlikely victory, that many cried openly on the air. Please allow that to sink in. Those were seasoned, nationally-recognized professionals, overtly baring their personal biases – biases they had spent a lifetime attempting to camouflage.

Regaining their bearings and shifting into attack mode, the media tirelessly repeated the lie that half the country was racist – that had to be the only explanation for Trump's success. The media added that the population must be deprogrammed. So outrageous was the clamor, it was almost unfathomable that anyone but the most extreme partisan would believe it. Yet, brainwashed by the tidal wave of half-truths and out-of-context, contrived, worst-case-scenario fabrications, many believed it.

Today, we hear a great deal of talk about unity and coming together to heal from the wounds of the Trump presidency, but that is laughable when one looks at the facts through an unbiased eye. Almost immediately after the 2016 election, the opposition – made of the media and elitist members of both political parties – worked tirelessly to dismantle the Trump agenda before it even commenced.

When Trump claimed that his campaign was being spied upon by the party in power, he was discounted as a purveyor of lies. Later, we found out he was correct. When Congress met to certify the election, Democrat after Democrat rose to object. Almost 70 members of Congress boycotted Trump's inauguration. That fact failed to make the news cycle.

As the inauguration grew nearer, massive protests were planned for the capital. Riots ensued and fear was omnipresent. Celebrities advised us that they were thinking about blowing up the White House. So dishonest was the media that they even lied about the crowd size of the inauguration. As if it really mattered – and in a display of gross stupidity – Trump lowered himself to their level and engaged in a public debate over the size of the assembly. Neither party was correct. The crowd was much larger than the media-manipulated photographs portrayed, but not nearly as large as Trump boasted.

I attended the inauguration, so I have firsthand knowledge of the facts. There was indeed a shroud of fear over many in attendance as rioters had burned cars the evening before. I was but a block from the riots; and while I could not see them, I could hear the pandemonium. Protestors shackled themselves to turnstiles in an attempt to restrict access to the National Mall.

I found Trump's acceptance speech uplifting and inspirational. In a setting similar to Reagan's inauguration 36 years earlier – it was a dreary day with on-again, off-again rain showers – the skies opened, and the sun popped out for just a minute when Trump placed his hand on the Bible. At that point, I reflected that God was well pleased. But upon returning to my hotel that evening, I learned from the media that the speech I heard actually was Hitlerian and dark. Hateful opinions jammed the airwaves, poisoning the minds of as many people as possible.

The discordant animosity became so acrimonious that many in the media, along with leaders from both sides of the political spectrum, aligned in their zeal to bring the president down. They instructed their followers to attack those who supported the Trump agenda. Many Trump supporters were harassed and abused with vile, hate-filled attacks. #Resist became the battle cry concerning anything or anyone related to Trump, and we experienced the most uncooperative period of my lifetime. We were subjected to a constant cavalcade of contrary positions that appeared to be taken for the sole purpose of opposition. The most idiotic example might have been #piegate. The internet exploded when Sarah Huckabee Sanders posted a picture of a pie she had made for Thanksgiving. April Ryan, a White House reporter, demanded that Sanders prove she had made the pie. Some joked that if Trump cured cancer, the resistance would report that he stole jobs from doctors.

No Saint, to Be Sure

Trump, a man with his own demons to face, waded into the fray with fiery language of his own. His language was regularly taken out of context and used as sound bites to further discredit his presidency.

His impulsive vocabulary appeared to be limited, and his choice of wording was at best bombastic, making it ripe for criticism.

One of literally hundreds of typical examples came from his comments over the people who kneeled for the National Anthem. He referred to the kneelers as "sons of bitches." I have heard that idiom used thousands of times in my life, and have even used it myself with great regularity. The media chomped on it like a rabid dog, and twisted its intent to indict Trump for his racist rant that called Black mothers of kneeling football players bitches. While I cannot with 100 percent certainty state that no one ever used that phrase with the intent as claimed by the media, I feel confident that the vast majority did not.

So, the battle was repeated daily for four exhausting years. As time went on, the feud intensified almost to the point of complete and utter idiocy. Every joke was taken out of context to malign and discredit the president, and he dug in and claimed the press was the enemy of the people. While that statement on its face feels outrageous, there is no question that the dishonest journalism devolved to an unprecedented low. In many ways, it felt like one of the last scenes in *Rocky* – with the two fighters beaten bloody, but both refusing to fall. Unfortunately, in the real-world scenario there was no bell to end it.

A Man Full of Flaws

With Trump's apparent inability to consider any sort of concession of wrongdoing or misstatements, his lavish defenses enraged the media and others who found him offensive. While I can understand his hesitancy, I believe public opinion would have favored him if he had admitted his missteps. I believe that the media and opposition would have piled on the criticism even deeper and wider than before; but had he risen above it rather than slogged through it, I believe the results would have been more advantageous. I see it as a missed opportunity.

While I found Trump's bravado revolting, the results he and his team delivered were incredible. He arguably had the greatest record of any presidency of my lifetime. It is an odd paradox that probably one of the most controversial presidents oversaw one of the best presidencies. The fact that Trump was able to accomplish what he did with a constant shroud of fabricated scandal besieging him is extraordinary. The most outrageous case was the Russian accusations. Most people would agree that he was exonerated; but he endured the accusations for years and they continue in some circles to this day.

Many in the media were lying in wait for any inkling of some sort of information that would tarnish the presidency. When a rumor was circulated there was no vetting – there was no fact checking. In fact, almost every principle of journalistic ethics was cast aside as the deeply partisan press core shrieked in jubilation. When negative rumors were found to be false, the silence from the media was deafening. Like a wounded animal, they would cower in the corner, awaiting a tasty bit of innuendo to reinvigorate their passions of hatred.

Trump's accomplishments were noteworthy and spanned a wide spectrum. Many in the media have created false impressions – and while they are entitled to their own opinions, they are not entitled to their own facts. The most outrageous example of distortion involves Trump's handling of the economy. In the view of any person who is looking through an unbiased lens, the accomplishments, pre-COVID, were nearly unprecedented. I will not list them here, but the facts remain. It was an economy where almost everyone won. When COVID debilitated the world economy, it took a huge toll on our country as well. Partisans attempted to paint a picture of a failed economic plan, and that was likely one of the more disgusting displays of dishonest behavior ever in our history.

The Once-in-100-Years Scourge Leads to Defeat

In Trump's handling of COVID, a significant number of mistakes were made. In my view, the biggest was Trump's refusal to wear a mask, with many of his team following suit. I saw that as a dangerous and disgraceful failure of leadership. To be fair, we must remember that many in the science and medical community advised us not to wear masks, so there definitely were mixed messages in play throughout the initial months of the crisis.

Never in my lifetime has the medical and science community been more wrong. This is not an indictment of them in general, but an acknowledgement that many mistakes were made. Such is the reality when dealing with the unknown. Much like a military theater of operations, the dynamic nature of the virus created chaos. The constantly changing information made it almost impossible for government officials to be consistently correct. However, when the recommendation came out that masks should be worn, Trump and his team should have worn masks as a matter of effective leadership. Inexplicably, he refused, further dividing the country.

At the same time, in a classic case of hypocrisy gone wild, the politicians and media who wore masks on camera and demanded that the population do the same (while condemning Trump) were regularly shown to be maskless when they thought the cameras were not rolling. Trump's mask policy was indeed ill-advised; but all can agree he was not a hypocrite on the matter.

The other major misstep was much more understandable. In an attempt to quell fear, Trump repeatedly made statements that turned out to be false. Placing a positive spin on reality is not anything new. During WWII, Churchill and Roosevelt regularly rallied their citizenry with unsubstantiated claims. It is called crisis leadership, and it is an effective tool to motivate and reassure. When hope is lost, disastrous consequences usually follow, as those impacted simply lose their will to fight. Where Trump made his mistake was his refusal to concede that he had been wrong. Most citizens would have welcomed the honesty and candor.

I believe that the COVID virus emanated from a lab in China, and a growing number of experts are coming to share that view with each passing day. Many feel it was an intentional act, while most believe it was released by accident. We will likely never know the truth. What we do know is that the Chinese government covered up details about the virus, costing millions of lives. In a display of borderline-treasonous hate speech, many spun the lie that the blood of the dead COVID-infected Americans was on Trump's hands. I imagine that Beijing marveled at the rhetoric.

While many mistakes were made in the handling of the COVID pandemic, there were many significant successes. Partnering with industry was one significant win, which allowed unprecedented, rapid development of the vaccines. Depending on whose version of the truth you believe, it was accomplished between three to ten times faster than considered possible.

The Accomplishments Continued

Trump's work on prison reform was also impressive. Even though his policies overwhelmingly benefited minorities, Trump's reward was to be regularly condemned as a racist. The term "racist" has become so ubiquitous, and for many it has lost all relevance. It has become nothing more than a virtual whip to punish the populace. Many of

Trump's other accomplishments could be viewed through multiple lenses, and as such – depending on your perspective – were very good or very bad. I will share a few and provide my perspective on why I think they were so important.

His most controversial work was on immigration reform. Interestingly, views on the topic of immigration illustrate how the crafting of words makes so many people suspicious of the motivations of others. We have laws on the books that determine the legality of a person's residency in the United States. Since millions are in violation of immigration laws, they are actually illegally in the country. Some, apparently comfortable with laws being broken because they disagree with the laws, just refer to those people as undocumented. While there may be plenty of sympathetic rationale for immigrants breaking the law, their activity remains illegal.

Trump's economic success became an enticement for hundreds of thousands to attempt to enter the country illegally. However, his strident policy was helpful in curbing the activity, and construction of the wall he promised was another triumph. It is hard to estimate how many young girls and boys were spared lives of cruelty and abuse through Trump's border controls, but there is little doubt that the efforts curbed sex trafficking dramatically. The border security also deterred illegal drugs from entering the country – drugs that kill our citizens at an epidemic rate.

Removal of the United States from the extraordinarily dangerous Paris Climate Accord was another hotly contested Trump achievement, as was the reduction of regulations that allowed the United States to become energy independent for the first time in a half a century. The Paris Climate Accord might have been the most asinine agreement ever contemplated. Allowing China and India to remain essentially unencumbered in their use of fossil fuels for 20 years while saddling others with debilitating commitments is not only terrible for the environment, it is devastating to national security. One of the facts that never gets discussed is the relevance of pollutants emitted from the use of a unit of fossil fuel. Due to superior environmental policies in place in the European Union and the United States, among others, a unit burned in those countries emits far less pollutants than the same unit burned in China. Adding costly regulations and limiting use of fossil fuels in the U.S. and Europe will shift a higher percentage of fossil fuel usage to countries like China that use suboptimal systems. That would create a more toxic global environment. Moreover, the shift of manufacturing to China will only serve to strengthen its economy and provide the Chinese with more power and influence on the world stage. Both developments are dangerous for the United States and the world – possibly with fatal consequences.

If one is willing to be equitable, Trump's accomplishments abound; it is worthwhile to research some unbiased accounts of his administration. In fairness, many of Trump's specific feats could be viewed differently when examined through an opposing lens. One example might be Trump's ability to get the USMCA (United States-Mexico-Canada Agreement) passed. If I were a Mexican national, I would categorize that development as negative as compared to its predecessor NAFTA. The North American Free Trade Agreement was a significant benefit to Mexico and its economy. The United States Department of Labor has certified that 950,000 US jobs were lost due to NAFTA; other accounts would state the number as much higher.

By far, one of Trump's most astounding accomplishments was the work on Middle East peace. In a brilliant strategic move, he changed the rules of the game. For decades, it was believed that the Palestinians would need to be courted for any possibility of progress. Trump simply outflanked them and removed them from the mix. Provided that Trump's work is allowed to stand, the world could see previously unimaginable progress in the near future.

Bitterly Divided

As a final commentary on Trump's presidency – after he was elected, we were assured that there would be a nuclear war, because Trump was too unhinged to manage our arsenal. Nothing could have been further from reality. In fact, he defeated the ISIS caliphate and over-saw four years of relative peace, with almost no outside terrorist activity in our country. Amazingly, the president we were told to fear led the most peaceful four years (in terms of military conflict) that many can remember.

Ironically, internal citizen-against-citizen conflict exploded. With the exception of the Civil War era, never has there been so much division and hatred in our country – and Trump needs to take his share of the blame for his role in the bitterness. That noted, the constant false attacks he endured will probably alter the presidency forever. Two partisan impeachments, with the second possibly having some merit but rushed through without regard for any Constitutional consideration, have opened the door for others to follow. Our political class considered putting a private citizen on trial for conduct that they saw as unfit.

In many ways, it appears that any time the opposing party has the majority in the House, impeachment will be a risk. The Republicans were discussing articles of impeachment for Joe Biden before he had even taken office. But it is worth remembering that a number of Democrats did the same before Trump's first day in office.

A Voice for the Voiceless

It is amazing that so many are shocked that Trump is a hero to so many others. Most of our elite class, whose voices have dominated the public square for decades, find it incredulous. For as long as I can remember, there has been talk about the silent majority. Now, unwilling to raise their voices themselves, Trump spoke for them.

That massive group of patriotic Americans – the ones who send their sons and daughters to war to defend the country – seek safety, fairness, and the ability to live their lives unencumbered. They finally had their voice heard. They simply want to see a better world for their children than the one they inherited. Many – either immigrants themselves, or descendants of immigrants – know too well the past horrors of life outside of the United States. They believe that the United States of America is unequaled as an ideal.

They believe that all immigrants should be welcomed, but only through a fair system that does not allow cheaters to skirt the law and then be rewarded. They want their jobs to stay in the country, and not be shipped off to forigen lands for the sake of corporate profits. They know that a dangerous world requires a strong America to keep the peace.

I have yet to meet anyone who embraces all of the tactics employed by Trump, but his uplifting message exhilarated them. Trump, with his flaws acknowledged, gave them something they never thought possible – a voice. He became the voice for the forgotten men and women who are the heart and soul of the country.

We Watched in Shock

It would be a gross injustice not to cover January 6, 2021. Trump rallied a large assembly of his supporters in Washington in an attempt to challenge an election that he believed was stolen. A small percentage of the protestors became rioters and breached the Capitol. The activity cannot be justified under any circumstances; but like an old 1950s record that you have heard many times, the media and political class amped up the rhetoric to paint it as an insurrection that threatened the Republic. As awful as it was, it did not rise to the level of a coup or revolution. A handful of protesters – who did not brandish guns or any other meaningful weaponry – rushed the Capitol and, facing very little resistance, gained unlawful entry to the House chamber. One protester even took a seat in the Speaker's chair.

I am not justifying the action; but as inauguration day approached, we witnessed National Guard soldiers sourced from every state in the union assigned to protect the Capitol in unprecedented numbers – they had been educated that the enemy is their fellow citizens. Other than the Civil War, this is likely the most outrageous example of state-sponsored action against a segment of our citizens in our history.

Opinions run the gamut, but I believe most people would say that Trump's actions were, at best, ill-advised and that his legacy will likely be tarnished as a result. Since politicians and the media now write most of the history books, Trump will likely be treated very unfairly. I see that as tragic. With all of his blemishes acknowledged, he gave a voice to millions of forgotten men and women, and it should be recognized and chronicled accordingly. Indeed, as President Biden has predicted, a dark winter approaches – sad times, to be sure.

Chapter 6

The Path Forward: Calling Culture Warriors

★ ★ ★ ★ ★ ★

WHEN I IMAGINED THIS book in my mind, I thought it would become an inspiring tome of hope and promise. It was to be the story of living a life of abundance, the life that God wants for all his children. I fervently believe that all of that is possible and likely probable; but as I surveyed the current environment, and as I searched my inner being, I realized that we are at a precipice – a true tipping point.

Once upon a time, in a place just like this one, only a few decades ago, we were mostly an aligned people. Generally, our enemies were known to us: Iran, North Korea, China, and Russia. While Communism was still an orthodoxy that most considered a threat, it had been supplanted by radical Islam as the primary danger.

Today, bitterness has blinded our citizenry. We see two (or more) factions within our own nation that threaten our very existence. So vile has the rhetoric become, that we see our leaders categorizing significant segments of our population as enemies. In doing so, those leaders offer aid and comfort to our true enemies. Stop and think about how destructive this ideological battle has become.

The path forward will not be an easy one, but the strengthening and protection of a country so ordained by God is worthy of our efforts and dedication. It will take a herculean effort, but the stakes are so high that we must try. I will never advocate for violence as we move forward. Violence will solve nothing, and only serves to widen the chasm. The rule of law must be maintained, and if we do not like the law, we should seek to have the laws changed. To be successful, we must align around a common message and call to action. I refer to this message as, **Wake Up**, **Speak Up**, **Step Up**. In the pages that immediately follow, I will describe the elements of this vital plan and the issues that are the impetus for the plan.

Wake Up

Unless you have analyzed what has transpired over the past year, you may not have noticed that there is an omnipresent threat to our civil liberties. While trampling the Constitution, authoritarians have placed undue regulations upon the population without regard to the rule of law. Under the guise of public health, and throughout the pandemic, they have selected winners and losers based on their political ideology. Churches have been shuttered, while abortion clinics have been left open unimpeded. Gatherings of more than 10 have been forbidden, while rioters in groups of thousands have been enabled by our leaders' silence. Not surprisingly, as one ideology feels empowered, their representatives have engaged in an infringement of free speech. They have been self-selecting the criteria without consideration of a bit of equity. Their discriminatory practices censor some speech, citing that it is hate-filled and dangerous, while allowing equally and often more inciteful speech to remain unfettered.

Regardless of your ideology, all of this should petrify you. In a world of "what's in it for me" beliefs, one side cheers while the other shrieks. Unfortunately, the political winds blow two ways, and today's celebration might become tomorrow's anguish. Further, as restricted speech provides cover for those with evil intent, the specter of a hidden agenda looms in the shadows. You might be okay with them cancelling the president, but when your son or daughter is denied employment – or worse, imprisoned – because their speech is restricted by an anonymous tribunal, you might feel differently.

During times of crisis, the line between 'truth and lie' often blurs, as do the gradients of right and wrong. Retired General Stanley McChrystal is publicly comparing Trump supporters to al-Qaeda and referring to them as the enemy. Michael Beller, legal counsel for PBS, is recommending that children of Trump supporters be taken from their families and placed in re-education camps. These are not extremist crazies. These are notable people who have influence and power, but who are so blinded by their own disdain for their fellow citizens that they have become unhinged. While it appears unlikely that any of that vile rhetoric will take hold, the silence of opposition to such disgusting commentary is deafening. Every fair-minded American should be screaming from the rafters. Silence is acceptance – and if unchallenged, that type of extremist mindset seeps into the category of normalcy.

Racism – a Slippery Slope

Racism has been a hotly contested issue for my entire life. Hatred between groups of people from different ethnic backgrounds has been occurring since Biblical days. In United States history, racism usually refers to Caucasian and Black race relations. The abomination that was slavery is a blemish on the history of this country – one we cannot forget. The segregation that followed was yet another tragic chapter in our history.

On a percentage basis, our poverty problem tends to impact Black Americans more than it does white Americans. The limited opportunities during segregation placed Blacks at a significant disadvantage. This certainly has played a role in the economic disparity we experience between the races. However, despite these truths, fanning the flames of acrimony and further dividing the country along racial lines is extremely dangerous.

Most of my life has been filled with government programs that are targeted to make up for the injustices perpetrated upon Black people over our history. Most of those programs have had the opposite effect of their intention, and racial tensions have risen as a result. Amazingly, our leaders fail to recognize that we have a generational poverty dilemma that is much more disturbing than our racial one. Poverty knows no race – it is color-blind, and it is debilitating. When well-intended programs are structured to favor Black people, under-privileged whites become enraged and they lash out. In no way am I justifying their anger or actions. I am stating it as a fact.

Having never been Black, I have no idea what it is like. I have had many close friends who are Black, and I have experienced multiple awkward moments in their presence. Most of these moments have been caused by individuals attempting to reach out and failing miserably in the endeavor. A fear of being seen as insensitive through their silence creates genuinely uncomfortable situations.

Still, we hear other stories of true racial hostility that assure us that there remain fringe elements within the country who truly hate the other race. We have experienced plenty of examples in both directions. There is evil in the world, and all of those hatemongers would fall into that category. No one knows what is in another's heart except that person and God. We cannot say with certainty that a person is racist, nor can we know their motivations. I do think there are a great deal of racial biases, but those biases do not necessarily rise to the level of racism.

If we are honest, the rhetoric of our leaders makes most of us uncomfortable. I suspect that my reputation will be sullied for raising the topic; but the deterioration of race relations is far too injurious to our future, and the topic must be addressed. In just the past few years, the myth of systemic racism has spread throughout our nation, and it is bolstered by the vicious lie known as white privilege. It is an epidemic – a virus so much more deadly than COVID-19. It poisons the minds of all who hear it. If one repeats a lie loud enough and often enough, people tend to believe it. Our youth become brainwashed and they lash out in anger, hating the country that has provided them everything. Our youth take to the streets, waving Soviet Union flags that symbolize an indictment of our country, while youth in Hong Kong and Japan rally around the American flag as a beacon of hope. This may indeed be the paradox of our lifetime; meanwhile, the waiting list to enter the United States balloons.

Racism is a significant issue in America – and sadly, a growing one. The constant drumbeat of accusations is, in actuality, inflaming a significant part of the population until ill feelings toward our fellow man develop. We must remember that this growing scourge is not the fault of people with different skin color or nationality, but rather the responsibility of the purveyors of lies and accusations, who seek to gain power and divide the country.

Martin Luther King Jr. said, "I've decided to stick with love; hate is too great a burden to bear." When he was assassinated, a justifiably angry Alveda King admitted that she wanted to blame all white people. Unimaginably, at only 17, she had lost her uncle – a civil rights icon. But she said that her father consoled her, saying, "White people did not kill your uncle, the devil did."

My heart cries out for leaders of such stature; there are so few remaining. Hope has been supplanted by rhetoric that fuels hate. Talk of love and peace has been supplanted by cries of, "No Justice, No Peace."

Winnowing Through the Emotion

The Merriam-Webster dictionary defines racism as follows: *a belief that race is a fundamental determinant of human traits and capacities and that racial differences produce an inherent superiority of a particular race.* Recite that definition a few times in your head and remember it, as it will likely be altered to reflect the activities currently afoot. Stating that one race of people commits more crime than another is not racist, if indeed it is a statement of fact. Following that logic, if you question a person of a certain ethnic group while investigating a crime, that act does not make you racist. You may indeed be a racist, but the mere act alone should not be an indictment.

We all have biases, and when the news is filled with an outrageous story, most make some judgments that regularly turn out to be wrong. A shooting in a bar is widely assumed to be of the hand of an Islamic terrorist until we learn that it was a jealous boyfriend. There were 3,261 shootings in Chicago in 2020 and 769 homicides. Most of the victims were Black, but we hear barely a peep from our leaders, who appear hapless and helpless. Chicago's numbers are up almost 50 percent from the previous year; it is a terrible tragedy, but it just does not get much attention. It seems beyond comprehension that such an epidemic of death is left mostly underreported and unaddressed. Reasonable minds should agree that this cannot stand.

The factors leading to this reality are complex, and it would be unjust to attempt to offer overly simplistic reasons or solutions. However, one major contributing factor is generational hopelessness. Hopelessness is not a malady owned by any race; rather, it is owned by all who believe the system is rigged against them. Our leaders promise solutions – solutions that never come – in exchange for loyalty at the ballot box. When a person feels hopeless, leaders reassure them that it is not their fault as the system is rigged against them. That is simply a panacea that crushes the spirit and rips their God-given optimism from them.

A House Divided Cannot Stand

On June 16, 1858, Abraham Lincoln delivered the now-famous speech that included the line, "A house divided against itself cannot stand." He was speaking of the decision to allow states to choose whether to permit slavery. The speech was so controversial that many of his friends encouraged him not to deliver it. Imagine an America with some states allowing slavery. Slavery is abhorrent in any view now, but it was an issue that was hotly debated at that time.

Lincoln lost his bid for the Senate for suggesting that slavery should be stopped. Inspired from scripture, Matthew 12:25 and Mark 3:24, the notion seemed almost revolutionary at the time. The decision to end slavery divided the country and resulted in a bitterly-fought war, killing over 600,000. That amounted to 2 percent of the country's population.

Today, our leaders are intentionally dividing us over something that cannot be changed – our heritage and skin color. I come from Czechoslovakian, English, and Scottish descent. No law nor outside influence can change that fact. There are countless vital topics on which we can disagree, debate and ultimately solve. Skin color and heritage is not one of them. Our leaders seem to have forgotten history and have opted to highlight the unalterable. In doing so, they make something that is unsolvable the defining issue of our times. Apparently incapable of addressing root causes, our leaders stoke an eternal fire, and are creating a division that cannot be reunified. The potential outcomes of this dangerous activity will most assuredly weaken our country. In the end, our standing is indeed in question.

Family and the Lessons Learned

I was born into a lower, middle-class family. My father's chronic illness when I was a small child strained the family finances. Cardboard was placed in the bottoms of shoes when the soles gave out, and receiving hand-me-down clothing was a welcome event. My parents always assured me that better days lay ahead; they taught me that just by being born in this great land, I would have every opportunity I would ever need. Through hard work I could rise to any position – even to president. I was instructed to respect and honor the police and other leaders. Even though my parents differed in political views, we were taught to revere the president with no exceptions.

Equipped with that education, I persevered through many tragedies. The more desperate a situation appeared, the stronger was my resolve to push through to a successful conclusion. It is certainly unfair to compare my upbringing with those of the chronically and generationally impoverished. However, the proper messaging from parents and political leaders today would go a long way to bring hope to the downtrodden. A hand up beats a hand out every day.

A Cruel Brainwashing

Returning to the current crisis, there is a strong movement afoot to require our children to be taught a new history and a revised thematic view of themselves and their families. If your child is Caucasian, they will be instructed in the theory of white privilege and will be urged to repent for their whiteness. Known broadly as Critical Race Theory, it over-dramatizes and sensationalizes some of our socioeconomic issues. The theory creates an untenable situation where self-loathing is encouraged. I cannot think of a more cruel or psychologically-damaging falsehood for our children and grandchildren to endure.

Further, with the number of biracial babies tripling in the last 30 years, and with that trend expected to continue, we should expect some significant confusion in the future. For example, if I am the product of a white and black union, am I to hate half of myself and pity the other half? We need to educate ourselves on this issue and other related issues, so we can discuss them intelligently and without emotion. Critical Race Theory is a real and present danger to our country's future.

Unbridled Power Left Unchecked

Historically, the press has been one of the key arbiters of truth. Once representatives of a noble industry, reporters' innate curiosity drives them to seek the truth wherever the story leads. It is generally considered a certainty that, over the years, most journalists have exhibited some bias and that some of their stories were likely motivated through personal prejudices. Joseph Pulitzer put it best: "The power to mould the future of the Republic will be in the hands of the journalists of future generations." That means that the press has the capacity to tell the populace how to think. Educating the population is a virtuous endeavor, which is why the press is so vital to our future.

Tragically, the vast majority of today's journalists exhibit biases that are so blatant and so bigoted that it renders them very dangerous. Since almost all in the traditional media have moved so far to the left and have become cheerleaders for left-wing causes, we have seen an emergence of far-right media outlets. Unfortunately, they appear to have taken an approach of fighting fire with fire, rendering their viewpoints as ineffective and dishonest as those of their opposing colleagues. We all love to hear stories that support our deeply-held value systems, but it does us little good to get swept up in the excitement that fawning words elicit. Only by sorting through all the opinions and biases to get to the real story do we find growth and become more educated.

Recently, I was reading an article that appeared to have some interesting facts within its content, but then the authors shifted into a dishonest oratory that attempted to convince the reader that suspect theories are facts. In the article, the authors claimed that President Trump had spread lies for weeks that the election was tainted, and that he incited a riot. With nearly half the population believing that skullduggery was afoot, it cast a shadow over the election results. Others claimed that Trump's speech had no impact on what happened at the Capitol. The authors were overtly attempting to influence the reader in what became an opinion piece.

There is no question that suspicious activity abounded in the days leading up to the election, and in the days after. While I do not know if the election was free and fair, I believe that reasonable people would want a few basic questions answered. When people act in a certain way to cover up actions, there is cause to be concerned. Trump's speech on January 6 was ill-advised; moreover, I believe he could or should have known that it would trigger a potential unintended action. That noted, I do not believe he intentionally set out to incite a riot, as the article claimed.

Although it is a belabored point, it is vitally important. As the history books are written, it is essential that they are not tainted, or that future generations are educated with a lie. It is true that history is written by the winners, but in this historic situation, we are witnessing an unprecedented example of what I would classify as poor winner syndrome. Not satisfied with the victory, the victors appear intent on crushing the defeated.

Modern-Day Monopolies

Big Tech may now be the most powerful force in the world. Protected from scrutiny by laws safeguarding their companies, passed by politicians who feast on their donations, Big Tech firms have the ability to control almost every aspect of our lives. Sadly, they are mostly run by ideologues who have a globalist view. They seem content with their companies profiting from goods resulting from the labor of children forced into work camps in foreign lands. They appear to have no issue with the brutality of hate-filled policies prevalent in those lands that execute or reprogram dissenters, force those from religious groups into internment camps, and allow environmental atrocities to occur unchallenged. One of the most severe examples is the treatment of the Uyghur population and other mostly-Muslim ethnic groups in the northwestern region of Xinjiang at the hands of the Chinese government.

At the same time, Big Tech leaders feign moral outrage over activities with which they disagree. Asking biological men to use a specific bathroom is viewed as a heinous act, while state-sponsored forced child labor is unopposed. It is an unthinkable double standard, allowed to thrive by our acquiescence. Google, Twitter, and Facebook have influence over our activities and our thinking, as we unwittingly give them admission to our words, thoughts and deeds. Speech that they find objectionable is promptly removed from their platforms, while other more divisive commentary is allowed to remain, according to their ideology. If you own a smartphone, computer, or other internet connected device, you have most assuredly allowed them entry into your life. I am also guilty as charged, because I find myself unable or unwilling to inconvenience myself.

Initially lulled into compliance by the marvel of technology, we have become addicted to it. Never contemplating that it would be used to control every aspect of our lives, we revel in the delight of the convenience it offers. "Too much of a good thing" is the beginning of an old adage, as is "Be careful what you ask for." We find ourselves with no clear pathway forward. It is a dangerous slippery slope, and we are all skidding downhill.

Great Educators in a Flawed System

Becoming an educator is another admirable profession. Usually underpaid and underappreciated, most of our teachers are to be lauded for their commitment. Equipping our children with the tools they need to live lives of abundance and compete at the apex of their abilities cannot be overstated. Tragically, our education system is deeply flawed. Influenced by decades of ideological dogma, it has become marginalizing. Far too much emphasis is placed on educating our children according to the ideals of those in charge of the education system.

Once, our children were taught the building blocks of "reading, writing and arithmetic" – to use an often-repeated phrase. Schools focused on civics and history, while ensuring that our children received a balanced education through the addition of the arts and physical activity. Every student understood why our republic's governance was superior to any other in the world at that time, or throughout history.

Today, those leading our educational system have created a system that poisons our children's minds through the rewriting of history. Once, we celebrated the founding of our country by Christopher Columbus, citing the fact that he embarked on a dangerous journey and ended up in the Americas. All of that is true, but today's history vilifies Columbus as a bloodthirsty murderer who set forth to destroy the lives of indigenous people. It is appropriate to engage in a discussion of the implications of colonization on the land; however, to present an extreme view promotes an aura of self-loathing. That is catastrophic to our children.

Revisionist history is but one example of the malevolence repeatedly driven into our children's tender minds. Celebrations of amoral behaviors, political hate speech, and fabrications about race relations are taught repeatedly, molding our children into a compliant flock that can be much easier controlled as they become adults.

When I was a student, I was subjected to a theoretical program that suggested that we not grade children's work from A to F. Those letters were supplanted by pluses, checks, and minuses. In my view, that program did little damage, as we all knew a plus was an A, a check was a C, and a minus was an F. Though uncertain, I seem to recall check-pluses and check-minuses added into a broader system.

The program was ended, as it was later determined to be asinine. No real harm done. I wish the theoretical programs of today were so simplistic and unimpactful.

As our children migrate into adulthood, many end up attending colleges and universities that are ideological think tanks, masked as centers of higher education. Degrees such as gender studies fuel the fires of division, failing to prepare our youth to compete in the real world. Such programs leave the students in significant debt and angry over a system that let them down.

Conservatives left the field of education years ago, making it ripe for a sociopolitical hijacking; the system now exchanges education for idealism. It is an idealism that jeopardizes the future of the nation, sucking out the lifeblood of patriotism and injecting perfidy in its place.

The True Tragedies Go Underreported

The true tragedy is the fixation on racism, transgender rights, and the type of straw we drink from, and the false belief that these are the most important issues of our day. By emphasizing those topics, much more dire concerns are unreported or underreported. Statistics tell us that within an hour of you reading this sentence, five baby girls will be born in the United States who will suffer the terror of sexual abuse before they turn 18. During that same hour, two girls will suffer the horrors of being sex trafficked and seven people will die of an overdose. Also in that same hour, one veteran will take his or her own life. Within four hours, a child will die because of abuse.

Homelessness is at an epidemic level. The mental health crisis is growing. There appears to be no end to generational poverty. None of the atrocities mentioned in the previous three paragraphs relate specifically to race, creed, sexual orientation, or color.

Just as the Rev. Alfred Daniel Williams King counseled his daughter, the devil is to blame; we have an awesome responsibility to wake up and act. Responsibility is two words in one: response and ability. We have the ability, so what is our response?

I do not intend to discount the importance of focusing on equality for all and on the environmental issues of our day, but when they steal the focus from other issues that are as important or more important, it feels away from goodness. It is hard to understand how the use of plastic straws can supplant the abuse of a little girl as an important issue of our day.

While I have focused on examples of domestic issues so far, on the international stage there is an extraordinary collection of dangerous events that threaten our very existence. We are so busy focusing on our disdain for each other that the distraction puts us in great peril. The fiery words in this section were carefully selected to emphasize the importance of this moment in history. I urge you to become educated on the issues and to form your own opinions. While the situation is dire and requires all our attention, it is not hopeless.

It is time to wake up, and wake up we must. The time is now, and now is the time.

Speak Up

Speaking up falls into three categories. The first category is persuasion, which is the art of gently nudging people's perspective through conversation. No one ever persuaded another with an opposing viewpoint by threatening, mocking or provoking them. Simply stated, those tactics are not effective if our objective is to foster unity. Sadly, we are immersed in an environment where we see that kind of approach repeated ad nauseum by our political leaders. While negative rhetoric is effective for rallying the base supporters, it leaves a significant segment of the population angry or afraid – often, a mix of both.

Admittedly, this book is packed with fiery language and might leave many readers wondering how to square the seemingly incongruous messages. My language has been carefully crafted to highlight a tiny segment of the population that lights the matches that stoke the fire of division. My quarrel is not with the people with whom I disagree, but rather with those who spin the truth to unjustly create chaos. It is the Saul Alinsky acolytes that I find so objectionable. If you are unfamiliar with the scourge that was Mr. Alinsky, I invite you to learn more about him and his tainted ideology.

An Approach Based in Self-Awareness

We should always look in the mirror and reflect upon how we would react to the opposer, if he or she seeks to inflame us. We need to adopt a standard of discovery where we can have a true dialogue that leads to learning. Most of our conversations should start by being prepared to listen. It is easy to say – but much harder to follow. By listening, we can explore areas for common ground and begin to build some bridges for our journey.

We also need to commit to asking questions and to be prepared for answers that may make us a bit uncomfortable. Take, for example, the George Floyd death. Many are confident that Mr. Floyd was killed by the police officer simply for the "crime" of being Black. Others see him as a criminal, whose unfair treatment by police led to his death. Still others think that Mr. Floyd's death was due to an overdose of drugs. With many opinions so hotly held, there is a significant risk for an unproductive outcome from a conversation on the topic.

How did we get here? It appears that the recent wave of dissent began with the death of Michael Brown. Initially, we were assured by the media and many in our government that Michael Brown begged for his life on his knees with his hands up. The idea that such an incident could happen revolted all decent people. But soon, we learned that much of the story was contrived. A firestorm started after it was revealed that Mr. Brown refused to follow the officer's orders. He then lunged for the officer's gun, and was killed. It was a tragic event, but much more understandable when we learn the facts. None of those facts brings Mr. Brown back.

How do we discuss such an emotional topic? We need to start by asking questions. A logical first question for someone with an opposing viewpoint is, "Why do you feel the way you do?" We can then probe for clarity, and offer "what if" solutions.

Since the race issue is such a divisive one, I will continue to follow that track. We ask again: How did we get here? We must peel back the onion and search for root causes. My belief is that we have a generational poverty problem. That problem knows no race, creed, or color, and has no sympathy. It does impact Blacks as a higher percentage of the population – but there are millions of people from other races affected just as negatively. Why is that the case? We must acknowledge that our history has blemishes, and some of those blemishes have created an imbalance. For example, the segregation that occurred through the first two thirds of the last century placed a significant percentage of Black children at a distinct disadvantage. Educational opportunities were inferior for African Americans, as were many of the employment opportunities.

Worse yet is the underlying psychological damage that might understandably result in Black children feeling either inferior, or that there is little hope for a bright future. When those kinds of feelings creep into one's psyche, it can result in thoughts of hopelessness. Hopelessness, in turn, fuels anger. Anger blinds us, and the result is often that we focus all of our energy on anger, leaving little room for productive thoughts and actions. The fact remains that these feelings do not have a correlation to one race. We must forget the messages of "You cannot" or "The system is rigged against you" – they do nothing but add to the acrimony.

Those enduring generational poverty often see no way out, and as such, the patterns repeat again and again. Probably with good intentions, the government provides some support to the poor – but only up to a level that is neither mentally nor physically healthy. We must start a conversation that provides hope to those mired in poverty, along with a clear path forward.

First, we must stop identity politics. We need to talk to the poor as a group with the goal of lifting them out of their circumstance. Leaders must give the message that there is hope, and they should work tirelessly to eliminate the optimism-killing lies that give rise to so much anger. Messages are easily stated, and we have heard them hundreds of times. "Stay in school – do not do drugs – do not have children until you are in a healthy and productive relationship with two parents…" and on, and on, and on. It is easily stated, but extraordinarily difficult to instill. A great start is to transform the goal into a very personal mission instead of an anonymous program. I suggest a mentoring program that partners the impoverished with guides who will help them make more productive decisions.

Productive Communication

The second element of speaking up consists of talking with individuals and groups that are like-minded, imploring them to let their voices be heard. Before we can send a group of impassioned folks into the public square, we must educate them on the skill sets required to engage in difficult, yet productive, conversations. There are many volumes available that detail how to engage in productive conversations, and I urge you to seek them out.

Active listening includes asking questions and exploring areas of commonality. Questions designed to improve understanding are a good first step. Exploring possible resolutions is a logical next step. Once the issue is framed and potential solutions are explored, progress can be made. Good questions are, "Have you considered _____?" or, "Do you think _____ would help?"

It is important to repeat back what you hear – for two reasons. First, it is to ensure that you indeed understood the respondent's position. Second, equally important, it is so that the respondent feels that you care enough about their opinion to state it. Next, we can follow up with questions such as, "What would make it better?" or, "Would _____make it better?" Positive words will facilitate the tone and tenor of the conversation.

Should the conversation become heated, we can turn it around by using a few tactics. If there is total disagreement, we could say, "How fascinating? Please tell me more." Another approach could be to use the phrase "It feels to me..." prior to making a statement. Most reasonable individuals would not object to you voicing your feelings. In a matter of 10 minutes or less, we can determine if the topic is something that is addressable. If it is unaddressable, we could move to a different topic and state, "We can agree to disagree on that one." Adding a chuckle at the end usually keeps the conversation on track.

Body language is the unspoken part of communication that accounts for 50 percent of messaging. Over 40 percent is tone and tenor, with the actual words accounting for less than 10 percent. Having control over body language and keeping the tone and tenor positive are essential elements for productive conversations.

Educate Yourself

Becoming educated on how to use the tools for productive conversations is essential. Using those tools with a style that complements your personality will be most effective. Being genuine is the final element. Most people will sense a phony, and insincerity will turn them off when the conversation is covering issues that matter to them.

We may also interact with others who either are unaware of the issues at hand, or have not considered the issues important enough for their consideration. In those conversations, we will need to personalize issues where we seek productive engagement. If a person has children or cares for other young people, we can effectively introduce the consequences of inaction as they would relate to children. It is important to note that we are not attempting to use the topic of children as leverage, but rather to share a genuine concern for the welfare of children. For example, during the writing of much of this book, many schools have been closed for more than a year. Pointing out the damage that will do to our children's future comes from a true concern about their well-being.

Becoming world class communicators – equipped with the facts – will move the needle on public opinion and facilitate a solution. We should be careful to keep an open mind, as many of the best solutions come through collaboration with those with different views.

Casting an Informed Ballot

The third element of speaking up is casting an informed vote at election time, and doing so up and down the ballot. Frankly, I have been guilty of not paying enough attention to local governance, and now realize that – in many ways – local political leaders are far more powerful than I had ever imagined. We are witnessing a potential disaster, as local governments make ill-advised decisions that result in decreased public safety. Since most politicians will provide lip service, one needs to dig deeply into who they associate with and into what their core values are. A good example of a topic is open borders and the current fight for securing them. Frenzied rhetoric does little to facilitate a solution; we should all want illegal immigration to cease. We may disagree on the number of immigrants that we allow to enter, and which countries we should allow immigration from, but we all should want to curb the rampant sex-trafficking and dangerous drugs that pour in through our porous borders. Border security is a good bellwether issue about which to ask questions.

Most politicians engage in the same practices, so we are often left to select the lesser of two evils – a sad testimonial. We need to urge others to vote but only if they are able to cast an informed vote. There are many issues that plague our country, and there are good arguments on both sides. Carefully listening to the arguments and researching them to uncover true root elements of the issue is a tedious but essential task. We simply cannot trust our politicians or most members of the media to tell us the truth, so we must conduct the research ourselves. With the current climate of free-speech censorship, it is becoming harder to determine the facts so we can make informed decisions.

It is time to speak up and have your voices heard. It is a vital exercise that must be conducted through a process of informed debate, empathy and respect.

Step Up

Stepping up is a call for action. Each of us must be willing to do our part for the greater good – for the survival of the country. I recognize that may sound severe, and even a bit sensationalized, but I truly see us at a tipping point in history. Historically, our country has usually had a foreign enemy that has helped us unify around our own great land. Now – tragically – we see the enemy as each other, and our hatred for our brothers and sisters exceeds that for our true enemies.

In my lifetime, we had the Soviet Union, Red China, North Korea, and despots in the Middle East, among others, as common enemies. Today, the news barely speaks of any of those threats. Instead, the media opts to divide the nation – much to the delight of our enemies. Most of those nations or entities do not allow for internal dissent, so they can focus on the objectives that are in their best interests.

Certainly, the ability for us to debate and disagree is part of the freedom we have always enjoyed in our nation – but when it supplants national security, it becomes fatally damaging. This is the environment in which we find ourselves today. We are divided as a nation. Members of opposing parties do not even attempt to cover their revulsion for their opponents. They sow fear and division, implying that those who disagree are akin to criminals.

One of the biggest mistakes we make as a society is that we incorrectly assume that those from other cultures think as we do. When considering individuals from other cultures, we must be cognizant that there are both seen and unseen differences. The unseen differences of other cultures' customs and ideals can be compared to a towering tree with an equally extensive, underground root system.

For example, in most Asian cultures, there is a past-orientation culture; however, the United States is a future-orientation culture. Therefore, people from the United States inadvertently insult their Asian counterparts by discounting their rich traditions. Similarly, we wrongly presume that mothers in Islamic countries would be horrified if their children died in a suicide bombing, because that is how American mothers would feel. Quite the contrary, many mothers in those Islamic countries would see such an event as a significant honor for their child.

Stepping up means that we must make inroads into the areas of largest concern. There are a few avenues that will be effective.

Recapturing the Public Voice

Many conservatives gave up on the education system and journalism decades ago. Nevertheless, we must urge our youth to consider following paths into these fields. I see going into those fields as important as a call to the ministry or the missionary fields. Much of the current viewpoints that are threatening our country's future are based on atheistic principles. Historically, dictators eliminate God, and with His elimination goes hope. The absence of God renders the population more malleable and controllable, and expands the power of those in charge.

We must facilitate a government action that addresses the Big Tech monopolies. The Sherman Antitrust Act of 1890 addressed price-fixing and other atrocities undertaken by large monopolistic entities. However, in today's arena, we see Big Tech engaging in "thought-fixing." In my view, that is a far more dangerous practice. While politicians might be hesitant to act, due to the influence-peddling that is commonplace within government, we must support and elect individuals who will buck the trend and rein in those companies.

At the same time, we need to encourage future generations to infiltrate those entities and their successors, and to balance the hidden agendas that the companies promote. As similar spinoff companies emerge, we must have talented individuals – who share our vision of faith, family and freedom – prepared and ready to lead. Stepping up means we will take action that will send a clear message to any company who seeks to injure the United States: we will not tolerate such action. Companies such as Nike are the poster child for such malfeasance. They engage in hypocritical virtue signaling, feasting off the backs of people doing low-wage work in foreign lands to make goods for the U.S. market. These workers live under cruel and inhuman rule. Conditions in those countries would make even the most hardened of us wince if we truly examined the realities.

An Essential Investment

Finally, stepping up means investing your resources to help the effort succeed. Whether it be with money, time, prayer, or another available investment, we must push through to victory. It is my sincere hope that what we are seeing now is but a blip in the history of this great land. I hope that, as in the past, when the pendulum swung too far in one direction and then recovered, we will find a way to move it back toward the middle. Whether our time represents a historic paradigm shift that will send us into an abyss, or if we are merely experiencing a swing of the pendulum that is destined to return to the middle, the principles of Wake Up, Speak Up and Step Up remain of great value.

A fair question might be: how does all of this translate into you enjoying the fruits of a life of fulfillment? The answer is simple. In all of history, there has been no environment more ripe for a migration from fear to fulfillment than the United States of America. Freedom is not free, and neither is fulfillment. The decline of this great land and her ideals is the biggest external challenge we face. Protecting the United States is paramount.

THE BLOCKBUSTER

Introduction to

Book II

★　　★　　★　　★　　★　　★

BOOK II EXPLORES HOW the beliefs and principles outlined in Book I can play out in a life, through the sharing of vignettes from my life. Every family has a story; some families' stories are blockbuster movies. Most people underestimate the impact of family and the uniqueness of family stories – each is singular, and chock-full of memories, experiences and education. As sure as each snowflake that falls on a winter eve is unique, so is each person. Individuals, combined with others in their orbit, come together to create a distinct and unique cadre known as the family.

I have always been known as a storyteller. Friends and family members have bestowed ample compliments upon me for my ability to breathe life and humor into what they perceive as everyday events. I imagine each event as an extraordinary set of circumstances that can create one-of-a-kind explanations. I employ these rather ordinary occurrences to entertain, educate and excite. Many who have heard my "you cannot make this stuff up" stories marvel at my ability to weave a tale.

Still, I regularly endure listeners' challenges to stories as I tell them. My response is always, "It happened just that way." And often I add, "You do not need to fabricate when it is this good." One such story involved a woman's clandestine leg-lengthening surgery, performed in Cairo during Ramadan. A member of my audience questioned its credibility, but I produced the surgeon's X-rays of the procedure. I explained, "The woman wanted to be three inches taller." One of the other people there appeared to be genuinely perplexed, and addressed her colleague: "Of all the stories he told, you chose not to believe that one?"

My belief is that everyone has dozens of great stories, yet they fail to recognize them. I see that as an epic tragedy. Significant portions of my marvelous life are captured in such stories, and I delight in sharing them. Most families face struggles, and many have secrets. Mine is no exception. When I was younger, my parents referred to these stories as "the dirty laundry," and we were regularly counseled not to "air" it. I have since learned that the events that my parents found so horrendous were rather commonplace in other families. Every family has "**stuff**," and as my pastor likes to say, "Those who think they do not have stuff likely have **really bad stuff**."

Family is a word that extends beyond bloodlines. We can find the closeness of family in a church, at work, or in a social setting. Family connotes an intimacy and an alignment with many of the values we hold dearly. While we cannot select our blood family, we do select our chosen family – those people to whom we gravitate. A significant part of achieving fulfillment is finding those souls with whom we will share our lives.

The tales in Book II are woven into the fabric of my life. I invite you to experience how my everyday life encounters have helped my evolution *From Fear to Fulfillment,* and how God, my Dinosaurs, and our great land have enhanced my life story.

Chapter 7

The Dinosaurs

Our mentors are akin to loving potters who mold us into the people we become. With each purposeful action, they help create the blockbuster that becomes our life story.

W E ALL HAVE THOSE important people in our lives who contribute to our character development. I refer to those influencers as Dinosaurs, because the influence they bestow upon us is singular. When they pass away, their unique perspectives are lost to history, but their manifestations live on through our lives. It then becomes our task to carry forward their mission and perspective to the next generation. Who were your Dinosaurs? How did they bless you? Are you fulfilling your vital role as a mentor to the next generation?

God blessed me with many Dinosaurs on both sides of my family – and with another group who were not related by blood, but by value systems. My father had seven living brothers and sisters; six of them were married. They were 13 examples for a young lad to watch and emulate.

God's Salt on This Earth

My father's brothers and sisters were great people who, on the surface, lived rather ordinary lives. Dedicated to the principles of faith, they quietly went about living productive lives; yet, each left a distinct and indelible mark on me. I think all would agree that their collective legacy was their children, grandchildren, nephews and nieces.

My Uncle Mike was a gentle and reserved man. The eldest of the eight, he accepted the mantle of leadership, but managed to do so without a hint of dramatic bravado. He was an entrepreneur who owned and operated a Texaco gas station. He was the family fisherman; and he taught me much about the sport on trips that took us deep into the Canadian outback. Those trips were among the fondest memories of my teen years. They took us to islands miles from the nearest roadways – each one included rustic cabins, no electricity, and no running water. We awoke each morning eager to board our boat, and we ended each evening with a rousing card game that was illuminated by propane-fueled lanterns. *This is heaven on earth*, I mused each evening as I drifted off to sleep.

My Aunts Mary and Ann were the eldest of my father's sisters. They were so much older that their children were parenting children of their own who were nearly my age. They each had three children, and all six became extraordinarily successful. They were the pride of the family and included two very successful businessmen, a decorated Air Force pilot, a NASA scientist, a Washington beltway engineer, and a stunningly beautiful daughter, who – along with her brilliant husband – enjoyed an abundant entrepreneurial life. They embodied the American dream, and my father reveled in their success.

My aunts had deep convictions in their Byzantine faith and were ideal mentors. Their strong commitment to the Lord poured out of them with each action. I do not recall ever seeing either aunt exhibit any outward anger. These two bright lights were so similar that they lived within a block of each other, and I delighted in walking to and from their homes while visiting.

Even at a young age, I had already grown to love the family traditions. I believe they were hard-coded within me from birth. At age 9 or 10, when I boarded the bus bound for Cleveland, I was filled with anticipation. After a short half-hour ride to Garfield Heights, where both my aunts lived, the ritual could commence. It was just before Easter, and I had been offered the opportunity to help prepare for the annual Easter feast.

Easter was the most sacred event of the year. Preparations included the making of Hrudka, an Easter egg cheese. Its leftover liquid was used as the basis for the Paska, which is a delightful Easter bread. I was able to participate in the traditional preparations, and then we donned our dress clothes to attend Mass, where all the food would be blessed by the priest.

Both sisters were skilled in the art of lavishly decorating the eggs that would adorn the table on Easter morning. A single egg might take several hours to complete. Equipped with beeswax, a pin inserted into a thin wooden dowel rod, and a candle, my aunts' skilled hands and keen eyes would go to work. Each invisible stroke of the beeswax-laden pinhead would reveal beautiful art as the eggs were submerged in the various colors of dye. Excess wax was removed through the practice of candling, as the warmth of the flame returned the wax to a liquid state. Once the wax was removed, the process would begin a second time with another color, and the result would be a wonderful mosaic. Some eggs were done in one color, while others boasted four or five colors.

My parents, with my brother in tow, arrived in Garfield Heights on Sunday morning to a fully-prepared feast, steeped in tradition. All food was served cold – everything had been blessed – and we feasted on the bounty that had been prepared the week before.

During my childhood, this annual celebration of the risen Lord was so vital to the family that only a few ever failed to attend. It made a lasting impression on me; each year, 26 members of my generation (including spouses), along with their 14 parents, and a growing number of the next generation, all gathered for the sacrosanct occasion of Easter.

The men all wore dark suits with thin ties, and the women were attired in beautiful dresses. The event screamed reverence and tradition, and those two driving principles have served me well throughout my life. By the time I was an adult, the Easter gathering that had continued for over a generation had slowly slipped away, and was supplanted by an annual summer family reunion. That event transitioned into a once-every-five-years extended reunion that included my grandfather's siblings' descendants. Those people are now gone as well. It felt like the reunions simply vanished as the last members of the generation who had organized them passed into their eternal rewards. That once tight-knit group bolstered by faith and family has scattered as falling leaves might on a cool autumn day.

When I reflect upon those events, and on the souls that made them so special, I am deeply stirred by mixed emotions. I am filled with gratitude for having experienced such life-shaping gatherings; yet, I am disheartened that they disappeared with such little acknowledgment. Gone – just gone.

Stewardship and Sacrifice Personified

With the exception of my mother's brother, my mother's family all lived in their homeland of Canada. My Uncle John, both a medical doctor and an ordained priest, was called by the Lord to Liberia and resided there for 12 years. He spread the Word to a populace eager for hope and also provided important medical services. Due to his calling, we did not know him well, but he was the most respected and revered member of my extended family. The few times that I had the opportunity to visit with him, I found him to be quite insightful. A quiet man of faith, he followed strict spiritual disciplines. During one meal he ordered hot water to drink, and I questioned him. He believed that he needed to remove coffee from his daily ritual for a time, and the substitution of hot water was to remind him of his commitment during every meal.

Here was a man who might have followed a path of fame and fortune, but he chose to answer God's calling. So strong was his faith that he moved to Brockville, Ontario, and supported a Christian school there until his death. Anything that God has called me to do pales in comparison to the life's work of this extraordinary man. But his example has been a light that has illuminated my journey, even during the darkest stages.

My mother's sister, my Aunt Barbara, created the role of outspoken octogenarian in my family, and was an incredibly focused and disciplined soul. She was more set in her ways than anyone I have known. Rather opinionated, and with a sharp and sarcastic tongue, she let you know where you stood with her. Much like my mother, she was consumed with family tradition. Once you pierced the crusty exterior, you would discover an inner goodness ensconced within an ocean of kindness and wisdom. She was a skilled entertainer and the quintessential cook; she prepared lavish meals that were always served on china. The presentation normally exceeded the flavor, but the experience was always noteworthy.

Near her death, she asked that I accept some of her most prized family possessions and keep them for future generations to enjoy.

Among them was the cup and plate that my grandfather used to offer communion to the injured and dying soldiers on the battlefields of World War I and World War II. When I hold the set, I can feel the soldiers' sacrifice; it is a powerful reminder that freedom is not free. For his service, my grandfather was highly decorated – even receiving acknowledgment from King George VI.

Skills to Enhance the Journey

Aunt Lillian was not blood-related, but she was every bit as much of an aunt to me as the closest relative. She was of the generation before my mother, so she was a great-aunt to me. She, like so many of my elderly relatives, appeared like she had just emerged from a 19th-century play. She was a spinster, as they were known in that day, and she lived in what had been her father's home in Hamilton, Ontario, with her two sisters, Maude and Jessie. I recall the house having the feel of a museum, and I sat rigidly during every visit for fear of breaking something.

Aunt Lillian taught me to sew; she believed that it was a skill that every gentleman needed to master. Specifically, she felt that I should be able to make repairs on my clothes if necessary. At age 5, I spent hours hand-sewing pieces of fabric together and then sewed dozens of buttons on each. Hundreds of buttons were secured and later removed, as the practice was repeated again and again for good measure.

Lillian was also a bit of a pack rat, and she provided me with thousands of stamps from old correspondence that seeded my love for philately. As she winnowed through boxes containing memorabilia up to 100 years old, I was the regular recipient of a plethora of stamps and related trinkets. Upon her death, we inherited boxes that had yet to be sorted, and they became a treasure trove of historic delight.

Empathetic Leadership in Action

Meanwhile, at work, decades of grossly incompetent negotiations had resulted in unprecedented tension between management and the labor unions. So bitter was the relationship that it was common for management to use the contract language as a harsh cudgel to inflict justice. At the same time, the union employed different contract passages to disrupt operations. The situation was intolerable.

The first time I met Ralph, it was quite evident that he did not care for me. That was a significant problem, because he was my supervisor. He came to lead us during the time of strife between management and the unions, when financial losses placed the very future of the business at risk. In addition, we were all grappling with the death of our previous leader. Emotions were raw.

Ralph's reputation was one of a no-nonsense hard-charger, and his actions after assuming his position were a confirmation that he had earned the standing honestly. We were so afraid of him that we decided not to advise him that the solid grey, crew neck sweater he donned one day had a beautiful pattern. Regrettably, he had put the sweater on backwards and only those behind him could enjoy its beauty.

After months of favorable results, his hostility toward me seemed to ease up, and our frosty relations thawed a bit. Soon, I realized that this man was one to emulate. Comfortable in his own skin, he even laughed when I finally shared the then-months-old sweater story with him.

In Ralph, I found an inner goodness that contradicted his notoriety. In each action he took, empathy poured out. During a meeting with our Teamsters union, one of the drivers lamented that a tree next to the plant entrance had a branch that made exiting the plant in a tractor-trailer extremely unsafe. It was high and blocked the driver's view of the heavily-trafficked street.

Ralph took the time to survey the situation, and at 7AM the next day, the man who ran the entire operation revved a chainsaw and remedied the unsafe condition – all while wearing a suit and tie.

Fast-forward five years: I channeled him as I found myself scrubbing the urine-stained walls and floors of a workers' bathroom that was so disgusting that I found it unusable. Management, on the other hand, had its own facilities that were under lock and key. "Treat people like animals, and there is no limit to the disappointing behavior one can discover; treat them like men and women, and the potential is limitless," I advised management. I closed the management bathroom facilities, forcing a leveling of relations.

As one might imagine, despite Ralph's inner goodness, there was no easy solution to the company's struggles. Slowly, however, we made progress – and our efforts paid off with improving numbers.

Despite the fact that he was exhausted from the tumult, Ralph elected to host a holiday party in his home for all the management staff and their spouses. But it was not a company sanctioned event; rather, it was Ralph's personal outreach to the team of men and women who he had asked to labor so tirelessly. The party was unique, as there was none of the structure of typical corporate events. Instead, it felt more like a gathering of friends sharing a laugh.

After the holiday party, I witnessed a softening of tensions between competing department heads, which resulted in enhanced operations in the workplace. We went from being a collection of individuals who were focused on watching our own backs to a team that had each other's backs. "Selfish" evolved into "selfless." Following Ralph's example, I made similar parties part of my regular leadership style for the next three decades – with stunning results.

Twenty years later, a veteran employee was reassigned to work under my leadership. During his first annual review, he had the courage to admit to me that he had hated me for years. But then he said, "Now I get it, your team always wins because you turn them into winners."

I corrected him by saying, "Everyone's a winner; most just do not realize it. I simply convince people that they deserve to win, and they do the rest." The employee closed the review session by advising me that he loved working for me. That kind of feeling was made possible by adding a personal touch to our relationship. And a personal touch could start with something as simple as hosting an employee party, even though you are exhausted.

A year or so later, Ralph was reassigned, as was I. So close was our friendship that I made a two-hour trek to visit him at least once a month for the next year. He offered me sage advice that covered a wide range of vital topics. When I decided to make a career change, it was Ralph who guided me. We stayed in contact for another five years through phone calls and visits, but finally the years took their toll, and we lost touch. A decade later, I learned through a personalized Christmas card that he had died. I wept uncontrollably at the loss of a man who had reminded me that it is okay to be genuine, and that – regardless of position – treating every coworker with dignity and respect is an essential attribute of a great leader.

A Southern Gentleman Teaches Benevolence

More lessons came from a man I called Mr. Victor, out of respect. The first time I met him, he was seated at his desk. When he rose to greet me, I noted that his chair, although rather simplistic in its design, was beautifully crafted. A plain but exquisitely constructed structure corresponded to the character of the man who rested upon it. In fact, Mr. Victor's entire office was simply, but tastefully, decorated. On one wall was a picture of Ronald Reagan's first inaugural. It had been personalized to read, "Dear Vic, Thanks to you this moment was possible, Ron."

Mr. Victor was a man of great wealth and singular wisdom. He was the embodiment of a Southern gentleman and he dressed the part too, often sporting thin leather suspenders that he hooked his thumbs behind. I soaked in his Southern charm as he taught me the customs of the Deep South. He possessed a quiet confidence that was the perfect counterbalance to my more bombastic leadership style. Within weeks of our first meeting, I felt as if I had been adopted as a surrogate son, and we engaged in deep conversations on topics that ranged from politics to faith. Looking back, I doubt that there was a topic that was taboo.

He had sold his business to my new employer, and had secured office space and a small stipend for a five-year period. Having no direct responsibilities within the organization, he assumed a role as a mentor, and I marveled at the opportunity to learn from him. I soon made a deep connection with him. The fact that it was fostered in less than four months made it even more astounding. I met him in October and was reassigned to Long Beach, California, in January the following year; it felt like a whisper of time for such a lasting relationship to be cemented.

During my very short time living in Biloxi, some amazing life lessons were learned. One of my team members, Bridget, had worked for the company for a decade but succumbed to brain cancer very quickly. During my arrival in late October, there was no mention of any illness; however, by my departure in January, she was clinging on to the last vestiges of life.

At some point during that brief period, Victor called her into his office and asked me to join him. Bridget knew the end was near, and as a single parent, she was deeply worried for the welfare of her young son. Victor provided reassuring counsel, and concluded with a promise that her son would be educated in the finest schools possible. Moreover, a trust fund would be established for his benefit. It was an amazingly emotional moment, and I have always felt that her anguish was eased by Victor's great generosity. What greater gift can a person bestow upon one who is dying but a reassurance that a loved one will be cared for?

Mr. Victor and I stayed in close contact for another 15 years. Some personal strife in my own life precipitated a period of self-induced exile and I lost contact. I have attempted to reconnect, but to no avail. I suspect he would be close to 90 now, yet my mind still reflects upon his counsel. I am heartened by the memories of his advice.

God's Messenger In The Flesh

During my time working in corporate America, moving was a regular part of the progression up the corporate ladder. In fact, during a 10-year period, my family and I lived in nine houses in four states, and I was temporarily assigned in a fifth state. A move to northern Kentucky in 1994, a relocation that promised to be a longer-term assignment, was welcome.

As part of each move, I found myself church shopping. Normally, the search consisted of finding the closest church of my preferred denomination. This time was different. I was an executive, and had come to believe that an executive-style church was a requirement. Because of that, I passed the small wooden church structure not a mile from my home for months, never giving it a second thought.

Left uninspired and deflated after a fruitless search, I entered the structure on the corner, which was nestled in the heart of the village. There were less than 20 in attendance that day, and the thought of being conspicuous frightened me. Then, the pastor began his sermon, and I realized I was home. This was the place where I was destined to worship, and I did so for five years.

Every congregant became a close friend – we truly were the **Family of God**, and we even sang the second verse. To elaborate, for all of my life I had attended churches who had referred to Christians as the *Family of God*. Regularly, we would sing a short hymn of the same name. I had always considered it part of the weekly ritual. Here, at this new church, we sang it with meaning – and we included all of the verses that, in turn, inspired a much deeper feeling within me.

The small congregation took the job of God's work seriously, and the light of the ministry shone brightly on the surrounding area. These were not people who just attended church on Sunday morning; almost every member carried God's message with them constantly, and their individual ministries were impressive.

The pastor was an amazing man, and he – along with his wife – brought a vitality to the church that was unparalleled in my experience. One reason for his vitality may have been that our pastor was following the path that God had planned for him, including running a successful psychiatric practice where he employed his talents for the betterment of others. He is also a gifted orator and truly preached the inspired word of God. It was his words that, for the first time in my life, led me to believe that Jesus wanted me to win. God was offering the same salvation to all of mankind and was not waiting to smite me for my sinful shortcomings.

My pastor had three passions beyond those that one might expect from a man of his spirit. The first was Kentucky basketball, and he seeded his love for the team within me. I continue to be a fan today – I attended their last appearance in the NCAA tournament finals. The second passion was a love for model trains; and I recall an impressive room at his home with trains and related memorabilia. His third passion was running, and he ran dozens of marathons in his 60s and 70s.

Despite his busy lifestyle, he decided to walk across the United States to raise money for the United Methodist Home for Children in Kentucky. The walk was an amazing one, and both he and his wife penned books about the experience. He planned his route to begin in Virginia Beach and end in San Francisco.

The journey took him through Colorado, and due to some extenuating circumstances, he found himself walking between Fort Collins and Walden on a day that was not originally part of his itinerary. Soon, he spied a group running toward him. After exchanging pleasantries, they all agreed to meet later in the day to share stories. The group was running from San Francisco to Boston for the benefit of Boston Children's Hospital.

When they met later that day, he learned that the group of runners were off their route as well; weather had compelled them to make a change. During their conversation, my friend the pastor shared his love of running, and his decade-long desire to run in the Boston Marathon. As the Boston Marathon is an invitation event, he lamented that his running pace would not be fast enough to earn him a spot in the race. One of the runners immediately said, "You're in next year." As it turned out, the person in charge of the Boston Marathon was part of the group of runners.

Two entities – both raising awareness and funds for children, both on the wrong route, on the wrong day – happened to meet. Blessings abounded. The story is hard to comprehend, but God's hand is all over it. In true God-fashion, those who choose to follow His path and bless others are themselves blessed. It is a surreal scenario that is repeated time and time again throughout all our lives – we only need to look.

My pastor's walk to benefit the United Methodist Home for Children ended as he placed his feet in the Pacific Ocean. At the conclusion of such a feat, many people of his age – 67 at the time – might have taken a rest. Not this man – his mind focused on *What is next?*

Now 84, he has completed 82 marathons in the past 30 years. He continues to have a thriving practice, inspiring young and old alike, while he engages in writing another book.

His story is an amazing one. His life's accomplishments are singular and impressive. Skilled enough to have ministered to a flock of thousands, he was led by God to serve in the humblest of settings, and my life has been ever enriched by his friendship. More than 20 years after my departure from that Kentucky community and the little church, we remain in contact. I bask in the memory of his wisdom every day.

Opportunities Discovered

God has an amazing way of nudging us in a direction that will provide fulfillment and blessings. Returning to my connection with that little church – it had initially seemed far too quaint and uninteresting, yet the people proved to be genuine. Their expectations were grounded in an unflappable faith and they reveled in the smallest of blessings.

Shortly after I joined that small congregation, it was announced that one of the members had been called on a mission trip to Uruguay. I had barely met the man, but it was clear to me that undertaking the mission was a strong passion for him. Unfortunately, making the trip also felt like an unscalable mountain to him, with the limited resources available to fund such a venture.

I hardly knew the church's lay leader, but I telephoned her the next day and offered to anonymously fund the man's airline trip to Uruguay. She remained silent for an extended moment; then, choking back what appeared to be overwhelming emotion, she thanked me graciously. Then, she asked, "How do you suppose he would get home?" Her question shocked me, because I had presumed that she would know I was planning to cover the return trip as well.

I reflect upon that cadre of Christians with great regularity. Expecting nothing, they had everything. God had seen to that.

Educators in the Classroom

I have always admired those who made the sacrifice to become educators. We hear much in the news about laziness motivating such a choice – "summers off, short days, and plenty of extended holidays" are common refrains. While there are some teachers who choose their work for less than principled motivations (just like in any profession), the vast majority are committed to their craft. They sacrifice their time and potential for better earnings in another field to help educate our children.

In addition to teachings in academic fields, life lessons taught by educators become ingrained in their students and remain for a lifetime. I was blessed to have six exceptional educators guide me – two in high school, and four during my time in college. From them, I learned about passion, humility, humor and commitment. Their words encouraged me and helped mold me into the man I have become.

Another, whose course I never took, became a lifelong friend and mentor. Our entire family admired him greatly. He was a passionate educator, fervent historian, avid outdoorsman, and a man of deep faith. As a teen, I anticipated his regular visits to our family store, hoping to glean a pebble of wisdom – and I was rarely disappointed.

After our store was sold, I found excuses to repeatedly visit the history professors' office complex, where I gained wisdom and inspiration – not only from him, but also from many of his colleagues. It was there where my passion for all things educational was formed.

As I moved beyond my college days, my busy lifestyle supplanted our regular connection. I lamented over the distance that had formed. I wondered if the regular connection that I sought with the professor would ever be rekindled, and came to believe that it was an impossible desire. As is regularly the case, God had different plans.

My family moved to a small village, and upon entering the tiny church there one Sunday, I spied my old friend sitting in the choir box. We learned that his wife was the pastor of the church, and a deeper and more fulfilling relationship developed. When I reflect upon the geographic realities, coupled with the fact that less than 100 congregants regularly worshiped in that church, the word "miracle" comes to my mind. The entire experience with the educator was a complete blessing for me and my family. To this day, over 30 years later, he remains an inspiration not only to me, but also to both of my children.

Thank Them for They Likely Do Not Know

In 1997, while on a plane from Kansas City to Cincinnati, I had the great fortune to sit next to a man who was a committed educator and a university chancellor. Our conversation migrated to education and educators. I regaled him with my feelings about the importance of those educators who had an impact on me. This lifelong educator asked me one vital question: "Have you ever thanked them?" I answered that they must know, and his response was chilling: "If you have not told them, then they do not know."

His words cut through me, and before the wheels touched ground in northern Kentucky, I made a commitment to right that wrong. Three weeks later, I found myself on a plane from Cincinnati to Pittsburgh; after a short one-and-a-half-hour drive north, I was sitting in the faculty lunchroom with two of my former university professors. It was a short but deeply therapeutic reunion. As one might expect, both were too humble to accept my thanks without demanding that I give myself a bit of the credit. *They are still teaching me after 30 years,* I thought, as I drove away from the campus.

Nearly a decade later, I found myself visiting a family member who was an interim resident of a skilled nursing center in a small town. At the end of my visit, I spotted a wheelchair-bound person who looked oddly familiar. I queried him and discovered that he was my high school chemistry teacher. He was up in years, and I was concerned that he might not remember me.

When I told him who I was, his face lit up. I took time to thank him for his mentorship and explained how much it had helped guide me though some of the challenges of life. He smiled and responded, "It was my pleasure; you were one of the top 10 chemistry students I ever taught." I thanked him for the kind words and departed. While I was still within earshot, I heard him call my name rather frantically. I returned to his side, and he uttered, "Top five, top 10 was incorrect, definitely top five." I laughed and thanked him again, but it was clear to me that he was not joking. He had given the matter some thought and wanted me to know how he felt.

When I took the time to thank those who had helped me early in my life, it resulted in significant blessings. Those blessings have remained with me, and I smile as I type this.

Who shaped you, and how might you thank them?

Dinosaurs Abound

So many Dinosaurs, and so few pages. There are another dozen or so Dinosaurs thundering through my mind as I pen these words. Mostly gone now, they all played integral roles in the development of the man I have become, complete with my blemishes. Two remain physically, but all the others live on in my mind; and their legacy is on full exhibit with every step I take.

Certainly, my parents, and those you have met – or will meet – in these pages, all played significant roles in my life. They are essential parts of the narrative that have become my story. It has been their influence that helped me construct my life plan, and calibrate my moral compass. It has been their influence that instilled within me the courage to push through the hard times, which led to my fulfillment. It has been their influence that has fueled my passion to share my story; and in doing so, I can help others to live lives of abundance. I hope that you, too, will share your story for the betterment of all who hear it.

Chapter 8

Dirty Laundry

Fear crushes dreams and stifles opportunity. Only when the iron curtain of secrecy is lifted can healing begin.

E VERY FAMILY HAS **STUFF**. Our family **stuff** remains hidden within the confines of our immediate loved ones' minds. Fear of embarrassment or misunderstanding often drives us to bury this "dirty laundry" deep inside our brains. Tragically, doing that often exacerbates the issues. Piercing the veil of secrecy and seeking support renders the laundry much less offensive. There is hope and there is help; everyone is dealing with issues in some form. What is your dirty laundry? How can you air it? How can you gain fulfillment from coming to terms with the realities of your circumstances?

Mental illness is among the most misunderstood maladies of our times. It is not that different from those chronic physical illnesses that plague the lives of millions. Through no fault of their own, those afflicted with mental disorders often carry an unfair stigma – a stigma that can ruin a life or a livelihood.

I am comforted by the evolution of thought surrounding mental illness. Once considered "untouchable," those afflicted hid their disease for fear of harsh, unwarranted treatment. Still, to most, mental illness remains a hidden ailment and more must be done to lift the veil of secrecy.

I have come to believe that we all suffer from some sort of mental disorder, and that most mental illnesses are not necessarily clearly-defined. I think of mental health as including a wide spectrum of behaviors, with out-of-bounds conduct bordering both ends. Most of us live the majority of their lives within the margins. Those who struggle with chronic mental illness wander outside normal boundaries with great regularity. Thankfully, medical treatment and counseling can help more socially acceptable behavior to blossom.

Since almost 15 percent of the adults in the United States report being on some mood-altering medication, you probably have a close family member or friend who is suffering. If an illness is undiagnosed, there is a high likelihood that some level of chaos touches your life. Such behavior might even create a chasm between loved ones. I like to suggest that we hate the affliction, love the afflicted, and pray for patience and courage.

My family has been ravaged by bipolar disorder. Also known as manic-depressive illness, it is a brain disorder that causes unusual shifts in a person's mood, energy, and ability to function. It is often hereditary. Often skipping a generation or two, it can affect almost any unsuspecting family. It is easily misdiagnosed, and diagnosis also becomes difficult when people refuse to admit that family members suffer from the disease. Since no test is available, confirmation of the affliction is challenging, and individuals can suffer with it for years without treatment.

My mother's father, an extraordinarily successful man in both position and deeds, passed on the gene of mental illness. During a rather deeply personal exchange with a cousin, he shared that out of 10 grandchildren, I was the only one who had been spared the torment of some manifestation of the illness. While I have no way of knowing if that is true, I thank God every day that the disease has seemingly passed me by.

Tragically, my brother has struggled with it most of his adult life. My brother has led an amazing life, with escapades that could fill multiple volumes. By most standards, he has been extraordinarily successful. He has an unequaled work ethic and a kind heart that is packed with empathy. His lifestyle has been defined by wanderlust – he has lived in over a dozen countries, and has visited 100 more. In true bipolar fashion, his actions mask his inner goodness; he may appear rather self-absorbed and aloof, unless the topic of conversation is of great interest to him.

Although we see only each other a couple of times a year (normally in conjunction with medical treatment), we are in constant contact. Since my mother's passing, I have assumed a role as one of his caregivers. It is an exceedingly stressful task, but one I have taken on without regret.

Please join me on a journey of discovery as I share the details of my early childhood. Look to see if you notice signs of illness along the way.

Humble Beginning

My brother and I were the result of a great deal of prayer. We were born into a normal lower-middle-class family. Our parents were divorcees, unique in both their families. My father was a "condemned to hell" Byzantine Catholic, and my mother was the daughter of an Anglican priest. Since my father's status was negligible in the Catholic Church and my mother had been brought up in a strict religious household, we were baptized and raised in the Episcopal Church.

Our parents were loving and nurturing. While we did not have much in the way of assets, I always felt exceptionally lucky to have such a great family. My mother had our lives planned out for us. I was to be an attorney and my older brother was to be a doctor. Of course, there was always president as another career option. This was the United States, post-World War II, and either of my mother's children could become president. All you had to do was decide that you wanted to do something, and it could be accomplished. That kind of advice and imprinting has served me well, but it has also placed unbelievable pressure upon me.

The Seeds of Fear Sown Deeply

I arrived with little fanfare on June 5, 1958, and my brother, 25 months my senior, was none too happy about a new member of the family who unintentionally stole the limelight. He immediately became jealous. While I only know the stories shared by my parents, evidently my brother wanted me gone so much that he placed me into drawers in my mother's dresser. I still question how a 2-year-old could have mustered the strength to accomplish that, but my mother testified on multiple occasions that it happened with great regularity. I never gave the subject much thought; but as I write, I am amazed that my mother allowed me to be alone with him.

What I do vividly recall is that my brother would regularly throw me into the bathroom and close the door. With no lights or window, I would become frantic, and he would hold the door knob closed until one of my parents arrived to save the day. I was terrorized by the practice. What unthinkable deed did I commit to elicit that action?

Nothing. It was merely something my brother did to break up the boredom of his day.

After a year or so, I learned to simply turn on the light switch while in there, and I felt quite stupid for having been so traumatized. My brother was not to be deterred, and the bathroom scare chamber was exchanged for the hallway cedar closet tomb. Illumination hung just out of my reach, as the lone light bulb had a rather short string. So, the terror continued. To this day, I remain quite frightened of the dark; while I cannot be sure, it seems reasonable that recollections of these early encounters have contributed to my fear.

Since we were the classic struggling, economically-challenged family, belt-tightening was a way of life – but I never realized it. We had everything we needed. It was not until well into adulthood that I understood how dire things had been. I received hand-me-downs and was happy to have them. My mother shopped at JCPenney for our school clothing, but she bought only the clearance items – and darn few of them. It never bothered me, but my brother found that extremely galling, and complained regularly about what he felt were "unacceptable" garments.

My brother always seemed to thrive on competition. He was driven to reach a point above and beyond. Everything he did, he attacked with zeal and passion. There was no second place. Failure was never an option – but when it came, temper came with it. To my parents' horror, the end always justified the means in my brother's mind. That translated into cheating. I remember playing the game of Life with my brother, and he cheated to win – a bitter metaphor.

My brother reveled in rivalries. One day, my parents decided to take a rare afternoon out and we were left with our first-ever male babysitter. Not long after my parents' departure, my brother began to wrestle with our guardian, and the result left a scratch on my mother's new buffet. It took my mother a day to discover the imperfection – but in no time, my brother and I were seated on the couch, where my mother said we would remain until the perpetrator confessed. It was clear that my brother, two years my senior, would be stoic in his refusal to admit to any wrongdoing. He probably realized that if we waited it out, nothing would or could be done. At 6 years old, I decided that it would be better to lie and claim responsibility than to sit in isolation forever. To do the unthinkable and tattle on my brother was out of the question. The physical and verbal abuse that would be unleashed if I tattled was too terrible to contemplate.

I admitted to the crime and prepared to receive my punishment, but my father was not buying it. He knew I was making the whole thing up; and, when he insisted that I show him how I had done it, I could not come up with a good enough tale and was spanked for lying. As my tears flowed, my brother remained unfettered – and then I blurted it out. I told the entire story, and my brother was sent to his room in tears – the recipient of a robust, repeated, open hand across the bottom. As I lay in my own room, sobbing, I contemplated what further pain would be inflicted upon me, but this time at the hand of my brother. It took a couple of days, but my tattling beating came – and actually, it was unremarkable. It was just another day that was typical in the early years with my brother.

The Stabbing

My brother had a propensity to get bored, and when he did, his temper usually followed.

I was a quiet child and suffered from great insecurity. Alone in the safe haven of my room, I played penny basketball. I was John Havlicek. One night, when I was playing "under the lights" at the "Boston Garden," I launched my official NBA penny toward the paperclip rim and it bounced in – yet another seventh game win in the NBA finals and I was in glory! But my brother decided my victory was to be short-lived, and with one quick swing of a lamp, my satisfaction was shattered. The pain reverberated in my head as I hit the carpeted floor.

What was my crime? What had I done? I had been happy – and that was unacceptable. I do not remember picking up the pencil – but I had had enough, and I remember sinking it deep into the flesh of his right arm. That was followed by a blood-curdling scream and the familiar "What in the hell is going on?" from my father. He turned the corner and entered my room, and with a quick **thwomp** he pulled the pencil out of the fleshy bicep that it had freshly punctured.

My brother was frantic, and I was in trouble. I braced for the pain that was sure to follow – an open hand across the face. It never came. Instead, my father just looked disgusted and screamed, "What in the hell am I going to do with you two?" He examined what appeared to be a three- to four-inch chunk of fat hanging out of my brother's recently impaled appendage. As my brother panicked and wailed, my father's ire turned to him. "You big baby, it's just a flesh wound." But my brother was convinced he was dying of lead poisoning, and after a Band-Aid was applied, he retired to his room to contemplate what he was sure were the remaining few minutes of his life.

Throughout the ordeal, the shattered lamp, and my head – which had broken it – were both forgotten. (Throughout my youth and into my teenage years my body "broke" countless lamps, brooms and ladders.) I lay in bed wondering if my brother was indeed dying, and if I was going to go to prison for killing him.

Shortly, my mother returned home. As the quintessential RN, she knew way too much of the horrors of what could happen to unsuspecting people with injuries. A quick inspection, coupled with a frantic retelling of the "attack," resulted in a strained, "Frank, this child needs to be in the emergency room immediately."

Before I knew it, I was in the back seat of the car and we were off to the ER. Now we were both crying, and my mother was furious. "What ever possessed you to stab your brother?" she asked. I hid my head in the seat and cried, and could only get out a weak apology. Had I been older, I could have managed a, "He broke a lamp over my head for no reason," but I was only thinking of what prison I would be going to.

As it turned out, my brother was fine, and the hospital put a Band-Aid over the hole. That is when I realized that my Dad could do anything. He had done exactly the right thing. He had done what the doctor had done. His position as the smartest man I knew rose another level. As for the "pencil incident," as it came to be known, similar encounters were a regular part of my life. Of course, in those days, no one ever thought anything of it. It was written off as competitive spirit. Or, it was a case of sibling rivalry. Nothing more.

Physiological Torment

My brother seemed to find great satisfaction in causing me physical and emotional pain. He went to great lengths to convince me that I had been adopted. He fabricated detailed and believable scenarios that were convincing to a young, vulnerable mind. As confirmation of his story, he pointed to the fact that there were almost no pictures of me as a baby anywhere in the house. I was petrified; and, despite my mother's continued reassurances to the contrary, I prayed to God every night that I was not adopted. But later, after my brother was diagnosed with bipolar disorder and I learned that the terrible disease was hereditary, I began to pray that I had been adopted.

Another of his fabrications was a story that we had an older brother who was kept in the basement. I was actually smart enough to realize that this tale was pure poppycock. But in an unbelievably ironic twist, unknown to both of us, my brother's imagination had not been too far off. We did indeed have a half-brother. It was not until after my father's death over 10 years later that we learned about my father's previous marriage and son. Father and son had been estranged due to yet another set of remarkable circumstances, and the child was not to be mentioned. One thing was for sure – he did not live in our basement.

Hypochondria Abounds

My mother had an antique table in her bedroom. It had been hewn by hand and the craftsman's expertise had created intricate patterns. Swirls, openings, and ornate stalactite-like appendages adorned its surfaces. My brother and I took turns dusting it. Its lower shelf was home to one of my mother's medical treasures – the Physician's Desk Reference. The PDR could diagnose almost any ailment, and my brother took to zealously reviewing its contents. Every headache became an inoperable brain tumor, and each stomach ache emanated from a malady too horrible to imagine. Every breath of air that filled his lungs contained the potential for funeral preparations.

Despite the plethora of terminal conditions that threatened my brother's very existence, he was driven for success and obsessed with winning. He was an Eagle Scout at 12 years old; to this day, one of the youngest ever. But that was not good enough. By the time he was 13, he had a palm (five additional merit badges), followed by another, and another. Next there was the God and Country award. Shortly thereafter, he was named Alawatsakema Chief of the Order of the Arrow. He attacked Scouting as he attacked everything. Hard work, focus, dedication and desire were paramount, and nothing would get in his way when he was in the zone.

A Battle for the Ages

As puberty made the scene, the winds of war between my father and brother began to blow briskly throughout our humble 1,000-square-foot ranch house. My father was a strict World War II-era man. His favorite line was, "Do as I say, not as I do," and he meant it. He lived by the "spare the rod, spoil the child" adage, but other than the occasional slap across the face, his discipline was a hand across the bottom. In fact, my father never hit us with anything other than an open hand. If the truth were to be told, it was always deserved, and it usually happened only after willful misconduct.

Puberty also brought a myriad of illnesses, and I remember my brother suffering from multiple obscure maladies. It seemed that he was forever taking medications, and he repeatedly complained about stomach and cranial disorders.

We rarely took family vacations, other than to visit my mother's relatives in Canada. My father rarely ever made these trips, claiming that he was far too busy trying to eke out a living. I later found that he found such trips uncomfortable, because he never felt that my mother's family totally embraced him. So, when my father announced that we would be taking a trip to New England and the Maritime Provinces, I was in shock. It would be a real vacation – and we were going to stay in real hotels and eat in real restaurants.

My brother was unimpressed; at 15, he would have preferred to stay home and spy on the neighbor girl undressing next door. Besides, he was suffering from a severe case of abdominal discomfort. Regardless, we loaded up the Bel Air and headed across the newly-completed Interstate 80.

When we arrived in Rhode Island, we found our way to the first of our hotels. My brother was suffering, and made sure everyone knew about it. After he was calmed, we were off to my first-ever New England dining experience. My father had me excited about trying clam chowder, and I could not wait. As we parked along the road that fronted our destination, my brother announced that he was far too ill to dine with the family. My mother, the consummate peacemaker, tried to prompt my brother into joining us. But my father's patience was gone, and he demanded that we leave my brother in the car.

As one might imagine, dinner was far from enjoyable, and my mother was convinced that my brother would be taken by lobstermen running amok. And her worst fears seemed to become a reality – when we returned to the car, my brother was missing. My father remained composed, and after driving a few blocks we found him. He had begun to feel better and had decided to explore. Another disaster averted.

The next night we were in Bangor, Maine, and the change of state did not improve my brother's condition. After another on-again, off-again day of ailments, my father and I found ourselves walking the streets of Bangor at 2 o'clock in the morning looking for milk. My brother was a milk fanatic, and my mother was convinced it was the only cure for his abdominal problems. In the days before 24-hour convenience stores, finding milk at that hour was a daunting task. Why we walked I do not remember, but amazingly enough, we found a coin-operated milk vending machine. We returned with the miracle liquid to a sleeping victim.

The balance of the trip involved a number of unsubstantiated maladies endured by my brother, but we all survived. I never remember my brother being cured, nor do I remember an official diagnosis; but he seemed to – as my father predicted – grow out of it.

I only saw my father cry twice in his life. The second time was when he said goodbye to me as he was dying. I frequently wonder if he cried more often.

After 63 years, I find that tears often come to my eyes, but I will never forget the first time he cried. Even as my father and I grew closer, he and my brother were on a path for conflict. One afternoon, I remember my brother and my father arguing in our front hall. It was over a motorcycle my brother had purchased. This was not unique; but for some reason I decided to slip into the living room for a front-row view. Voices became shrill and the inevitable battle was in full swing. Just then, something that had never happened before occurred. My father, frustrated to the nth degree, screamed, "Okay, if you're so tough, take your best shot."

My afternoon entertainment took an unprecedented turn as I saw my brother's left fist clench, followed by a punch careening in the direction of my father's head. My father's quick duck followed by a counter to the left temple, and my brother bounced off the entrance doorway, falling into a crumpled ball on the floor. My father turned and wept openly. He sobbed and repeated over and over again, "I never thought I would raise a fist to one of my children." We were taught that you did not cry when you were a man – yet his tears flowed – and I was aghast. The incident was never spoken about again; but I was amazed by the fact that my brother had pushed my father, the stalwart of control, to uncontrollable rage. Still, there was no question that there was something in the recesses of my brother's mind that kept him continually on the **edge**.

Our last years in our modest home were filled with other seemingly unrelated oddities. Our house was the one that was vandalized on multiple occasions, when others in the community were left untouched. Our lawn seemed to be the one that motorists would unintentionally drive onto, and leave the grass torn apart. Were we a lightning rod of bad luck? Was there some unseen code in our 415 house number? No, nothing quite so dramatic. As it turned out, my family was being punished because some of the young men in the community had taken issue with the way my brother conducted himself. I never knew the details, and did not ask. I was uninvolved, and too young to be consulted.

It remains unclear to me if my brother's early conduct can be attributed to his since-diagnosed condition, but now it is so easy to draw parallels – to see the signs. We were a proud family, and mental illness was something that happened to other people – in other communities. We were God-fearing Christians, and those kinds of things were not possible.

"How could we have been so blinded?" my mother was heard to say frequently in her later years.

Two Memories in Utter Conflict

Oddly, my brother had a very different view of our childhood. I find this fascinating, as events that are so clear in my mind appear to be starkly different from those in my brother's mind.

My brother is convinced that he was beaten regularly by a belt-equipped father; but I distinctly recall my father advising me that if he ever felt the need to use anything but an open hand, it would be a very dark day. I do not recall any such darkness. I have racked my mind for anything to support my brother's claim, and can only come up with an incident where my father accidentally struck me with a wiffle-ball bat during a spirited game of horseplay. The inadvertent swat resulted in a broken finger.

The other stark, disparate recollection between us is the memory of the front hallway exchange. My brother is convinced that it was he who leveled my father, teaching him a valuable lesson on how to parent. My recollection of the event is so vivid that I see his version as almost impossible, yet I suspect that my brother's memory is equally clear. How odd! Evidently one of us is wrong; maybe both of us are misremembering.

The outrageous experiences that have become knitted into my brother's life story could fill many volumes. In fact, in 2006, I wrote a 100,000-word volume that only scratched the surface. Since its writing, another 100,000 could easily be penned as an epilogue. But so raw are my recollections, that I am unsure if the story will ever migrate from my hard drive to the page.

If you or a loved one are suffering with some sort of mental illness, I urge you to seek immediate professional advice. There is hope and no one should suffer in silence. Now medicated and under the care of physicians, my brother is leading a productive and fruitful life. It is probably not as exciting as it once was, but it is definitely safer.

Chapter 9

The Cottage:
A Passion Instilled

Passion is one of the strongest paths to fulfillment, and the passions of our youth often fuel us throughout our life journey.

S LIPPERY ROCK IS SUCH an unlikely name for a town; it is named for nearby Slippery Rock Creek. It is not the town, but the creek to which I feel most connected. Nestled in western Pennsylvania, the waterway earned its name from the rocks that adorn its bed. The rocks are said to have facilitated the escape of Colonel Daniel Brodhead and his men from attack by the Seneca Indians during an expedition in 1779. According to reports, the Seneca, wearing moccasins, were unable to pass through the stream due to the slickness of the stones, while the soldiers' heavy boots afforded them unimpeded passage.

My father was self-employed, and he struggled with chronic health issues most of my life. He was stricken with one such illness when I was 4 years old, and it prohibited him from working for months. With declining income and no safety net, my parents tightened their belts and added yet another scoop of water to our soup.

My mother, a registered nurse, returned to work on the midnight shift at one of Pittsburgh's hospitals. But then my father, a dedicated and disciplined man, returned to health and attacked his work with vigor. Following the promise of the American Dream, our family regained its footing – and in four years, we began having discussions about upgrading the 1,000-square-foot, one-bath ranch house.

My father, an outdoorsman in his heart, convinced my mother that a summer cottage could supplant the desire for a more enhanced home. We launched a search for the perfect hamlet, a search that took us in a one-hour transit radius from our home in Monroeville, as that felt like a reasonable commute for a proposed weekend getaway.

Disappointment Leads to Opportunity

House hunting was not an activity that was high on the list of preferred activities for either me or my brother. My father would include subtle bribes as enticements for good behavior on house hunting trips. One such inducement included a proposed picnic at Rock Falls Park; my father hyped the park as an amazing place for everything fun. We were crestfallen when, instead of going to Rock Falls Park, we found ourselves at an old picnic table next to a spartan and uninteresting cement-block edifice in the middle of nowhere.

The structure became our new summer home. It was a two-room building that boasted a beautiful, raised fireplace, flanked by a red brick backdrop. I have never seen anything quite like it, before or since. The house was a cold, dank place with cement floors and a small slate porch.

My father, by no means a carpenter, paneled and insulated the room that would become the bedroom. He also assembled a makeshift divider with open cupboards and a formica top that provided welcome counter space in the open-style kitchen. Within a year, wall-to-wall carpeting was installed, and that was followed by the construction of a screened-in porch on the rear of the house. Unfortunately, it did not boast a view of the beautiful creek that fronted the property. A mile-long private road led to the remote cabin; the road seemed to always be in a state of disrepair, which limited the number of visitors. Amazingly, the bread and milk delivery trucks arrived each week without any issues.

Heaven on Earth

In my preteen mind, the place became heaven on earth, and I loved summering there. It was a place of firsts, and the vast majority of them involved the great outdoors. I found a small, round metal tin container on a ledge in the pump room (which was in the bathroom) and discovered some fishing hooks inside. Neither of my parents had ever fished, but my father tied one of the hooks to a piece of kite string and provided me with some day-old bread.

Lying face down on a dock with a hand extended to hide the sun's glare, I could see fish darting through the waters below. The water was crystal clear; at the time, I did not realize that pollutants that hindered some aquatic life were also responsible for the water clarity. Microorganisms that often clouded the water column were as adversely impacted as the fish. Nevertheless, a few species of fish flourished, and among them was a 12-inch bullhead catfish that was the first catch of my life. That success unleashed a lifelong passion for fishing, and I fueled it almost daily from the banks of beautiful Slippery Rock Creek.

A Lifelong Passion Is Seeded

In June of 1972, Hurricane Agnes made the scene, and I watched with horror as the stream, swollen to five or six times its normal size, took on a chocolate milk color (due to the soil that had been swept into the torrent). Uprooted trees and other debris were racing past our home in the ravaging waters below. But the most disturbing sight was the millions of dead fish that had succumbed to the acidic waters from nearby coal mines. That day, I became an environmentalist, and I have continued in a fight for reasonable and commonsense ecological policy since.

My summers became synonymous with tree houses, long canoe trips up and down the creek, late-night campfires, overnight campouts, excursions into unknown territories in search of blueberries and blackberries, and all related activities. In many ways, those were some of the best times of my life. As I neared the age of 12, I found myself sitting on a log in the snow for hours, waiting for a deer that would never pass my way. I repeated the procedure multiple times every year, and each evening I returned to the cottage to rest so I could do it all again the next day. Since the only heat source in the cabin was that fireplace, "cold" was the operative word during visits.

Many nights were filled with large card games; families from neighboring cottages would gather and play for hours. Bingo at the fire hall in the nearby town was another regular event, as were Saturday night auctions. Every week, I would return home with a box full of treasures that I had bought from a man holding a gavel and a microphone while talking rapid-fire.

Above all else, the creek itself was the major appeal. My friend and I spent hours in our old row boat with fishing rods or a .22 caliber rifle. We were either catching fish or shooting frogs. I learned to swim in the waters of the creek, and I also trained for the mile swim event there. To me, the waters held a magical appeal. In them, on them, or next to them, I felt a bit closer to heaven. Over them, we engaged in a fun activity as we swung on a bull rope, clinging on long enough to release ourselves into the waters below. Then, we would hurry back up the hillside to do it all over again.

During my teenage years, the cabin became home for a short while, because my family had purchased a small convenience store about five miles away. The cottage became a retreat for my friends and me to host classic teen parties. Shortly after my sixteenth birthday, my friends and I secured a case of beer, and we had just gotten down to business when lights from a car approached. The place was so remote, and the road leading to it was in such poor condition, that almost no one ever ventured there – and never at night.

We scrambled to hide the beer just as my father entered the cabin. He claimed he was just checking on us. He remained for about five minutes and then left, advising us to have fun. It was so odd. We were not adept at subterfuge; we sighed deep breaths and partied heartily. The next morning, at about 11 o'clock, my father returned. He claimed he had accidently taken the keys to the only vehicle we had. He returned them with no explanation.

It was not until years later that I realized he had taken the keys to ensure that we did not decide to go for a joy ride while in a drunken stupor. I have reflected on his act many times since, and have reveled in the brilliance of his recognition that teens will do what teens will do. I suspect that in today's culture, his rather unique gesture would be met with significant scrutiny. So it is with the passage of time.

The Unthinkable Is Upon Us

The cottage became synonymous for adventure and fun. In 1975, it also served as the recuperation center for my father's recovery from surgery. When I reflect on that time, I see a true paradox. There was no place on earth that I would have rather spent time; yet, I believe it might have been the worst venue for a critically-ill person's convalescence. It was damp, had no phone, and not much of a television. I do not believe that there was even a window in the bedroom. In many ways, it served as a temporary tomb for the man whose body would be permanently entombed just a few short months later.

Shortly after my father's death, my mother – suffering from intense depression – left for her homeland and I became the sole inhabitant of the cottage for the better part of a year. With our family in crisis, time seemed to fly as we buried ourselves in a mountain of distractions rather than coming to grips with the pain of the grieving process. What I describe as "shortly after" was in reality nearly two years. Dragging my way through college and with no parents and no hope, I made many, poor life choices. I endured a rather tumultuous period with the cottage as my backdrop.

The cottage was refurbished the next year when my mother returned from her self-enabled exile. We added heat and a telephone, as well as a second bedroom – which I built. With carpentry not being my strong suit, the room left a bit to be desired – but it worked – and it even had a window. I pulled off this construction marvel all while finishing my senior year at Slippery Rock State College.

New Beginnings

Immediately after graduation, I married and the cottage became home for my bride and me. With few resources, we were unable to afford heating oil, so we purchased a wood stove with our wedding money. My early-morning ritual included a first-breath exhale from the warmth of our twin bed to check for the water vapor that would confirm that the room temperature had dipped into the 40s and that the fire had not lasted through the night. For nearly 10 months, I played house-husband while I attended some follow-up schooling, chopped wood, trapped, hunted, and crocheted blankets. For a significant part of that time period, I was making the life changes required to become an officer in the Air Force, a story detailed in a later chapter. My job search had been fruitless, and I rested my career aspirations on a military commission.

On June 2, 1981, the cottage phone rang about 10 a.m., and it was the Air Force. My final interview had been canceled due to a bureaucratic snafu. They still wanted me, but my commission would have to wait until the fall. I returned to my chair and started an earnest conversation with God. I recall it starting with something like, "Why do you hate me so much?" Suffering from what I called **deity harassment**, I had convinced myself that I was destined to fail.

My rant lasted for most of four hours, and then God answered in the form of a phone call. It was a prospective employer; I had interviewed with them four months prior. They wanted me for another interview on the upcoming Friday.

A mix of excitement and fear tormented my mind. The next three days were filled with conflicting voices – some assured me that it was the solution I sought, but others promised that I would somehow come up short. I was so nervous that I drove the 70 miles to the interview the day before, to ensure I would correctly estimate my transit time.

God Changes Everything

The cottage was the place I left to get my first real job. It happened at 7 o'clock on the morning of Friday, June 5, 1981. I had arrived over an hour early for the job interview to ensure I would be prompt, and that I would have enough time to prepare myself for another arduous interview experience. In an unprecedented moment, God filled me with courage – a courage I had never believed possible. I convinced myself that I would not leave that location without the job I sought. It was my twenty-third birthday, and it was just under a year since my graduation from college. I had been stymied at every attempt to secure full-time employment. This time was going to be different.

Prior to that date, fear had filled my life and I allowed myself to be controlled by others. I had always wondered if I was good enough, smart enough, or strong enough to compete. I had spent a large part of my teen years trying to fit a mold of others' expectations. *Never again*, I kept telling myself, as I ascended the stairs to the reception area. *I simply need to be myself and sell my unique blend of skills and talents.* Ironically, every concern that had plagued my prior interviewing experiences left me that day. I did not give a thought to any competition; I did not anticipate how to answer any questions so I would sound smarter or more engaging than other candidates.

As the time drew closer to what turned out to be a series of round-robin interviews, many of my classmates filled the empty seats in the reception area. Previously, I would have crumbled at the thought of such stiff competition. Not this day. In fact, I felt sorry for them as I thought of their plight to find the right job to begin their careers – because this one was mine.

The interviewing process was intense. I met with five different individuals, and was invited for a plant tour. Shortly after what would have normally been a lunch break, I found myself in the office of the senior on-site manager. He had invited the other four interviewers to join him in his office.

"We like you," I recall him saying, and he added, "Do you have any other questions?"

I responded that I had appreciated the breadth of the educational experience, and my only question was, "When do I start?"

He laughed and said, "We need some time to think about you and the other candidates we have interviewed, and we will get back to you Monday."

The words came out of my mouth before I even could catch myself. "Sir, I promised myself that I would not leave here without a job, and I would really appreciate you giving me the opportunity to prove myself, starting today."

"I like your confidence," he responded. "Provided you pass the physical, the job is yours."

"Can we arrange for the physical today?" I pressed further.

Within the next two hours I found myself at the doctor's office, and was approved to start my career the following Monday. It was a long drive home, but I recall thinking, *I will never be afraid again. God has me*, I thought.

More than 40 years since then, He is still in control and always will remain so.

Tears of thanksgiving and joy washed over me as I returned to the cottage as a career man. Now my picture had earned its place on the wall of my grandmother's apartment.

The cottage was sold, and with it the best part of my youth. In all, I believe we enjoyed seven or eight summers there. Oddly, in my mind, it feels like it was decades of happy memories. It was an age of innocence – followed by a coming of age that quickly turned into some of the darkest times of my life. A paradox, to be sure. Joy was eradicated by fear; I then fell prey to anger, and along with it, destructive behaviors. Throughout the turbulence, a courage was seeded within me –then it nurtured and it blossomed, serving me well all these years of my life.

I regularly reflect upon the watershed and its ability to rejuvenate. My passion for our environment, one of my strongest compulsions, was born there by the creek. God has bestowed upon mankind dominion over the environment, and with this great blessing comes critical responsibility. The environment of my youth was on the precipice of devastation; but man has learned from his mistakes. We are now working in more environmentally responsible ways to enrich both the environment and ourselves. Once-struggling ecosystems are now vibrant environments, teeming with life and providing essential elements for all the creatures that call them home. Just as Mother Nature rejuvenates, we can find rejuvenation through God's grace. No matter what pollutants we allow to seep into our lives, God is there to cleanse us and make us new again.

Chapter 10

The Paradox of My Life: Corner 8

Storms can ravage your life. We must learn to be storm-proof navigators as we transverse the rocky seas of life.

MY FATHER WAS AN entrepreneur who believed in the American Dream. He had been in and out of his own businesses for most of his working life. His unique, charismatic personality, Sicilian features, large stature, and inner goodness created the perfect purveyor. My mother was a born businesswoman. She was intelligent and quick. What she lacked in charisma, she made up for in dedication and loyalty. She had a way of growing on people, and would eventually become an acquaintance's most genuine and dependable friend.

My brother took a business class in tenth grade and became enamored with the idea of being a businessman. The class unleashed an entrepreneurial spirit and a wanderlust within him that would remain for a lifetime.

As for me, I loved to fish and hunt, and at 14 years of age, I dreamed of owning a hunting and fishing empire. I could see myself emerging from nature and bringing my singular expertise to a successful establishment that would be involved in all things outdoors.

With those qualities in play, how could we fail? In October 1973, we purchased what became the Corner 8 General Store. My brother was going to be operations manager, my mother was going to be the business manager, and I was going to be in tenth grade. It was a tough life. The business was far too small to support our family, so my father also continued to operate his collection agency.

The 10-acre site of our dreams consisted of a small convenience store, a gravel parking lot containing three gas pumps, an old grease pit used by the original owner to perform minor automobile maintenance, and a small residence attached to the rear of the store and layered above a sparse storeroom. A half-door that swung both ways separated our private struggles from our public personas. My father saw opportunity in every crevice and corner. Each pebble of gravel in the lot was a gem of prospect.

A Double Life

My brother and I attended Slippery Rock Area High School. My brother was in the work-study program as a senior, and his position of store operations manager was tailor-made for the curriculum. I was a full-time sophomore, and found myself friendless and the target of taunting from my classmates. I never understood why I had earned that distinction, but I fulfilled the role admirably.

Running the business was a difficult life. There was none of the excitement that the scholastic business textbooks had promised. Life was pumping gas, stocking shelves, and slicing the chipped ham that every customer wanted in a particular way. My personal favorite was thinly sliced, but not jumble stacked. By Christmas, my brother had grown tired of the business life, and his working days in the store were behind him. Since I had no friends, hated school, and loathed just about everyone my age within 50 miles, I gravitated to the store. It was my comfort – my oasis. Here, I was somebody and the customers seemed to like me, and I liked them. These were my people. Forty to 50 hours per week netted me all the chipped ham I could eat, and $10.

The business was a mix of triumphs and defeats, as we were saddled with insanely bad luck. Shortly after our grand opening, the gasoline world was turned upside down as OPEC decided to restrict oil sales. That delivered a crushing blow. Our government's response was to ration gasoline and institute a national speed limit of 55 miles per hour. In addition, the government eliminated Sunday gasoline sales, and established odd-numbered and even-numbered license plate gasoline sales restrictions.

In those days, almost all businesses were closed on Sunday. As a convenience store, we were open, and it was our biggest sales day of the week, often doubling revenues. The governmental action devastated our business. My father, however, remained stalwart in his commitment. With his dazzling personality, he pushed through, and the business thrived despite the challenges.

My Father's Brilliant Idea

In February 1974, in the midst of the tumult, my father approached me with an idea. Seemingly unfazed by the challenges we faced, he wanted to convert the old grease pit area to a bait and tackle shop. That shop would be mine to run. Not yet 16 years old, I would not be able to satisfy all the governmental regulations. But it was mine. My father named it Elliott's Bait and Tackle Depot. He and I went to work – renovating the building, sourcing shelving, and procuring minnow tanks. The minnow tanks were my favorite feature, as they were made of old water-bath, soda-pop coolers that had become obsolete with the advent of refrigerated units.

In March, we attended the retailers' sportsman expo in Pittsburgh. My father had agreed to fund a $10,000 stocking allotment, and I agreed to pay him back as soon as I was able. The host was shocked when my father instructed him to work directly with me. While I walked the show floor and selected the items I deemed essential to stock, my father feasted on the sandwiches that were available.

The bait and tackle business was an overnight success. By July, I was able to return the entirety of my father's loan while keeping a fully stocked establishment. One of the categories of items I stocked was ammunition; I was venturing into the hunting field. I saw it as a natural extension to the fishing category. Ironically, I was selling something that, at my tender age, I was not legally allowed to purchase.

Rocky Road Ahead

Concurrently, disaster loomed. My mother fell ill with a disabling neuropathy. After unsuccessful surgeries, she was hospitalized for weeks. The nearest real hospital was over an hour away, so it created quite a predicament.

My brother had enlisted in the Air Force, leaving just my father and me to handle the business along with our great employees – most of whom became my friends. My father had always been my best friend, but that period cemented our relationship. If he was afraid of the challenges facing our family, he did not show it; in fact, his singular brand of optimism seemed to swell. Most days we were exhausted, and we traveled the 12 miles to the all-night truck stop to get dinner at 11 p.m. after we had closed and settled the receipts.

Despite the tumult in our lives, along with the disastrous government regulations in place, the business continued to grow, and we saw revenues swell sixfold. But heartbreak was not finished with us yet – far from it. On August 3, 1975, my father underwent what was to be routine surgery. His once-vibrant body was riddled with cancer, and immediate and drastic treatment was required. The treatment darn near killed him. During all the havoc, my mother requested a hardship discharge for my brother from the Air Force, and he returned to assist with my father's care and the store operations.

It all happened during such a short period of time, but it seemed like a lifetime in hell as I was enduring it. On December 24, we bought a new car so my father could be more comfortable on his drives for treatment. He and I drove the car home together and talked about the Christmas celebration planned for the following day.

Christmas morning came, and my father was unable to leave the bed. On New Year's Day, he took his second ride in the car, which was to be his last. The destination was the hospital that housed the bed he would die in. My mother, to her credit, sat in vigil by his side for two weeks. She returned home only to sign checks to cover bills.

After returning home again on a Sunday afternoon, he died early the next morning. She was devastated, and a significant part of who she was also died on that day.

The next year and a half was as ugly a period as one could imagine. With our personal lives in total disarray, much like sailboats that lose their rudders, we careened through a rocky sea of despair. Despite our personal struggles, the business continued to thrive, and we doubled our sales again. The relationship between my mother and me suffered catastrophically. My father had wanted the business to be saved for me, but my mother found that she hated every aspect of it. Those rough seas sent us aground, and the business was sold just two years after my father died.

My father's one-hundred and third birthday would be tomorrow, I realize as I type. Gone 45 years – I miss him every day, and nothing I have experienced has ever come close to the utter grief I endured when he passed. We all will face anguish in our lives. I suspect that I have my share ahead, but feel incredibly blessed to have suffered the four years that was the Corner 8. In many ways, the tribulations and triumphs crafted a character that has served me well over the years.

Chapter 11

The Dinosaur's Dinosaur

The legacy we leave is dependent upon our life choices. We often have no idea of the impact that our example can have on others.

I LEARNED THE STAGES OF grief at far too early an age. Anger at everyone and everything manifested as anger at God, and then as resentment toward the deceased. As the fury subsided, grief quickly took its place. Anguish and hopelessness became sadness etched with hopefulness. Those feelings transformed into a lifelong mission to celebrate life. Having been fortunate enough to have that great man as my father, a gratefulness to God dwells within me.

My father was my best friend. Stricken with cancer due to a 20-year relationship with cigarettes, he was gone far too early. I could write an entire volume about him and the impact he had on the man I have become; but the fact is that he lives on through almost every word penned in this book. The quintessential Dinosaur, he was steeped in tradition – and when he passed, my world collapsed.

High school felt much like a four-year prison sentence. My crimes had been **confusion** and **awkwardness**. Near the end of my incarceration in my senior year, the hell of losing my mentor buried the travails of teen life deep in the recesses of my mind, rendering them inconsequential.

My dad died on Groundhog Day. The groundhog saw his shadow that year, forecasting six more weeks of winter; but my winter was only beginning and would endure for years to come. It was the Ice Age of my life, to be sure.

A Miraculous Letter Arrives

Since so much of this book illuminates the brightness that was my father, I will leave it to an old friend (who shared his thoughts with me through Instant Messenger) to summarize my dad. Unannounced and unanticipated, the message appeared on my phone at 3:24 p.m. on October 5, 2020. This friend and I were quite close during our high school years. In fact, he was my co-worker at the general store and a source of great inspiration. We lost contact, and over the past 40 years, we had only spoken once.

When I reflect on many of the remarkable unexpected occurrences that have enriched my lifetime, this one certainly resides near the top. It is astounding that my friend chose to communicate with me 16,317 days after my father's passing, and probably 40 years after I had last seen him. It is a fitting and apt eulogy to my father, beautifully written.

168

Hi Elliott!

After we exchanged comments yesterday – you are very sensible and eloquent – I was watching football, and my mind started thinking of your Dad. I've often reminisced about you and our times at the Corner 8.

What a great guy and character he was! Devoted to the business and family, strict attention to detail, and an influential mentor. I always wanted to please him and worked at doing so.

Remember that awful limestone dust that would blow in from Branchton? Made it necessary to thoroughly clean all the shelves and the stock constantly. Your Dad would always give me a smile and say "Just like downtown!" which made it all worthwhile. Guess what – I STILL say that to this day!

Remember how he'd take us to Morgan's after closing Friday night, for the "all you can eat" fish? He didn't have to do that, but it was a gracious gesture, and always fun. Boy, you could really do damage there!

I think he gave you the responsibility for the "Bait & Tackle" venture as a learning tool – truly a stroke of genius. He was a very canny and empathetic person. I always listened to what he had to say and learned a lot.

I don't know if you remember this, or even knew about it. About a week before I went to France, he asked me to visit at the cottage. He was feeling ill. We talked for about 30 minutes. He expressed gratitude for my service at the store, and most of all for the time you and I spent together. I let him know my gratitude as well.

I'll talk about my memories of you separately, needless to say we had fun! A month or two into my French exile, I got a letter from my parents advising that your father passed away. I wept, something I've done perhaps 3-4 times since...

Your Dad was a remarkable man, one of a kind. I'm so glad that you've done well and are happy – as he undoubtedly is, from wherever we go next. And he must certainly be proud of the man you've become.

Sorry to be maudlin, I'm actually getting a bit choked up.

Cheers, my friend!

When I originally envisioned this chapter, I had intended to allow my friend's letter to close it; but after reflection, the spirit that is my father is far too bright and I feel compelled to provide some additional context.

A Mountain of a Man

At 6 feet, 2 1/2 inches and 240 pounds, my father was a mountain of a man compared to most of his generation. His olive skin that darkened to a deep brown in the summer, along with his jet black hair and chiseled facial features, rendered him a rather imposing persona. His rugged appearance belied his inner goodness and genuine love for almost everyone. He had a zest for life.

If I had to use one word to describe him, it would be kind. He was the kindest person I have ever known and he was generous with the one thing none of us can control – time. He gave his time freely and in abundance, and when I was with him I felt as if I was the most important person in the world. His generosity with his time extended to my friends, and we all loved being with him.

My father was a one-of-a-kind spirit who could light up any room he entered. His charisma was unequaled. He excelled at bringing happiness to others and was a maestro.

One Christmas, instead of buying himself new shoes, he made them last a little longer by filling their hole-pocked soles with cardboard. He was then able to make the holiday brighter for my brother and me with the gifts he bought with his shoe money.

He smoked Winston cigarettes, and at age 5 – through my mother's prodding – I climbed into his lap and asked him to quit. Just like that, he had smoked his last cigarette; but he commenced smoking Phillies Perfecto cigars instead. Three years later, I attempted a similar feat, asking him to quit smoking the cigars. He agreed again, and from that point forward he had smoked his last cigar. He possessed an amazing discipline.

A Unique Perspective

My father was a bill collector, and he had a unique ability to compel even the most challenging of people to make restitution. He was so skilled at his craft that I recall very little angst associated with his business dealings. If a client was not able to muster the cash to meet their obligation, my father either set up a payment plan or repossessed their merchandise.

Our house was filled with guns, movie projectors, and other items he collected as payment. Amazingly, I never recall any animosity – clients handed over their possessions without issue. One client took us deep into the Allegheny National Forest, and within what seemed like an instant, we were the proud owners of his prized hunting camp. Oddly, he seemed almost relieved to have the matter behind him.

My dad was uniquely intuitive. Within two years of when I landed the bullhead that launched my lifelong passion for fishing, my father had saved enough money to purchase an aluminum rowboat. Equipped with a Johnson 6-horsepower motor, it became our adventure vessel through the waters of western Pennsylvania.

One trip was abruptly cut short when upon catching a fish, I inadvertently swung it in his direction, knocking his glasses into the deep muddy waters of Lake Arthur. He was legally blind without corrective lenses, and we found ourselves in an unenviable situation. He quietly instructed me to pilot the boat to the dock, where we loaded it upon our car.

After a bit of contemplation, my father asked me for my glasses. Because I too suffered from severe myopia, the glasses corrected his vision enough for him to safely drive us to our home an hour away. He never raised his voice or scolded me. Deep down, he knew I had punished myself far more than he could. So it was with my father.

He had a temper and my brother and I were skilled at testing it, but he always quickly returned to his jocular self and usually was back joking within minutes. Fishing, hunting, basketball, scouting, or homework – no matter what we were involved in at the moment, my father found time to be with us, and his love felt unconditional. Other fathers would golf with buddies or engage in any of a number of adult activities. My dad would just hang with us.

The Bet

Dad was an ardent Cleveland sports fan. But because I grew up in the suburbs of Pittsburgh, I revered the Pirates, and he teased me about them constantly. For some reason, I felt involved in, and connected to, their successes or failures. In 1971, my father bet me that the Pirates would not make the playoffs, and offered a 50-cent-per-game wager. The Pirates were 32 games over .500 that season, which netted me $16. That was over a year's worth of allowance.

"Double or nothing, on the NLCS," he barked. Two weeks later, I had $32.

"Double or nothing, on the World Series." With the Pirates down two games and looking like a defeated team, my father attempted to negotiate a $16 compromise, but I stuck with my team and was handsomely rewarded. After an amazing seven-game series, I won $64.

He paid me in quarters; more than six rolls of them. It was probably more than he earned in a week. He taught me a valuable lesson on losing with grace – enjoying the loss with added humor.

Despite his disdain for all Pittsburgh sports, for my thirteenth birthday my Dad took me to a Pirates game at the newly-opened

Three Rivers Stadium. These seats were not the normal $1 general admission seats. They were box seats, three rows from first base, where my hero Willie Stargell was sure to be playing. But Willie was not playing that day, and my father's disappointment was obvious. Those tickets likely represented the most expensive seats he had ever purchased. I do not think he ever realized how special I felt when I was with him, or that he knew that the day was still great for me, with or without Willie. My true hero was sitting next to me.

The Earthly Journey Cut Short

The cigarettes and cigars he had given up so easily got the better of him, and he succumbed to lung cancer less than a decade later. Historical weather data confirms my memory that February 3, 1976, was a bitterly cold day. The temperature in Harrisville, Pennsylvania, averaged in the mid-teens on the day that his funeral visitation was held. Nevertheless, hundreds filed past his flag-draped casket. Some waited over an hour in the frigid night air.

Men, women and children filed by and paid their respects to a community leader, each with their own memories to share. Near the end of the long evening, a man and a young boy, about 5 years old, made their way to our position. The father calmly stated, "My boy wanted to say goodbye to his friend Frank." Confused, the young lad asked where he could find his buddy.

"He's under the flag," someone responded. Confused, the youngster seemed deflated. It was most likely his first encounter with death; he had not quite grasped the gravity of the situation. His **giant hero** was not to be seen, and he cried quietly. It is a haunting, yet illuminating memory that defines the impact my father had on young and old alike.

46 Years and Forever

He has been gone nearly a lifetime, and a day does not go by that I do not miss him. I feel his presence in good times and bad. He is with me wherever I go, and always will be.

During my post-collegiate job interviews, a common question was, "If you could have dinner with anyone living or dead, who would it be?" My answer was always the same: "My father." When an academic advisor informed me that my answer lacked depth, I was shocked. Taking his advice, I modified my answer to the following, "I've been advised that answering, "My father," lacks depth so since he is not in the running, I'd pick....." My normal surrogate was Ronald Reagan and, while a fine man, not quite who I was thinking about.

The patriot, businessman, husband and warrior embraced his favorite moniker – dad. He unknowingly created the framework for my moral compass before I knew I needed one. Faith in God, care for family, and love of country was hard-coded within him – and through him, in me.

Chapter 12

Unlikely Accidents

Unplanned events take on the role of vital educators, as inches and seconds are the difference between inconvenience and disaster.

A CCIDENTS CAN BE DEFINED as unexpected or unintentional events, actions or conditions. Traditionally, when I think about accidents, my mind immediately moves to the automotive variety. However, accidents know no category – they occur throughout our lives and become woven into our life stories, adding important context as they occur.

Throughout my life, many "accidents" have befallen me, and I have experienced their impacts through any of a number of unscripted – and often unconventional – methods. At age 18, I fell through the ice while horseplaying on a thawing pond. The icy waters consumed me, and, in the darkness, I felt my life slipping from me. I recovered and smashed back through the ice in an unlikely example of amazing, great fortune.

In the past 40 years, my vehicles have been involved in six accidents. The last two were not particularly noteworthy – in both cases the car I was driving was simply rear-ended by a distracted driver. The previous four were a bit more unique; in all four cases, my car was parked with no occupants. The most remarkable accident involved two cars with no occupants and one fatality. Another involved a midnight birthday party toast, followed by what felt like a great explosion. Prior to that 40-year period, my accident-to-personal responsibility ratio was significant. When I was a teen, I made some poor life choices. Many of them occurred in a new black Chevrolet Blazer for which I paid cash while still a student at Slippery Rock Area High School.

Like others of my age and experience, I felt bulletproof when I was behind the wheel. That feeling of invincibility resulted in a trifecta of accidents in a relatively short time. In addition to the accidents on record, there was a cavalcade of unfortunate events that left my prized possession in a ditch. The roads seem to have straightened a bit with the passing years, and the thoroughfares have become far less icy.

A New World Emerges

The winter of 1977-1978 was a significant one. Still reeling from the death of my father, my mother sold our store, which also served as our house, leaving me alone with our small, remote cottage. With no heat other than a fireplace, and on a mile-long desolate road boasting only one other off-season resident, it was a rather lonely existence. When the hunting season ended, I found comfort with a wonderful family who generously allowed me to stay with them at their farm. I was attending college in my hometown, and with over 20 miles of county roads on the commute, driving in the winter was challenging. I found myself sleeping at the farm, in my car, or at the cottage, with no particular pattern.

I recall that family and their farm as the perfect therapy for a grieving young man who was struggling with writing the next chapter of his life. It was on that farm where I learned how to nut piglets, milk a cow, scald a hog, and slaughter a turkey. It was there where we were awakened one night to a house full of smoke, and it was there where a litter of shoats shared the living room with me one frigid winter night.

The patriarch was a barrel-chested man with a hearty laugh and a rather rugged appearance. I knew him as a kind and jocular person. He was quick to provide advice on all topics from farming to life skills. At that time of my life, I had acquired a rather spirited tongue. He provided me with some extraordinary advice. "Be careful what you allow to come out of your mouth, as it is extremely hard to control," he said. "Controlling what goes in your mouth is far easier." I failed to heed his advice then, but 40 years later, the counsel continues to ring true. I have repeated those words regularly to others, and have been surprised to have never heard them from another person.

On February 16, 1978, I was exiting the long steep drive of the farm – I remember the driveway as being very long and winding. It had been the site of a previous incident, when an oak tree jumped in front of my vehicle. On this particular day, I was heading to a job interview. The type of job was not nearly as important as the need to have one. Since my family had purchased a store in 1973, my work life had been predetermined up until recently – but things had changed.

The drive was muddied with melting snow. I piloted my Blazer over the curb, stopped, and immediately spotted a car rounding a curve heading in my direction. The occupants were two elderly women, engaged in a discussion that had their full attention.

In my memory, time stood still as I braced for impact. I recall the horror etched on both of their faces as they realized a collision was unavoidable. Their car hit the left side of my vehicle ahead of the front tire, and the impact thrust my car about six feet to the right. Uninjured, I exited my vehicle and scrambled to attend to the occupants. Both appeared to be injured, and I panicked as the blood-splattered windshield created a morbid scene.

Unable to provide much help, I scoped the remote area for any sight of a possible lifeline. I spied a trailer down the road, and ran there. After pounding on the front door, I realized the trailer was unoccupied, and decided it was best to run back to the farmhouse. My interview-ready attire included size 15 platform shoes that boasted three-inch heels, and I suspect that I was quite a sight as I made my way along the mile-long muddy and icy path.

The police arrived, and both women were creating quite an uncomfortable commotion. They appeared to have made amazing recoveries, and both refused to enter the awaiting ambulance that had been dispatched at their request. I recall their profanity-laced outbursts as they lobbied the officer to have me arrested.

When the commotion subsided, I found myself alone with an inoperable car and a ticket for pulling out in front of another vehicle and stopping. It was an odd citation, to be sure, but the ticket was far more manageable than the back of a police car. Looking back on the incident now, I find it interesting that the officer failed to offer me a ride anywhere. Defeated and frustrated, I commenced the 20-mile walk to my "real" home. I do not recall ever returning to that farmhouse or the couch that I had called my bed for most of three months. Worse, I have no recollection of why I never revisited. Still, many of the family members remain good friends to this day.

Despite being a no-show for the interview, I earned the job – washing dishes and cooking at the Dog and Suds in Slippery Rock. It was the perfect position for a college sophomore who was footing the bill for his tuition and living expenses. Inconveniently, and through a comedy of errors, it took over six months for my car to be repaired.

Unfortunately, my preferred mode of transportation became tennis shoes and my right thumb. Kind friends provided rides from time to time, but mostly I walked. The restaurant was just over a mile from campus, and the cottage where I lived was about six or seven miles from either place. Donned in wet jeans after a midnight closing, it was quite a hike home that winter. I often reflect on how stupid I had been not to bring a change of clothes with me to work so I could avoid the frozen jeans scraping my thighs.

Shortly after I joined the Dog and Suds crew, the restaurant changed its name to Con Puckly's Family Restaurant. Gone were the skimpy red skirts modeled by the cute teenage waitresses; in their place were gaudy smocks. I always wondered if the change in attire caused revenue to subside. Certainly, the demographic of the clientele shifted to a more refined one. Other than the sign and the uniforms, nothing much else changed. Unchanged also was the owner's proclivity to seduce selected waitresses in his locked office. The rumored dalliances were confirmed when an unsuspecting waitress opened the office door to get change, only to find her co-worker changing the boss's demeanor.

In many ways, that winter and that accident represented a coming of age for me. I cascaded into the darkest period in my life, but I received a vital education in the realities of the real world. Until that time, I had lived a rather insular adolescence. When I worked for my family, I never experienced some of the realities that other teens had endured.

In my teen years I had worked long hours, dealt with the debilitating illnesses of both of my parents, and engaged mostly with people far older than I was. I had never imagined what it would be like not to have a safety net – and without one, I fell prey to some unsavory influences. I ended up nearly failing out of college and suffering from a significant drug dependency – my prospects were not great.

Regarding my workplace, I had never imagined that a respected, married business person would engage in dalliances with teenage girls in his employ as I was washing dishes less than 10 feet away. I had never felt how cold it could be when there was no heat source other than a fireplace. I had never experienced how long six miles could be when walking in subzero weather in wet clothing. I had never imagined what could happen to a young hitchhiker when he would enter the car of a stranger at midnight.

Throughout it all, I emerged physically unharmed, but mentally compromised. I grew much wiser that winter, and it shoved me onto a new course – a more productive one. I finished the final two years of college with a nearly perfect grade record, lifting my unimpressive 2.2 QPA (quality point average) to over 3. With new vigor for life and my future, I was able to complete college while holding down two jobs.

That winter at that restaurant, I met the girl who would become my wife of 28 years. She is an amazing person, an exceptional mother, and was a significant part of my successful transformation from fear to fulfillment. Sadly, 20 years of constant travel for work insinuated both physical and relational distance between us, and we divorced. We remain good friends to this day, and will continue to be part of each other's lives in the future. When I reflect upon that winter, I realize that God had me every step of the way. He allowed me to experience defeat and engage in idiotic practices, but never allowed me to be truly harmed. Many of the seeds of fulfillment were sown during that dark period.

Inches from Disaster

Nineteen years after the February 1978 accident, I was enjoying a midnight birthday drink with a close friend and our wives at a local tavern. As a nearly 40-year-old father of preteen twins, it was a rare night out. Our revelry had broken the solitude of this sleepy establishment only minutes earlier. Suddenly, we were scared into sobriety by what felt like a bomb going off in the establishment. After a few seconds, we realized that the building had been hit by a vehicle. We exited the bar and found a car embedded into the corner of the façade. In it sat two extremely inebriated young men.

As we checked on their well-being, the impaired driver and passenger stumbled out of the car. The driver, barely able to walk, attempted to reenter the still-running car. My friend beat him to it, extracted the keys, and advised the man that he was going nowhere. Enraged, the drunk charged my friend who threw the keys to me. As he turned his anger to me, I decided I did not need to be a statistic, and I tossed the keys toward the open car door. Amazingly, the keys landed in the slot of the armrest. The driver, thinking that the keys had landed in the tall grass surrounding the building, dove into the grass.

In the midst of all the rancor and anarchy, I allowed a light chuckle to slip out. Watching those two dimwits crawling through the grass as part of what appeared to be a demented scavenger hunt – while the keys lay clearly visible a few feet away – was quite entertaining. The passenger took on the role of an idiotic straight man as the two engaged in mindless babble.

After a half-hour the police made the scene, along with a fairly large number of bystanders – including a young lady who had clearly been fighting with her significant other. She was quite a sight in her pajamas. Making matters even more entertaining, her boyfriend appeared, demanding – in a profanity-laced rant – that she return home.

Finally, the two scavenger hunt participants realized that the police had arrived. The passenger appeared awestruck, and uttered, "It's Johnny Law." The driver engaged in a fruitless begging exercise that lasted about three minutes before the officer handcuffed him and placed him in the back of the cruiser.

The officer surveyed the scene, and asked who owned the green Intrepid that had been smashed as part of the incident. In all of the intensity of the moment, I had not realized that the driver had pinballed off of my car – parked on the street – before lurching into the side of the building. My mirth was quelled as I realized that I had an expensive stake in the debacle. Luckily, my car was drivable, and the drunk driver had ample insurance. So, other than creating some inconvenience for me, the incident was rather inconsequential.

A final twist in the story came when the officer was about to leave for the police station. The passenger asked the officer for a lift. The officer, ironically named John, explained that he could only drive him to the police station, and that he would be required to arrest him. Since the passenger had done nothing wrong other than to be an occupant in a vehicle driven by a drunk, there was no need for such an arrest. But after an extraordinary exchange, the witless drunk decided a night in lockup was a far better option than being left alone on the side of the street, and he tucked his hands behind his back to await a set of cuffs.

The next day, we learned an additional fact. The police had recreated the trajectory of the car. They concluded that, if not for my automobile being parked where it was and altering the drunk driver's course, the careening car would have been launched through the bar's plate glass window. The report advised that the car probably would have taken out a significant part of the seating area. The unlikely chain of circumstances likely saved my buddy and I, and our wives, from significant injury.

In a related stroke of luck, I now had a new tale to weave that did not require any embellishment.

I have often thought about what might have been if events had played out even slightly differently. The difference of even a split-second or a few millimeters can alter the trajectory of our life paths. Because of such occurrences, my belief that the hand of God guides us – regardless of the circumstance – is fortified.

The Unwitting Reunion

I spent the better part of 30 years racing through airports. This day was no different. I had departed Northern Kentucky early, destined for Minneapolis, where I had delivered a speech to a trade group. I then made my way to Pittsburgh, the site of the American Irish Fund dinner, where later that evening I was hosting a table of vendors and their spouses. For the small fee of $10,000 each, they were bestowed with the honor of being my guest.

As expected, my trusted limo driver was waiting for me, and we made our way to the hotel with a stop to retrieve the tux I had reserved. The trip was uneventful, and during it we discussed my departure early the next morning. After checking in, I entered a rather crowded elevator, where a voice I had known all my years called out. That voice belonged to my brother.

My brother and I had been estranged for years, and I was shocked by his presence. He followed me off the elevator, and asked if he could crash with me for the night. I quickly explained my evening's schedule, which promised to end quite late and would be followed by an early trip to the airport. As I changed into the tux, I gave him the options of either sleeping on the floor or requesting a rollaway bed.

I had not seen my brother in over a year. The most apt descriptor of our relationship would be "rollercoaster," and this particular period had been one of the deepest dips. As I pen this, I cannot remember where he was living at the time or how he ended up in Pittsburgh. Even more curious, how did he know that I would be there? There was no time for questioning or even light banter, as I was late for the event.

After I returned, he asked if he could hitch a ride to the airport with me. Because he was chronically late, I advised him that I was leaving at 6 a.m., and added that if he was in the lobby and ready by then, he could join me. The next morning started off with the normal rush through my basic ritual, one I had followed hundreds of times in the past. But this morning was different; my uninvited guest cast an uncomfortable aura over my proceedings. Throughout my life, whenever my brother had insinuated himself into my routine, anomalies seemed to occur with great regularity. Many were of his doing, but still others seemed to be completely circumstantial.

I was stunned; my brother was ready on time and without incident. Normally, my driver would be waiting for me; he was never late. On this morning, he was nowhere to be seen. I telephoned him and he apologized profusely. He had misunderstood the time, but was on his way.

Not one to leave matters to chance. I jumped into a Yellow Cab with my brother in tow. The driver appeared rather jumpy – to a point where normally I would have been concerned. But the morning was too chaotic, and I was focused on transport to the airport. The back seat of the cab became a get-acquainted chamber between the brothers.

Traffic was starting to thicken as we headed across the Fort Pitt bridge. Noting that the driver was in the wrong lane, I questioned if he was intending to take the "South Side shortcut," which was a longer route but could be faster during times of heavy traffic.

Without comment or warning, the cab driver swerved into the adjacent lane. He slammed into two cars, which in turn caused a chain reaction with 10 to 12 others, leaving them crumpled across three lanes. The cab ended up lodged in a tunnel abutment. After a few harsh words were exchanged, I phoned my driver. He reported that he would need to take a different route to retrieve me because the entire Fort Pitt Bridge was in gridlock. "No kidding," I responded. "We caused it."

Wasting no time, I demanded that the cab driver retrieve our luggage, and my brother and I started walking along a downward ramp toward Carson Street. Normally, that roadway would have been packed with cars, but today there had been an accident – our accident – that was blocking the ramp. We had unfettered access. It must have been quite a scene as we literally strutted down the middle of the lane, two abreast.

It was rather cold that morning, and neither of us had the proper attire. As we walked, the thought of freezing to death crossed my mind, as did the potential liability from leaving an accident scene prior to the arrival of the police. Both of those thoughts were quickly replaced by a strong desire to ensure that I made my flight, a feat that appeared unlikely.

It was not yet 8 a.m., so I surmised that my assistant was probably in transit to the office. Since cell phone use was in its infancy, I knew that contact with my assistant would probably not be possible.

My driver, notwithstanding the slip-up that morning, had pulled off many transit miracles in the past. He came through again and was waiting for us. He said that the lack of traffic had enabled him to make record time. I offered that perhaps the thousands of cars completely blocking the major artery to the area – again, because of our accident – was the explanation. He commented, as if it was an unrelated fortuitous event, "I'll bet that's it."

My brother and I said our goodbyes, and I boarded my plane. I often find myself in a state of reflection – and that rather quiet flight was no exception, for there was plenty to reflect upon that morning.

Later that morning as I sat at my desk, a few of my questions were answered. The cab driver had been impaired by some sort of mind-altering drug; he was discharged from his duties. My brother had found my whereabouts by contacting my company and securing my itinerary from the travel department. To this day, I believe he had pretended to be me, but I cannot be sure of that. He had one more surprise for me, though. As I perused my hotel receipt, I learned he had ordered a rather inordinate amount of room service and secured his evening entertainment through the "all access" adult channel offered on the hotel television.

I recall very little interaction between my brother and me during that time of my life, but in many ways, the hotel and car interlude marked a return to normalcy from a strained relationship. As angry as I was at the time, the unlikely series of events served as an important catalyst, leading to a more productive future.

I Don't Believe In No Ghosts

In June of 2000, I was wrestling with a significant life decision. I had spent the past decade constructing a career in corporate America. I had achieved what many would describe as success. I had earned a seat on the management board of two divisions of a successful Fortune 500 company. I was both the youngest and least formally educated member of both boards, a fact in which I took great delight.

But the company was enduring significant internal strife, and my immediate family was dealing with their own set of challenges. A decade of constant travel, punctuated by eight moves that took us to four states and me to five, had taken its toll.

After a rather bombastic meeting, I decided to change courses. Many would advise me that I was throwing a successful career into a blazing and terminal pyre. Still, it was a decision fomented through altruistic reflection, and one I was destined to make again a dozen years into the future.

For me it has always been about the greater good – fit and fulfillment, not wealth and status. I opted to follow my instincts; I accepted a significantly inferior compensation plan at a tiny entity. In doing so, a move to yet another town was upon us. We also faced a seemingly never-ending search for a new home. To be candid, the responsibility for that significant task fell upon the capable shoulders of my wife, as it had so many times previously.

After being in alignment for nearly 20 years on selecting our houses, we found ourselves at an interesting crossroads. The two remaining options could not have been more disparate. A relatively new home in the country with nearly 100 acres lost out to a stately mansion situated in a town that had fallen victim to a generation of societal transitions. Once a wealthy community that boasted one of the more prestigious colleges in the state, the town had experienced significant decline. Most of the town's lavish mansions that had once hosted lavish balls had been transitioned to apartments or professional offices. This one had not. Known as the Louis Walker home, it had been built by a Civil War-era colonel who had patented the zipper.

If life could not have been more complicated at that time, my brother badgered me into taking ownership of his year-old Chrysler

300M. He had secured an interest-free loan, and I was maneuvered into taking over the payments because he was suddenly moving to Europe. I do not recall exactly how it transpired, but we were able to take over the obligation, license the car, and insure it without taking actual ownership. While it seems incredulous, it is a factual and important element of a broader story.

As my wife planned our purchase of the albatross that became our home, we learned that it was known around town for being haunted. While I do not believe in the paranormal, it became yet another interesting piece of the story.

During that period, cell phone technology was new. Most businesspeople found cell phones essential, but they had not evolved to everyday personal use. As such, when the realtor's cell phone rang as she and my wife toured the home, it came with some level of fanfare. One question was asked – did the prospective client own a gold 300M? There had been an accident, and both my wife and the realtor were summoned to the scene. Shortly thereafter, my cell phone rang, and my panicked wife apprised me of the details. There had been an accident involving my brother's car – no one had occupied any of the impacted vehicles, yet there was one person deceased and many bystanders rattled.

The scene was pandemonium. On the side of the street lay the covered body of a lifeless man, who evidently had been run down by a driverless van that careened across the street. The van was still running, wedged into the rear corner of my brother's car. It had been traveling at a high enough speed that after striking the man, it continued its course another 100 feet. The damage rendered my brother's car inoperable.

As I made the two-hour drive to assess the situation and bring aid to my stranded wife, I learned a bit more about the incident.

Evidently, the van that had been driven by the deceased man. The vehicle had experienced a mechanical problem, and the driver decided to stop the van and crawl under it. It was unclear if the van was running at the time, but the transmission had evidently been placed in the Park position. Did the car mysteriously start itself? Did the car jump from Park to Drive without anyone at the helm? Two questions that likely will never be answered.

Nevertheless, while the driver was under it, the van mysteriously shifted into Drive and began to accelerate. It crushed the man, killing him instantly, and then raced across the roadway – striking the 300M. Witnesses claimed that the van was in full acceleration as it unsuccessfully attempted to continue its path that was blocked by the parked car.

When I arrived, the scene was quiet, and the only remnant of the accident was a lone police cruiser and a chalk outline of the man's body etched in the blacktop of the parking lot. It was a stark and uneasy visual.

After hearing the incident related by others multiple times, my attention turned to short-term future planning. My wife needed transportation, and I had yet to announce my decision to leave my employer for the new position. After a series of now mind-hazed events, I found myself traveling south alone in a Ford Expedition that would ultimately become my new company vehicle. As I traveled, I contacted a close friend to regale him with the unlikely accident story, and I conflated the accident with the background of the haunted mansion that was, up to that point, not obligated to me. I convinced myself that some force beyond the mortal plane had caused the accident, and that proceeding with the purchase would be unwise.

It was dark when I entered the underground garage of the building where I had a temporary apartment. The building, a converted train station near downtown Pittsburgh, was situated in a rather unsavory section of the city and boasted a robust security system. To enter the garage, a pass card was inserted into a kiosk that lifted a barricade arm.

In my emotionally drained state, I dropped the card, and it bounced off the ledge and rested under my car. Without a thought, I found myself in the prone position under the car, with my outstretched arms attempting to retrieve the card. A revolting sense of uneasiness permeated my body as I realized I was in much the same position as the decedent had been a few hours before.

Rattled and unnerved, I returned to my vehicle to the sound of a ringing cell phone. I answered, only to hear an intense booing sound – an effect that one might imagine emanating from a ghost. Because this was in the days before caller ID, I did not know who was on the other end of the phone. I admonished the unknown caller, and demanded that they identify themselves – to no avail. Now I was terrorized.

I entered the elevator that led to my temporary apartment. While going up, the phone rang two more times – and each time the call was dropped. As I approached my door, I convinced myself that a white cross had been painted upon its face.

The building, with an ominous façade and a storied past, was unnerving on the best of days. Under the current circumstances, preparing to sleep there became almost intolerable. As I unlocked the door, I felt I was living through a poorly-choreographed scene in a demented B horror movie. Now the phone was ringing inside the apartment. To my knowledge, no one who knew me had the apartment phone number, and this was before robocalls plagued our daily lives. Tentatively, and wrought with anxiety, I answered the phone. Relief filled me as I heard the voice of my now-concerned friend, apologizing for a practical joke gone horribly wrong.

The first phone call had been from him – and it was followed by three others that, due to the thick walls of the complex, had failed to connect. Somehow, he had secured the landline number from my assistant, who evidently had gotten it from human resources.

The next morning as I left the apartment, I surveyed the white cross that had warned against my entrance the night before. Viewed in daylight through a more unaltered lens, the door simply had two intersecting and errant paint strokes that had just been applied by the painters who were working in the building.

Later that day as I put the finishing touches on my resignation letter, I reflected upon the recent series of unlikely events. I now had yet another story in a lifetime of interesting stories, to be told and retold long into the future.

My reverie was interrupted by a call from our human resources department, alerting me to the fact that a Frank Haverlack's car had been in a fatal accident the day before. They queried if he was any relation. The improbable story had made the front page of the local paper; my company, in an attempt to get in front of any damaging stories about executives, subscribed to a service that scanned media outlets. *How fortuitous that I had never changed the ownership records,* I mused. I returned to drafting my resignation.

Despite the "paranormal" guidance, along with several other similarly-unexplainable warnings against it, we ended up moving into the mansion and called it home for a relatively short period of time. Even though there were many unexplainable events that transpired while I lived there, I remain unconvinced that ghosts roam the world. However, if they do, they definitely have 875 Grove Street among their homes.

The Accidents within Accidents

A heavy snow had fallen on a Thursday afternoon in late January 2004, adding a fresh coat of nature's paint to the rather dreary landscape of winter. We had recently released the "zipper house" albatross from around our necks and were residing in an apartment. Both children were off at college, and we were free for a getaway to our home on Lake Chautauqua. As I stood at the top of the rather steep outdoor stairway that led from the second story to the parking lot, I surveyed the beauty of the seasonal scene. But then, one errant step onto a snow-masked ice buildup, and I was careening down the entire flight until my left foot caught an open stair tread. That abruptly stopped my progress with a loud pop, followed by intense pain.

Unaware of my dilemma, my wife exited the apartment as I had minutes before. I had alerted her to the ice on the steps and she saw my predicament. After making her way to me without incident, she quickly ascended the steps to call for an ambulance.

Oddly, she appeared almost giddy as – much to my chagrin – she had recently joined an ambulance service (which I thought was a waste of time and money). Regardless of the cost, I was in transit to the local medical center. After triage, I learned that I had suffered a complete tear and detachment of the quadriceps. We were sent home with an inflatable cast and instructed to return the following morning for surgery.

At times, I wonder if our medical profession fully thinks through the details of each patient's unique living circumstances. It was now after dark, and we were left alone to determine how to forge our way up the nearly unscalable stairs into the apartment. And then we would need to descend again before dawn the next morning.

Life can be rather complex, and after the chaos of the afternoon and evening, I phoned my mother. She herself was recovering in Long Beach Memorial Hospital from surgery she had endured the day before. A chronic hypochondriac, my mother had chosen to have countless medical procedures throughout her lifetime. This latest one was to implant the latest-technology pacemaker, which would replace her current, fully-functioning one.

She sounded weak and nearly incoherent. I became overcome with guilt, as I had chosen not to make the long trip to California to be with her. So, I did not bother to inform her that I had just suffered an injury and was facing surgery of my own in the morning. There just did not seem to be any point in doing so. Neither did my wife or I inform either of our children.

The time for surgery prep came, and rather shockingly, my wife was allowed access into the preparation room. I was fully prepped with IV in place, and the phone rang. My attention was requested. It was my assistant, and my wife fumed. "My mother has died. It's the only explanation," I muttered as my wife approached the phone. No – my wife informed me that my daughter had been taken to the hospital. She had been accidentally knocked down a flight of stairs during an off-campus party.

With surgery scheduled within minutes, I did not have time to feel any normal sense of hopelessness prior to slipping away under anesthesia. The surgery was long but successful, and I awoke to a rather dull pain. I found myself attached to an apparatus that was keeping my injured leg in continual and steady motion.

I was awakened the next morning by my wife, who looked as if the world had swallowed her up. Fearing the worst, I inquired about my daughter. My wife assured me that my daughter was fine, but added that my mother was indeed dead. I am not sure if it was the narcotics talking, but I simply stated, "I knew that yesterday."

My wife, never a subtle sort, had blurted out the news in the presence of a nurse at the hospital – who appeared to be overcome with shock and grief. I consoled the nurse and added, "It's okay. I will never have to worry about hearing that news again."

I have often wondered if that nurse thought me incredibly cold-hearted; I believe that my reaction was not what she expected. For whatever reason, I had convinced myself that my mother had died, and the news came only as an expected confirmation rather than a cause for shock.

My mother's remains were cremated, but not before her brand-new pacemaker was extracted. Evidently, pacemakers do not react well to the pyre of a furnace. I was asked what I wanted to do with the pacemaker – to which I responded, "I do not know, but she doesn't need it anymore."

Six weeks into the yearlong convalescence after my surgery, I was released to travel to California. I would be handling my mother's affairs and attending a memorial service that would provide closure for her friends. Our family service would be held after the ground thawed in the spring. The entire trip was filled with a mix of fortunate and regrettable incidents, and was highlighted by some extraordinarily amusing events.

Dinner was cathartic, and included more drink than advisable. In attendance was my wife, my brother, and my mother's three best friends. My wife, the most responsible member of the party, had avoided the fruit of the grape and agreed to transport our guests back to their homes. In the meantime, I, with my leg immobilized and equipped with crutches, was unceremoniously placed into the back seat of my brother's car. *The vulnerability of the handicapped,* I thought. My brother made an unplanned stop, and as I sat shivering in the car, I watched through the window as my brother engaged the attractive attendant in the cigar store along East Ocean Boulevard. He had imbibed more than was responsible for driving, and the impairment fueled his quest.

I required a bathroom, so I formed a plan. Dialing 411 from my cell phone, I obtained the phone number of the establishment where he was involved in his tete-a-tete. It is rather surreal when you can see a person answer the phone from across the street, and then watch the shock on her face as you ask her to stop the conversation and send your brother back to the car.

Despite the unplanned stop, the evening had been extremely therapeutic. Emotions were running a bit high, likely fueled by the alcohol intake. My brother asked if we could stop into the hotel bar for a nightcap. Despite being in moderate discomfort, I agreed, but we found the bar to be closed. We said our goodnights and departed for our rooms.

Slumber came easily that night, and for the first time since my injury I fell into a deep sleep. But my sleep was rudely interrupted by a ringing phone. My wife answered, and with an ashen color overtaking her face, handed me the phone as if it had been infected.

It was the Long Beach Police Department. "Do you have a brother, Frank Haverlack?" they asked. Before I could answer, they advised me there had been an accident and that my presence was required at Long Beach Memorial Hospital. I asked about his condition and what had transpired, but my questions were left unanswered. The only information I could gather was that he was alive.

My emotions were high as my wife drove toward the hospital where my mother had been just six weeks prior. When we arrived, there was no fanfare and no police. Eventually, we were led to a room where my badly beaten brother lay on a gurney. As I entered, a single tear ran down his face. I was in total shock, as he was still attired in the clothing he had worn the night before.

During the beating or soon afterward, he had lost control of his bowels. This normally proud and impeccably attired man laid defeated in a blood-stained shirt and immersed in his own waste. I was ushered to a waiting room; to my horror, after an hour or two he was released to my care. His face had been beaten so badly that I barely recognized him; but other than extensive bruising and some fractures to the face, there was, in the hospital's judgment, no medical reason to admit him. *So is the way of a big city hospital,* I thought.

The story became much more complex at this point, but it is not particularly relevant. In the end, he was fine physically, but suffered significant post-traumatic stress symptoms.

The night before, he had elected to get that nightcap, and despite his impaired state he used sound enough judgment to employ a taxi. Many of the facts of the story remain in dispute to this day, but the evening's events ended with him being beaten with a blunt object and left in a ditch for dead. Somehow, he recovered consciousness and stumbled onto the freeway, where help was summoned.

As I took a bit of time to ponder the entire sequence of events from my fall to my brother's beating, I became overwhelmed with guilt. *How could I have allowed my mother to be treated in such a hell-hole with no one to advocate for her?* To this day, the thought sickens me; every time I see an elderly person alone in a hospital, the entire nauseating episode is replayed in my head.

My mother had suffered with debilitating fear much of her life. She had feared not having enough money for the entirety of my life, and that fear manifested itself into a fear of declining health in later years. She chronically overmedicated herself and regularly volunteered for experimental treatments. Ultimately, the fear that had controlled much of her life killed her. According to the man who performed her autopsy, her heart had weakened from decades-long cocktails of medications. He estimated that she had but 15 percent of her heart capacity, and the stress of the surgery simply pushed her heart beyond its ability to sustain her life.

The unfortunate events of my mother's decline and death fueled my passion to help lift others from the deadly grip of fear and to encourage them on the path to fulfillment. I believe my mother had a full and mostly happy life, but it could have been much fuller and more productive. At her death, her estate was valued in excess of $700,000, but she lived as if she was a pauper – a tragedy of epic proportions.

Preparation and Time

Time marches on, and in effect, it is the one universal thing we cannot impact. Nothing and no one of this world can stop it. Despite the series of unlikely accidents that become part of our life story, the clock continues to move forward, unaffected by the tumult. Despite the reality that none of us know when the next accident will impact our lives, we need to learn to master time management. We need to prepare ourselves for what the future brings, while engaging in clear decision-making that enables us to avoid accidents that are of our own doing.

When we commit to a discipline of planning our lives and striving for fulfillment, **accidents** are far less debilitating. Time becomes our ally, as we are more capable of using it to our advantage. Much as a conditioned athlete can leap hurdles on the track ahead, we can condition ourselves to overcome life's challenges – and in doing so, they are rendered more like inconveniences than like life-altering tragedies.

Chapter 13

The Unintended Miracle

God is in control. He has us; we simply need to trust Him.

NTERWOVEN WITHIN THE SERIES of accidents spanning over 40 years and detailed in Chapter 12, life marched on. July 31, 1985 – it was just another day. I was outside working on some project that had me using a circular saw, which, due to my extraordinarily poor carpentry skills, was never an optimal operation. My wife, who was pregnant and had been mostly bedridden for two weeks, came out of the house. She advised me that her water had broken. *Finally*, I thought, as I helped her into the car. Two weeks past her due date, she had been in utter misery for a month. As I recall, she gained 62 pounds during the pregnancy, and I was convinced something odd was afoot.

We arrived at the hospital around 6 p.m.; I left her in the capable hands of the nursing staff and parked the car. Upon my return to the building, a set of scrubs was thrown in my direction and I was advised that she was at seven centimeters. She would deliver at any time.

Sadly, I had gained more weight than she had. "Sympathy weight gain" is the unofficial term, and I excelled in gaining weight to support others. To say that the scrubs I was given were a bit snug would be an understatement. A baloney skin might be the most apt description of their appearance on my swollen body.

When I arrived at the room, my wife was wired up. If it had not been for the Lamaze classes we had taken, I would have likely freaked out. She did not look good. In fact, I thought she was in distress. What had been described as an immediate delivery transformed into a waiting game. When the Tonight Show came on TV, I realized the mother's ring was going to be adorned with a peridot in place of the strongly preferred ruby.

Shortly after midnight, the obstetrician recommended that forceps would need to be used to deliver the baby. The conditions were deteriorating; the delivery would require a spinal. My wife was devastated at the news, but we had little choice. I remember the doctor inserting the implement and placing his foot on the table, as he pulled with what appeared to be all his might. I think I entered a state of shock. He turned to me and advised, "I can try again, but if the baby gets stuck, I will have to break its collar bone." I refer to the baby as "it," since we did not yet know the sex of our new family member.

A Prediction in the Midst of Tumult

The only other option was an emergency caesarean, and so we departed for the operating room. Per hospital protocol, a pediatrician had to be on site to witness the procedure. As we walked to the operating room, I cried out to God silently. Still a bit raw from my father's death, I felt something bad brewing. I finally blurted out what

I had been thinking for the past two weeks. "Are you sure this isn't twins?" I queried the doctor.

His response was, "Guaranteed not; it's just one big baby."

As I stood by my wife's side, with a pediatrician as company, I awaited the birth. My wife, who had long passed her point of patience, icily commented, "You better hope this is the son you want; you are not getting any more." I knew she was not joking, so I started silently rooting for a boy. Within a few minutes, I was the proud father of a son. He had dark black hair and arrived screaming.

Unbridled Joy

The pediatrician advised me that something was terribly wrong. The baby was not enormous as predicted, but rather normal in size. Immediately the obstetrician mused, "Surprise, surprise, we've got another one." *Hope it's a girl,* I thought, and within minutes I was the proud father of a daughter. She was silent and had short, reddish-colored hair. Her silence was of great concern, and the nursing team went into action. Within seconds, she joined her brother in a chorus of screams.

Not to be outdone, the delivering doctor cried out, "I think we have a third." Evidently, I started to weave, and someone screamed, "Get Mr. Haverlack a chair, he's going down!" I honestly cannot recall if a chair ever arrived, but within seconds it was confirmed that I would not be the father of triplets.

At 2:02 a.m. and 2:06 a.m., a 6-pound, 6-ounce son and a 6-pound, 12-ounce daughter were born. Both were healthy and without blemish. The doctor asked my wife what she thought; her only response was, "While you have me cut open, please tie my tubes." That request was not honored.

I returned home and decided that I would take a quick nap – no need to bother the family in the wee hours of the morning. At 7 a.m., I commenced my calls. The first call was to my mother, who appeared oddly unimpressed that her first two grandchildren had been born. I concluded my round of calls around 9 a.m. just as the phone rang. It was my mother again. She asked if I had called that morning to share news that she had become a grandmother of twins, a fact that I confirmed. She had been sleeping, and thought the phone call had been a dream. Bubbly with joy, for an instant she seemed to have shed her normally reserved persona.

God's Hand Is All Over It

I was so overjoyed that it took a couple of weeks before I thought about how incompetent that the obstetrician had been. How could he have been so wrong and incredulous about the procedure until the birth of the second baby? Then it hit me – God had played a role in this entire episode. As a struggling young couple, the decision to bring a child into the world had serious implications. Obviously, having the capacity both financially and mentally to care for a human who will be completely reliant on you was paramount.

I had a good job and a reasonable career path. My wife held a terrific position that appeared stable. We had excellent insurance, and with hers as a secondary, medical expenses were not a significant worry. A new addition to the family, with an understanding that day care would be a necessity, seemed appropriate. Unfortunately, things changed. My wife's job ended unceremoniously after she was already pregnant; and my company made an adjustment to the medical insurance program, with a dramatic reduction in benefits. What had been a carefully-planned blessing turned into a more challenging endeavor.

Had I known to expect twins, I likely would have suffered great emotional strife. It might have created issues in my work and in my personal life. I was spared that strain and tumult. Now the father of surprise twins, I had no choice but to come to grips with how to manage everything. Amazingly, it all worked out with little issue. Our inability to bring twins home with only one car seat was remedied by a community collection. A neighbor lent us a crib, and a friend bought us a 60-day diaper service. We had plenty of help from family members, and we survived the first few months without major issues.

A few weeks into August, I was promoted at work. So, much of the financial burden was lifted. The only remaining issue was the hospital bill. We had planned for a $100 copay and it ended up being $2,400 – a hefty sum in 1985.

When the children were four months old, my wife contracted chickenpox – a very dangerous disease for both mother and infant. Shortly afterward, we had planned to take a reward trip that I had earned through my employment. My mother and her best friend agreed to babysit for the weekend. With the shadow of chickenpox looming, my wife and I boarded the plane. We checked in with my mother a couple times a day, a task that was a bit more challenging in the pre-cell phone era.

My mother was in her glory and having a wonderful time, or so she made us believe. We found out later that the first visible sign that both children had been infected appeared just as we were boarding the plane. We returned to two speckled babies, a relieved grandmother, and an exhausted best friend.

The day following July 31, 1985, was the greatest of my life. It was a new beginning, and a new generation had arrived. What followed has been a lifelong exploration packed with a panoply of emotion. The great honor of becoming a parent is one of those life events that is very hard to describe.

Unbridled joy, intertwined with gut wrenching fear, is commonplace in the early days. It is a cavalcade of firsts – first step, first tumble, first word, first day of school, first goal, first love, first heartbreak, first success, and first failure. Through it all, we parents are but active spectators with an awesome responsibility to guide, teach, lift up, and calm down. We laugh with them one minute, and cry for them the next. All along, we wish we could shoulder some of the pain, while realizing that they must endure it alone. All of these experiences are woven into the fabric of what is their unique journey.

Then, one day, we realize that our offspring have successfully overcome the travails of adolescence and have transformed into formidable, contributing adults. They too will leave their legacy for future generations. It is a parent's greatest blessing to witness and take part in that transformation, and I am forever grateful for having been so fortunate.

Chapter 14

The Rock

**How the ordinary becomes an extraordinary
part of your life journey.**

I N MY MEMORY, MY father's family was an outdoors family. We were constantly in the field or on the water, most likely at the edge of civilization. The reality, however, was far more ordinary. My father liked to hunt, as did one of his brothers. Another brother enjoyed fishing. But those three human influencers, fueled by my imagination, were enough to instill in me a love of the outdoors and a compulsion to commune with nature. Those impulses have manifested into almost a reverence for our environment.

Over the past 20 years, I have had the good fortune to experience what can be classified as world-class hunting and fishing adventures. From the Arctic to the Equator, I have hunted, fished, explored, and connected with nature. It has brought me great time for reflection, and the solitude has enriched my well-being. Despite the breadth of the fantastic journeys I have encountered, my mind always wanders back to a field in western Pennsylvania. The field and the woods that surrounded it are not particularly noteworthy. In fact, other than enjoying the sight of some deer who might be feeding there, the tens of thousands of people who drive Route 258 every year likely do not give it a thought.

The field was part of a non-operating farm that had been in my wife's family for over half a century. It included 128 acres, a house, and the deteriorating vestiges of outbuildings required for farming in that era. A distant relative did some planting from time to time, but the heavy work of caring for and nurturing the land had long ceased. The carefully-manicured furrows that had once provided protection for a variety of game, while also keeping the field's water table in check, had been allowed to atrophy. Depending on the season and recent rainfall, the field could be rather dry or could become an almost impassable morass. The conditions normally were the latter. So wet was the normal environment, those that hunted there began wearing 16-inch-high, insulated rubber boots. In certain years, even those boots failed to protect one's feet from the icy waters. One misplaced step could bring the water up over the rim of a boot.

Almost as if it had been placed strategically, there was a rather large rock that adorned the middle of the field. To the casual observer, it was merely an impediment. The farmers of the past probably found it easier to plow around than to remove. But to those of us who called the farm our hunting mecca, it was the obelisk of our entire hunting experience. It was the meeting point where fires raged, stories were formed, and life transpired. The Rock was so important to our hunting existence that those of us who were blessed enough to bask in its persona became known as the Rock Hunters. We loved the community-bestowed moniker.

Rites of Passage

The Rock became part of our spiritual landscape with the passage of time, and integral to the rites that occurred in the field down through the years. In order to truly reap the fruits of the experience, there was some lexicon that needed to be learned by participants. The terminology described geography and events, and included **deer parlance**.

Among the notable places that were part of the experience was **the swamp**. It was to the left of the Rock, and encompassed about 30 acres of nearly-impermeable goo; but it became a sanctuary for many of the deer once the season opened. Further to the left was the **gas line**. As the name suggests, it was a clearcut area about 12 feet wide and 300 feet long. Any deer that attempted an escape through the gas line area would be vulnerable.

The **railroad tie pile** was in the corner of the woods, and its elevated position was a great spot to spy deer sneaking through the trees. About 400 yards beyond the Rock, past the field, were the **tree tops**, which were the remnants from a logging exercise 20 years earlier. Due to the thick saplings that choked the area after the trees had been removed, this area was nearly impassable, making it another great hiding spot for our prey.

Activities included **posting, drives**, and **pushing**. **Posting** referred to taking a motionless position and being on the ready to fire at deer when they would run by. That role was part of a **drive** that included any number of hunters walking through a certain area, attempting to move deer. **Pushing** was the art of compelling the deer to move in a certain direction.

One of our most important terms was **Mooeh Grande**. That term was reserved for the legendary monster buck that was regularly seen, but never subdued. Either he was too smart for us, or our perception gave him a larger status than the reality. Those harvested bucks never seemed to measure up to the legend.

Four generations knitted the yarns of life, ensconced near the Rock. It was a place to enjoy a respite from more strenuous activities. It was a place of firsts: it witnessed the first deer harvested by my son, the first deer harvested by my nephew, the first deer harvested by dozens of friends and family members, and the first deer harvested by me. But the Rock was so much more to us than merely a hunting totem.

As the years passed, and as many of us migrated from youth to middle age and then old age, our lives were enriched while we enjoyed a warm fire and some roasted pepperoni – all in the shadow of the Rock. Children became educated, went to war, and had children of their own – and we told the stories heartily. Members of older generations succumbed to the travails that occurred in lives well-lived, and they were replaced by new generations of eager, hungry minds jumping at the chance to encounter the magic. Each year, for the two-week hunting season, those acres around the Rock were transformed into an oasis for dreams – past, present and future.

Now that I no longer go there, I think I miss the excitement most of all. Members of our hunting family embarked into the predawn blackness of the woods on those brisk snowy mornings. Each of us anticipated encountering the prize. Alone, as the earth continued its revolution, the skies would begin to brighten just a bit and, in the shadows, one could imagine the precious prey sneaking through the forest.

While we thought it was still far too dark to raise our gun barrels, the solitude would be broken as a shot would ring out from a neighboring farm. I would feel a mix of wonder – how could anyone actually see well enough to fire a weapon? – and excitement – thinking that the time had actually arrived.

Each season was a bit different and the actual individual experiences were fluid. At some point, one by one, the members of the hunting party would wander to the Rock for warmth and camaraderie. The tales of the day's marvels would commence, while frozen fingers were warmed over the fire.

Another important exercise that regularly occurred at the Rock was strategic planning. There would be discussions about the next tactical assault, certain to push an unprecedented number of deer within range of our skilled marksmen.What would the campaign's details include? Perhaps a two-person drive through the treetops, sending frightened prey toward a sharpshooter hiding near the washing machines? Maybe a lone soul would be brave enough to traverse the dreaded swamp, where the Mooeh Grande was sure to be hiding.

The swamp was so thickly packed with flora that passage was virtually impossible. Agreeing to go there would require the participant to unload his gun and allow it to hang on a specially-hewn branch; carrying the gun into the swamp would be futile and hazardous. That branch, of course, grew from a sapling near the Rock. "Pushing the swamp," as it was known, was a noble act that was always respected by the other members of the party. For it to be effective, it required a hunter posted on the gas line and another in the corner. It was also wise to place another shooter near the railroad tie pile.

Regardless of the agreed-upon offensive, one thing was required and sacrosanct. Someone had to man the Rock. His job was two-fold. First, he needed to serve as the last line of offense, should any deer attempt to outflank the team and cross the field to the safety of the Martins' property – a 40-acre strip of land impenetrable by hunters, due to the owners' strict policy. The second and equally important duty was to keep the fire stoked. Tactics were continually debated and executed. Some were accomplished successfully, while most failed to meet the intended objective. Regardless, each incident became woven into the fabric of the history we were creating.

A previous generation of hunters had strategically placed a few washing machines – ancient wringer models – throughout the woods. Their purpose was to serve as icy repositories for beers to be enjoyed by hunters. Many suggested that our Rock would have been scoffed at by the previous generation. Some of the older generation even dared to describe us as nonhunters. They had washing machines stocked with cool beer, and we had a Rock. From my perspective, they seemed like eerily similar monoliths.

Each day as the sun faded and the temperatures plummeted, the guns were unloaded, the fire was fueled, and the bourbon and brandy began to flow. Sure to follow was the recounting of stories both new and often-told. Jokes would fly, and good-natured teasing ensued. Finally, someone would suggest that we head back to the farmhouse, where spaghetti awaited.

Once inside the farmhouse, the tales would be retold to our critical fact-checkers, who ensured that the accounts contained no embellishment – or at least that any enrichments met the allowable criteria. Included in those allowable elaborations would be the transformation of a nice eight-point into a monster buck. That said, anyone concocting a story where a doe miraculously grew horns was required to stand in the corner until their eyes cleared.

Dinner was normally followed by a rousing game of contract rum. My nephew would insert any twos he was dealt into the temples of his glasses, announcing their existence to the other players. Twos were the vital wild cards that often led to victory, and the phrase, "look at the twos," was regularly heard as a player's cards were unveiled. In an attempt to intimidate the competition, my nephew delighted in allowing the competition to look at them early.

Days became years, and years developed into lifetimes, and the Rock stood unfettered and unaltered. Mindless banter converted into life stories, and they evolved into generational testimonies. Truth be told, most of us were faux marksmen, and our ineptitude led to exciting volleys of lead orbs that rarely hit their intended targets. It was not unusual for more than 20 shells to lie at our feet after such a barrage had concluded. I actually imagined the deer caucusing within the protection of the woods to determine who would make the run across the field to amuse the herd. My contrived version of a stag's game of chicken seemed rather plausible.

The Day I Had Dreamed Of

For decades, the first day of the antlered deer hunt in Pennsylvania fell on the Monday following Thanksgiving. For the vast majority of my hunting life, the antlered deer hunt meant that the only creatures legally allowed to be harvested during those two weeks were those with antlers of at least three inches. Traditionally, an antlerless hunt of two days followed the antlered hunt.

Opening Day was in many ways even more popular than Thanksgiving. Schools closed and businesses were shuttered, as over 1.3 million hunters took to the woods of Pennsylvania in search of the coveted whitetail. In many rural counties, the schools closed on the Monday following the end of the antlered deer season, because that day would begin the antlerless deer season.

The year 1987 was no different. The anticipation and preparation filled our minds and bodies. In 10 hours, all the members of our party would be sitting quietly in their positions, waiting for the darkness to cede its grip on the woods. This Sunday evening, as was tradition, the fish sandwiches and chili were being served by veteran barmaids who continuously poured the Wild Turkey. With each shot, an ice-cold beer to cool the pipes was added. Our favorite bar had become yet another integral part of our annual hunting regime.

As I recall, Monday, the opening day, came and went without any noteworthy revelations. A front was descending on the area as Monday became Tuesday, and with it came rain and dropping temperatures. We awoke Tuesday morning to a steady rain, and only two hunters remained. I recall debating if we should even take to the woods. The ancestors' guilt trip motivated us to slowly make our way through the soggy morass. I agreed to take the first drive, realizing that the rain would make it hard to push the deer from their beds. I also knew that the noise of the rainfall spitting on the leaves and surrounding foliage would render my ears useless. I agreed more out of boredom than any belief that there would be any positive outcome.

As I approached the thickest section of the woods ahead, I spied what appeared to be a branch. My eyes told me it looked like antlers but my eyes had deceived me countless times in the past while on the hunt. Hay bales had appeared to be herds of deer and movement of any kind had made my heart race.

This time was different. I followed those branches toward two ears, and finally, an eye. The deer was no more than 30 yards from me, nestled in the thick brush. He had apparently decided that I would simply walk past him. I raised my gun and fired one shot. Immediately the deer rose to his feet. Had I missed? That question remained unanswered, because before the deer had a chance to take a step, I had chambered a second bullet and fired it into his chest cavity. He fell where he had been lying.

The woods were so wet that, unknown to me, one of his antlers had become buried in the mud. As I surveyed the kill, I counted five points on one antler and did not see the other. I immediately was lamenting the loss of his other antler. Had it come loose and fallen as the result of a fight, or had it simply never grown due to some disease? Either way, this beautiful buck's rack would have been the largest I had ever harvested – had it had two antlers. *He'll be darn good eating*, I thought, as I grasped his rear two legs in an attempt to move him to a spot where field dressing would be more convenient.

As I lifted him from his mucky and brushy grave, a second antler, equal to the first, emerged from the gooey mud. A perfect 10-point – and my mind immediately raced to how great he would look on my wall. Indeed, his taxidermied head has adorned my walls in multiple houses, in numerous states.

The balance of Tuesday was caught up with those activities that one does when a deer has been successfully hunted. I performed the field dressing, which was followed by a long and tedious drag to the barn. There, the deer would hang and drain until he was ultimately loaded into a pickup for his final ride to the butcher.

Surreal, Yet Comical

The snow had already begun to fall as I said my goodbyes and headed for home around a quarter to 5 p.m. It was a half-hour ride home in normal conditions, so I knew it would be dark before I got home. When I arrived, the phone was ringing. Another deer had been harvested, but was missing in the Martins'. "He's huge," my brother-in-law exclaimed, attempting to catch his breath. "I hit him in the lung; there's foamy blood everywhere." I agreed to return and provide assistance.

The ride back was much more hazardous than the reverse route of an hour earlier. Six or seven inches of heavy, wet snow had blanketed the countryside. It was as if God had painted the entire world in celebration of the successful hunt.

As the snow subsided, the clouds gave way to a full moon that illuminated the entire woods. With God's lunar illumination as my guide, I headed out alone to find my brother-in-law. Much to my surprise, there were two sets of fresh tracks, neither large enough to be his, heading in a direction far different from the one that his description led me to imagine.

I rightfully assumed that my sister-in-law and nephew had been dispatched to assist in the ritualistic activities that follow the harvest. That walk to the woods was among the most surreal I have ever encountered. With each stride through the thick snow that masked the treacherous uneven ground below, I marveled at how beautiful everything looked. As it was a good two-and-a-half hours past sunset, I could make out every tree and every snow-adorned branch. I could easily see the snow-decorated corn stalks that dotted the field.

My solitude was rudely disrupted as I entered the woods; I unwittingly surprised a herd of deer napping nearby. A lone flashlight flickered in the distance, signaling the path ahead. Then, without warning, a shot rang out. *Holy shit*, I thought, *they do not know I am here.* I started screaming, "I'm over here. I'm over here." I followed those words with, "Don't shoot." My screams were left unanswered, so I decided to take cover behind a large pin oak.

A second shot rang out, and I saw a wounded deer run by my position and settle about 20 yards away.

"Over here," I screamed. "There's a deer over here."

"Is that you?" a voice called, and I yelled in response, "Yes!"

As my brother-in-law made his way to me, flanked by his son and wife, I admit I recited a little prayer of thanksgiving. Upon his arrival, he appeared perplexed and exhausted. "I've been chasing this deer all night," he panted.

"I think he's right over there," I said, and pointed.

A properly-directed flashlight confirmed my belief. In the artificial glow, we saw what appeared to be a beautiful young buck without flaw, but clearly too tired to move. The blood-stained snow confirmed that some unseen injury had contributed to the deer's inability to move from his spot. My brother-in-law squared his stance toward the deer, raised a .357, and squeezed the trigger. The deer jumped and moved about 10 feet.

"This deer won't die," he exclaimed in disbelief.

"You've got to hit it," I said, as I snarkily sneered.

My misplaced comment prompted my sister-in-law to chime in. "That deer is hurt. You need to kill it."

In position again but closer this time, my brother-in-law drew his weapon. The exhausted buck motioned his head feebly, thrusting his antlers toward us. A shot rang out, but the deer remained in his defensive position unharmed. The .357 was now out of ammunition and we were left with a dilemma. Quickly, I drew on my coon-hunting recollections, and recommended that we retrieve the rifle from camp and employ it with the guidance of a properly-directed flashlight. My nephew, not yet 12, was selected to retrieve the weapon and ammunition.

Upon my nephew's return, the deer was promptly taken from his misery. For all our faults, the lot of us were empathetic souls. The thought of a suffering animal haunted us, and drove us to search for hours into the darkness to bring the matter to a humane conclusion.

The incident stings in our memories to this day, even as we regale listeners with the comedy of errors that make it a story for the ages.

The Mind Is Willing, but the Heart Refuses

At 14 years old, my niece wanted to hunt. For some reason her father, a hunter himself, had declined to take her. I have always loved children and I delight in teaching. The satisfaction of helping young people learn has led me to tutor, teach and mentor throughout my life. I eagerly offered to take on the role. After successfully earning her hunter safety award, she procured the required license, and I began instructing her as to the finer points of handling the rifle she would use. She was a quick study and possessed a good eye; she quickly convinced me that she could easily harvest any animal that crossed our path.

A large willow stood in the corner of the swamp. It had been theorized that if a stand could be constructed in that tree, the results would be lethal to deer. Never a true carpenter, but skilled enough to attempt the feat, I began construction on a stand that would safely house both my niece and me. It would afford us the opportunity to shoot from a sitting or standing position, but it had neither aesthetics nor engineering excellence. In fact, had I not constructed it and tested it, I likely would not have considered using it. It probably did not even pass the most loosely-considered definition of a deer stand, but it got the job done.

The wind was blowing briskly on the morning that we first used it. Our elevation and the lack of any protection from the gusts created a bone-chilling environment. It felt exceptionally frigid. As the icy wind cut through my thermal layers, I reflected on the benefits of walls. As I had learned to expect, the skies began to brighten – and finally, we could make out the twisted paths that crisscrossed the thicket below. Alone in a tree, enduring the dark frozenness, a hunter's mind begins to wander. *Maybe the earth is off course and the sun will never rise* is a thought that has entered my mind upon occasion.

Since I was not alone and had some teaching to do, I banished any mind-wandering from my brain. My goal was clear: to have my niece successfully harvest a buck, any buck – if I bagged one too, so much the better. I had placed us strategically so we could survey an entire 360 degrees. Watching for any movement, I heard a light voice whisper, "One's coming," which she immediately followed with, "It's bigger than my dad's." Slowly, I turned and saw a trophy whitetail walking through the woods. He was completely unaware of our position and proudly displayed his impressive rack.

I quietly guided my niece to position the gun properly, and to ensure that she squeezed the trigger instead of pulling it. The deer was within 25 yards, and remained unaware that his life was to be cut short in the next several seconds. From my vantage point, the gun barrel appeared motionless. *Ice water is running through her veins,* I thought, as she stoically wielded her weapon.

Without warning, she announced that she was unable to shoot the deer. I examined her eyes and immediately knew that there was no reason to comment further. I instructed her to unload her gun. She descended the ladder without comment, and headed for the farmhouse alone.

I reflected as I sat alone in the tree. I replayed the scene in my head. It felt as if it had taken an eternity, but in fact it lasted less than a minute. I was not angry, I was not sad – I had become enlightened. The same reverence that fueled my passion to take to the woods in search of that special moment led my niece to decide that she could not take the life of such a beautiful creature. I lingered in that tree the rest of the remaining daylight hours and never saw another deer. In fact, to my knowledge, no deer has ever been harvested from that position.

Over 30 years later, my niece and I still have never discussed the incident. Not a hint or word has ever been uttered about it between us. Oddly enough, I have shared the story with other hunters from time to time, but it causes me no joy. I often wonder how I would have been judged if I had simply pushed her out of the way and taken my shot.

The Next Generation Takes the Field

My son's turn to make the journey into Rock legend came, and I was overjoyed. Hunting runs through the blood of some, while others' veins pump a different passion. I believed early on that my son was not destined to be a hunter, and I embraced his preference. Nevertheless, I was delighted when he agreed to join me on the first day of the season.

My youth had been full of the outdoors. I spent the lion's share of my summers on or in the water, or in the woods equipped with a .22, a bow and arrow, or a fishing pole. I hiked and explored, seeking new waters to fish and different glens to investigate. I would leave in the morning and often not return until after dark. Looking back on it all through today's moral lens, I suspect my mother might be classified as unfit, but I reveled in the freedom. Moreover, she had instilled within me a healthy respect for a broad spectrum of possible pitfalls, and that regard served as my protection. Indeed, she excelled as a model of great parenting in her generation.

From my perspective, my son's youth had been packed with sports. He participated in both soccer and basketball, and was quite competitive in both. In basketball, where he led the team on and off the court, he was an intense competitor. Clearly the best player on a subpar team, he always hustled up and down the court for the entire game. He indeed did leave everything on the court. His soccer career was much different. He was part of a juggernaut team that, through most seasons, dominated the local competition. His skills were keen, and he had a great command of the sport. It appeared to me that he was much more comfortable just being a member of that power-house, and was not compelled to vie for a leadership role.

One year, after losing 3-1 in the state championship game, I attempted to console an obviously dejected athlete. I commented that his team had won the silver medal, to which he reminded me that to win a silver you needed to lose the gold. Sadly, his team had only lost two games the entire season – both to the same team. The first encounter ended in a 1-1 tie and was lost through a penalty-kick elimination in the regional championship game. That loss put my son's team in the loser bracket in the state championship tournament. His team then had to play every team that had won their respective divisions. So exceptional was his team's talent that they handled the assignment with ease – but the rematch with the team that had beaten them resulted in defeat.

Sadly, genetics cut his career short. He was a late bloomer (as was his father before him) and when the high school teams were being slated, he was comfortable with turning his attention to other interests.

Despite our differing viewpoints on the excitement of the hunt, we found ourselves in a tree stand that had become the premier position to ambush unsuspecting prey. In the 10 years of its use, more deer were taken from that vantage point by bow and rifle than any other position on the farm. It became known as Elliott's Stand. Constructed by me, it clearly confirmed that my carpentry skills had not developed in the 15 years since I had erected the one on the willow tree on the opposite side of the swamp.

We climbed the ladder and took our positions. The Pennsylvania Game Commission, grappling with a 30 percent decline in license sales, had allowed for the harvesting of does by youth hunters – defined as age 16 and under. They believed that the new rule might stimulate more youth interest in the sport, and indeed it was a great motivator. As the sky began to brighten, a young doe quietly made its way toward us. My son simply raised his weapon, squeezed the trigger, and soon we were descending to the ground to survey the kill. I was as giddy as I could be, but my son seemed to take a very businesslike approach to the situation.

My nephew arrived to help with the field dressing, and announced it was the smallest doe he had ever seen harvested. He then tossed it over his shoulder caveman style. In fact, that deer never made it to the barn. At less than 40 pounds, we decided it would be optimal to grill that succulent fawn over an open fire.

My son tarried by the fire for a bit and then elected to return to the farmhouse for some rest. The 5 a.m. wake-up was always a rousing one, and since the intended mission had been executed successfully, he had earned some additional slumber.

The next year, when winds began to nip and the leaves started to fall, signaling another autumn was upon us, my son announced that he wanted to participate in the hunt again. Ecstatic, I began preparing for our second hunt. In our stand, we shivered as we awaited the onset of God's illumination. But I fell asleep; evidently the early wake-up call was too much for me. I awoke to my son whispering, "Here comes one." – to which I responded, "Let's wait for a buck."

Quietly, he confirmed that indeed it was a buck, and, in a flash, he fired his weapon. We descended to survey the slaughter. It was undeniably exactly that – an execution performed flawlessly. One shot, and the very respectable six-point had taken two steps before falling. We were out of the woods by 8 a.m., and to my knowledge, that was the last time my son fired a weapon.

Reflections of a Father

Later that afternoon, I reflected as I sat solitary in my tree. I had hunted seven years before I ever saw a legal deer, and another six before I shot one. My son had killed two in less than an hour of daylight in the woods. In fact, I believe that the time he sat waiting in the darkness far exceeded the entire time he spent during shooting hours.

I was as proud as I could be, and replayed his marksmanship in my mind 100 times that afternoon. I wondered how many deer I had missed in my hunting life due to falling asleep; more importantly, I wondered how I had never fallen to my death in doing so – no walls, you may recall.

Refreshment for the Soul

Another decade of hunts on the Pennsylvania farm passed, and it was chock-full of priceless moments. A friend of mine asked if he could bring his daughter and nephew to the farm to hunt. They both scored nice bucks, but with an interesting twist. My nephew, now in his mid-30s, who had become the best overall outdoorsman of all who had hunted those woods, pushed a herd through to the awaiting youngsters. Both of them fired once. After the normal investigation found no evidence of a successful shot, my friend's daughter was understandably dejected. She was sure that she had missed. We assumed that the buck taken by her cousin had been the same one and had not been so fortunate with his second experience with a hunter.

My nephew, convinced that there was more than one buck in the group, investigated. He found some disturbed leaves near where the young girl had said she took her shot. He announced that she had hit the deer, and despite the fact that there was no blood to be seen, the running pattern in the leaves was all the evidence he needed. As I recall, it took him an hour, but he came across a fresh kill that had been hit in the head; the shot had not been immediately lethal. Now, we had two bucks down and two ecstatic youngsters.

I marveled at my nephew's ability to know the woods, but more importantly, at his empathy for this girl who was distraught by what she thought was her failure. Although he had never met her, nor would he ever meet her again, he took the time and used his skills to discover her trophy.

One year, the Pennsylvania Game Commission – in its infinite wisdom – decided to allow buck or doe harvesting on the last day of the antlered season. In our sophomoric euphoria, we killed 10 does and one buck that day. In my post-excited, more rational mind, I realized that meant probably 20 fawns would not be born the next spring. We had over-harvested, and the hunting suffered for several years afterward. That was yet another life lesson, forged in the field.

The Joke That Became a Legend

One evening, after a bombastic day of missed opportunity, my brother-in-law questioned the future. I immediately assumed that yet another deep conversation concerning the generations would follow.

"Do you ever think of the future?" he asked.

Believing that the conversation would transition into the topic of aging, and ultimately to death, I responded, "Well, we are all getting a bit older."

"I'm not talking about our future," he snapped, and added, "One day, a thousand years from now, explorers will come upon this place and likely state, 'Brave men defended this rock, but from what, we have no idea.'"

As I surveyed the fire-illuminated glitter, cast from dozens of spent shells sinking into the muddy soil, I reflected upon the hundreds of cartridges that had been discarded in the surrounding ground throughout the decades. Along with a camp spoon or two, and a few knives, a couple of unfired bullets were probably hidden in the earth. Still, what had started as a joke transformed into a vital question regarding the enormity of human existence. Could our recreational passion possibly metamorphose into some salient theory created by future generations? Would they believe that our interaction with the Rock was essential to the survival of the species? Probably not – but as memories fade, many interesting and genuinely crucial historical events have been lost to history.

It has been a decade since I last wielded a rifle. Somehow, I lost the intense euphoria that had fueled my passion for hunting. I decided that it would be 'away from goodness' to participate further. And due to an extraordinary set of factors, none of the group that delighted in the visage of the Rock have hunted those grounds for over a decade.

The property remains closed to hunting. The generation that is now the age I was when I first stalked those woods has never enjoyed a minute there. It is possible that in 50 years, no one will remain who participated in the activities that I have just described. There may be no one left who listened intently to all those stories as they huddled around a roaring fire. For both the storytellers and the listeners who were there, I can still imagine them all laughing heartily as they think back on the stories surrounding the legend of the Rock.

I often think about returning to the Rock – not to hunt, but rather to instruct younger generations and revel in the camaraderie. Some of the greatest moments of my life were enjoyed at the Rock. If serendipity could prevail – and the Rock could become again a revered landmark for hunters old and young – I would be there in a flash.

Chapter 15

The Family Windows: An Epiphany

**God can be found everywhere and often shows up
in the most interesting ways.**

M Y MOTHER'S FAMILY TREE is laden with prominent individuals from established families tracing back to 1401. Her mother's side boasts the Howitt, Mickle, Curwen, and Ranson families. Her grandfather was an Anglican priest who grew to significant notoriety in his day, lecturing across Canada and the United States. Transcripts from many of his teachings remain in print today.

My great-grandfather, Fredrick Elliott Howitt, was born in Castletown on the Isle of Man. At age 10, he became terribly ill and was not expected to survive. While fighting through that illness, he made a promise to God that he would dedicate his remaining days to the Lord's service. A man of great wealth and status, he was known for his incredible generosity. He served as the rector of St. George's Church in Hamilton, Ontario – and ultimately, he was canonized.

As a young child during visits to Canada, I would worship in St George's, along with my family. We basked in the warm glow of large, stained-glass windows that were situated on the left side of the sanctuary. There were two sets of double windows that depicted significant scenes from the Bible. One depicted the road to Emmaus; the other displayed the empty tomb, and was titled *He Is Risen*. One set was dedicated to my great-grandfather and the other was dedicated to my great-grandmother. I reveled in the beauty of the windows and felt at peace while in their glow. The sun would shine through them and they sparkled with an almost heavenly aura.

Shortly after my mother's passing, I became immersed in a spirit of nostalgia and decided that my 19-year-old twins needed to experience the windows. So, we made the five-hour drive to Hamilton.

The church was smaller than I remembered; and to my shock, it had been converted to a nondenominational house of worship. The exterior remained much as I recalled, with its sturdy stone façade, but the windows were missing – in their place were clear panes of glass. I was devastated. Sadly, the doors were locked, and entrance was impossible. We tarried on the grounds for a bit, and as we returned to our car, left unfulfilled.

God Arrived, Just in Time

God has an interesting way of making the scene just when you need Him. On this day, He took the form of a kindly gentleman who happened to be walking down the street. I greeted him as I would any passerby, and he seemed oddly approachable.

"What can you tell me about this church?" I asked. He responded that he was the pastor, and he invited us inside. Once inside, I was crestfallen to see that not one historic element of the once-stately church remained. The pews had been removed, and all the beautiful woodwork that adorned the altar was gone. In the altar's place were folding chairs and an open stage that held a set of drums. We learned that the Anglican Church had decided to close and had removed the windows, along with all the other stately accoutrements. The remaining members of the congregation had commenced worshiping in the basement of a nearby Baptist church. This pastor's flock, who themselves had been worshiping in a temporary space, had purchased the building.

As we made our way to my aunt's house in Muskoka, I reflected upon the church windows and how much they had meant to my family. Upon greeting my aunt, I informed her of the status of the church and the windows. She seemed more angry than sad, which I found odd. I was sad and felt no anger.

When I returned home, I decided that I needed to attempt to discover the whereabouts of the windows. In my mind, the search became preeminent. Dozens of phone calls took me down fruitless paths, until I connected with the archivist for the Anglican Church's Diocese of Niagara. He was unaware of the whereabouts of the windows, but agreed to do a bit of research. He requested a week or two.

Ancient Inspiration Arrives

One Friday, I was at my desk and the phone rang; it was the receptionist. Most of my employees knew about my family and some of the more interesting elements of my history. The receptionist asked me to confirm that one of my ancestors was Mary Howitt. She explained that the quote of the day from her internet site had been attributed to Mary. On the computer screen there were seven words:

For visions come not to polluted eyes.

As I was reading the passage, my phone rang again. The windows had been found, and rather amazingly, they were available if I was interested in purchasing them. Immediately, I agreed.

A Quest for Reconnection

As we made the five-hour journey by car, it was possibly the hottest September day I could ever recall. We met the archivist and enjoyed a nice lunch. He explained that a funeral home in the city had purchased the windows but had never paid for them. They were to be installed in a yet-to-be-built chapel on the funeral home grounds.

We made payment, which was a bit complicated because a United States check in Canada creates some confusion. My wife and I made our way to the funeral home, and, once there, were led down a very steep set of old stairs past embalming tables to a dark and filthy cubby. This was no child's play area.

Left alone, my wife and I extracted the windows from their storage place, and schlepped them up a different staircase that led to the street. Sixteen trips in all left us exhausted and grimy. Regrettably, the dedication panes that noted my great-grandparents were nowhere to be found. I expect that we were quite a sight as we crossed the Peace Bridge, but the inquisition by the immigration officer was brief. I have never been quite sure why the officer asked us almost no questions, but it felt a bit as if God had filled him with the knowledge that the two grubby transients should be approved for passage.

I informed my aunt that the windows were back with the family, and she was quite pleased. Her demeanor turned to anger, however, when I advised her that I had been asked to purchase them. In her view, our family had paid for them once. So intense was her ire that she drafted a missive to the diocese, which in turn published it in their quarterly newsletter. The letter then found its way to the Reverend John Smith.

A Call for the Ages

I received Reverend Smith's call at my home three days before Christmas, and he had a fantastical story to share. His church was interested in acquiring my great-grandfather's windows. His congregation was what remained of the original St. George's assemblage, and they felt a very close connection to my great-grandfather. They had recently purchased another abandoned Anglican church building and had searched for the windows unsuccessfully.

The story became incredible as he shared the historical details of the church. Apparently, the church had been named St. Margaret's, in honor of my great-grandmother who had passed away. My great-grandfather had donated the money to acquire the land and to fund the church's initial construction. In another eerie connection to my family, my great-uncle, an ordained Anglican priest, had been the first rector of the church.

After a week of contemplation, I returned Reverend Smith's call and advised him that the windows were not for sale. However, I would happily donate them to the church in return for a promise that they would not be removed without a reasonable attempt to find a member of my family who might want them back. He eagerly agreed.

A few weeks later, two parishioners arrived at my home and we loaded the windows for their journey back to Canada. Ironically, the windows would be installed only a few blocks from the place of their original location. On this day, it was the windows' turn to have a surprise for me. During the time of the dismantlement of St. George's, the diocese had determined there was no value in the dedication plates, and they were left behind to be destroyed. But the congregants saved them, as they felt that the windows would, at some point, be rededicated in their new place of worship. And so, I was presented with the dedication plates from the windows honoring my great-grandmother.

The Blessings Within the Blessing

A few short months later, I found myself in the new St. George's, formerly St. Margaret's, surrounded by my extended family. The sanctuary was overflowing for the rededication of the stained glass windows. Among my family members was my aunt who had written the letter, and who the press had named the "outspoken octogenarian." A distant cousin, who I had not seen in over 20 years, was also among the more than 30 of my family in attendance. She learned that her father had been the first rector of the church and was overwhelmed with joy at hearing the news.

I had been asked to address the congregation as part of the dedication ceremony. I decided to carry my great-grandfather's pocket watch with me for inspiration. I had never carried it; I had only held it on occasion. On a wild hunch, I decided to wind its stem right before the service. I marveled as the hands of a watch that had not been wound in over 60 years began to move. After a rather impassioned talk to the audience, I returned to my seat. While holding the watch, the hands stopped. They have not moved since.

Five of my mother's generation, along with dozens from the two subsequent generations, gathered that day. It was a moment of family unity, as we remembered our past through the worship of God. That older generation is now all with God, but that day in Hamilton was a triumph made possible only through God's hand.

When I reflect upon the windows and their history, I see parallels to our life's journey. Conceived, manufactured, installed, dedicated, uninstalled, lost, recovered, reconditioned, reinstalled and rededicated within a few city blocks, in Hamilton, Ontario – the windows had quite a story, including a short three-month trip to the United States. Their warm glow inspires the faithful in their new home. *Just as God intended*, I muse.

I am steeped in family tradition, and have assumed the role of curator of my family's historical treasures. I feel a deep and almost reverent closeness to my ancestors, and hunger to learn more about them. Perplexed that others in my family seem rather uninterested in their history, I marvel at the treasures that I unearth as I continue my informal search. I feel a bit of sorrow over my family's apparent lack of curiosity.

As the story of the windows shows, so many of our ancestors – now mostly forgotten – were once part of a loving family. Their triumphs and their failures are lost to history, but their influence lives on. I see it as a tragedy of epic proportions that so many families know so little about their lineage. Today, the search for family history by so many has become big business, but most seekers only find dates and names. While those are nice records to discover, the richness of family stems from the stories that ancestors shared, and from the people and items that they held so dear.

I have recreated my great-grandparents' dining room in my home, and I find great comfort when I dine at their table and sit in the chair that my great-grandfather once used. The room is adorned with some of the artwork that hung in their dining room, along with many other items that made their dining experience so grand. It is a room of great inspiration and peace.

What relics of your past inspire you? Are there others to be discovered? Are you willing to search for them? How will your fulfillment be enriched when you take that step?

Chapter 16

The Epic Battle of the Bulge

We all face struggles and some can plague us for a lifetime, yet those struggles often strengthen our character. Struggles fuel our empathy, which leads toward fulfillment.

MANY WOULD DESCRIBE ME as large, both in size and personality. At six feet, five and a half inches, I tower over most people. My height is a combination of genetics and God's will. With no other member of my extended family taller than six feet, three inches, I am a bit of an anomaly. Depending on your perspective, you might say that my personality is either flamboyant or ostentatious. Some might say that I breathe life into a room; others might say that I suck all the oxygen from it. I surmise this emanates from my father's advice:

- Never leave a room forgotten.
- Remain true to your principles; it matters little how you are perceived.

In my father's view, being genuine was far more important than being liked. In fact, he loathed phonies.

Sadly, my weight has been the epic battle of my life. I have grappled with it since I was a child. In total, I have lost well over 1,500 pounds; and I have lost over 100 pounds on eleven different occasions. As is the plight of the yoyo-dieter, I have gained it all back in one form or another. I remain 70 pounds below my peak weight, but 60 pounds above my preferred weight, and 100 pounds above my doctor-recommended weight. Of course, at my doctor-recommended weight, most of my family would plan funeral arrangements, as they would suspect a terminal illness.

A Mother's Disappointment

My mother loathed my weight problem – she saw it as a lack of discipline that I should have been able to overcome. I was forced to consume untested home remedies that only embittered me. To this day, I have no knowledge of what was forced down my throat, but none of it seemed to improve the situation. The fact that neither of my parents ever darkened the door of a gym did not help, and then there were the starving children in China whose plight required me to sit at the table for hours until I finished every bite of my meals. I was also extremely uncoordinated, and my mother – convinced I had been stricken with a birth defect – forced me into orthopedic shoes. They further impeded any significant exercise.

By sixth grade, I was required to engage in a protein diet, the precursor to the now-famous Atkins or Keto plan. During the diet, I lost 30 pounds in just over two months; but with no proper planning afterward, I gained it all back within the next six months. In junior high, we tried the 1,000-calorie diet. When I entered my senior year, I was on the verge of 300 pounds; however, by the time I took the stage to receive my diploma, I was a skinny 180 pounds, earning me the nickname, "Stretch."

I gained, lost, and gained back another 100 pounds during college. After graduation and during the planning of my wedding, I ballooned up to over 350 pounds.

This Journey Led to an Unintended Place

On January 2, 1981, I decided I wanted to join the AirForce as a candidate for Officer Training School. I suspect that the colonel, who was responsible for ROTC and recruitment at my college, laughed a bit as I appeared and weighed in at 351 pounds. The target weight for eligibility was 230 pounds, and I needed to be at goal weight by June 1 of that same year.

It was peanuts for a pro like me. On May 1, the slimmed-down version of Elliott Haverlack, at two pounds below the goal weight, was presented to the selection committee. I had passed the rigorous physical requirements, scored perfectly on both qualifying tests, and had excelled in the additional required coursework – which included a class in differential equations. That course was notable, as it required three years of calculus as a prerequisite. Having taken none of the calculus courses required, the exception granted to me was, in itself, a bit of a miracle.

On June 2, I received the news that, due to a bureaucratic snafu, the start of my military career would have to wait until the fall. Later that week, I successfully found long-term employment in a bakery, officially ending my quest to secure military service. One might imagine that a bakery could be a difficult place to work for a chronically obese person – and they would be correct. I gained and lost over 100 pounds twice during my nine-year bakery career.

In 1989, I made a career change that ultimately took me to Scranton, Pennsylvania. There, I also contracted Lyme disease – and that, coupled with absolutely zero discipline and a ton of stress found me at my highest weight ever.

I had a brilliant plan to lose some weight, and I did – about 140 pounds worth. Again, within a few years, I had regained my rotund status. During an off-site meeting, my company's president – seemingly caught off guard – remarked to me and a portly co-worker, "God, are you two fat."

To which I responded, "Yes, exceedingly so, sir."

Later, during a board meeting, many were lamenting their weight status, and three members of the board had decided to give the Atkins diet a try. The president admonished them for not adopting the Weight Watchers program, as the company owned it. I piped up that I, too, was going on a diet, and would follow the company-owned program.

I think the president genuinely enjoyed my rather unsophisticated approach to most everything, and he issued a challenge that he knew I would never meet. If I could achieve my weight goal, I would be rewarded with dinner with the Duchess of York, our new spokesperson. Dinner was scheduled as part of a promotional tour. As a huge fan of the British monarchy, I was elated, and I achieved the goal. Unfortunately, an illness cut her tour short and I never did receive my reward. Still, I had become a much smaller version of myself.

A Life-Changing Decision

In 2004, my dieting journey took an important turn. As part of my rehabilitation from the accident described in Chapter 12, I was assigned physical therapy. After a few weeks, I realized that I was mostly unsupervised – and since I was approaching 400 pounds, I decided that maybe a fitness regime was in order. I visited and joined a gym for the first time later that week. I also hired a trainer, who became a very close confidant. As with most things, I attacked training with a jocular attitude. After six months, I had not lost a pound, but felt much better.

One day at the gym, while laughing at a funny story, a grouchy old man interrupted me. "You are wasting your time," he snarled. As it turned out, he was an elitist district judge who was so full of himself that he could not force a smile if his life depended on it. His remark was just the incentive I needed to jump-start my combined exercise and diet regime. My trainer guided me throughout a one-and-a-half-year program that led to me to weigh only two pounds over my self-appointed goal of 200 pounds.

With the exercise included in my life program, I was stronger and healthier than I had ever been. Unfortunately, my lack of body fat threw me into hypoglycemic shock, which almost killed me. Hilariously, my physician advised me to carry sucrose pills and gain a bit of weight. Since then, I have trained over 300 days a year with a trainer. Unfortunately, my weight struggles remain, and I suspect that they will for the rest of my days. I have often mused that I hope I will be a skinny angel.

It is rather amazing – with an intense exercise regime as part of my regular routine, I have reduced the deviation of my weight to a much smaller range. What often used to be a periodic need to lose 100 or more pounds has been limited in recent years to an occasional need to lose 75, or maybe even just 50.

From 2006 through 2011, I remained below 280 pounds. Two ruptured discs later, I found myself over 300 once again, and closing in on a score of pounds over that mark. When my daughter announced that I was going to become a grandfather, it gave me the incentive I needed to get serious about dieting again. On September 9, 2014, an excited and immensely proud grandpa met his new granddaughter, and did so at 250 pounds.

Shortly after the New Year in 2015, I received a call from my brother, who had been living in Egypt, Italy, and Turkey for the previous six months. My brother informed me that he was calling from the Pennsylvania-Delaware border. Evidently, police had surrounded his car with guns drawn, and he was unsure what to do. That incident set off a six-month series of events – to be the topic of a future missive – and the stress resulted in a 50-to-60-pound weight gain.

A second quadricep tear in 2016, a love of bar popcorn, and COVID-19 have sequentially stymied valiant attempts to return to my goal weight. I make honest attempts of 30-pound and even 40-pound losses, only to find the pounds again while seated at a favorite watering hole, enjoying Chef Vanessa's or Chef Nate's exquisite fare. It is an odd paradox – while it has been incredibly frustrating, it has also been a bit of fun.

A Cruel Reality

If you have never struggled with significant weight problems, you likely have never contemplated the implications of an overweight status beyond the immediate health risks. Having held the distinction of falling into every weight classification from morbidly obese through normal, multiple times in my adult life, I have an interesting perspective.

If there is a stereotypical profiling characteristic, it might be weight. It is amazing to discover the overt biases that come with differing weight statuses. Everything from body language to topics of conversation receives varying perspectives depending on one's weight. Such biases regularly lead to starkly differing outcomes. Weight is probably the most under-discussed prejudice of our times. As with other prejudices, most people who have it work tirelessly to cloak it.

Interestingly, when I find myself part of the **thin** classification, the biases are on full display. Since casual acquaintances have no awareness of my multiple weight statuses over the years, conversations regularly devolve into the most vile of topics when they believe I am just another normal guy. It leaves me wondering – if they knew I was really a fat guy, temporarily hidden in a thin body, would their choice of words have been so cruel? In many ways, it all has been an exceptional learning experience, as I even regularly find myself slipping into unfair biases on a number of topics. The **fat guy vs. thin guy paradox** serves as an important reminder that we need to check our biases on a continual basis.

Weight has been my Achilles' heel. Channeling my mother, I blame myself entirely for my lack of discipline. I could concoct dozens of excuses about slow metabolism and related factors beyond my control, but the fact remains that I am completely responsible for my weight status. I do not use the word hate often, but I hate being fat. Since I blame myself for the condition, in an odd Machiavellian way, I detest my weakness. If I find myself too weak to beat this condition, how will I find the courage to take on the issues of the day? In many ways, this is a primary reason that I worry so much about the future, and about the implications of the current environment on my descendants. In order to become the warriors we must become, to take on the challenges facing our great land, our bodies and minds must be kept in tip-top condition. The physical and mental distractions of a lifelong struggle like combating obesity stands counter to our objective.

I urge everyone to strive for kindness and understanding. Those attributes that make us different from others should be celebrated, and met with love and compassion. One person's struggle with weight might be the next person's battle with addiction. Physical and mental disabilities – seen and unseen – challenge many of our citizens, as well as those who reside outside of our borders. Embracing those characteristics that make us unique leads to fulfillment and well-being, enhancing our journey, and the journeys of so many others.

Chapter 17

The End of the Earthly Journey

For God So Loved the World . . .

E VERY JOURNEY HAS A first step, and also a final one, reminding us that **it is the stuff we do between those first and last steps** that defines us and leaves our legacy. Most people do not like to speak about death or dying. It is an uncomfortable topic, to be sure. As we age, we realize that death is inevitable.

As a young man, I recall being very uncomfortable with the topic, particularly when an older loved one would broach the subject with me. Now I am the older loved one, and suspect that I might be repeating history.

Billy Graham said, "Many people say they do not fear death, but the process of dying. It's not the destination, but the trip that they dread." I share Reverend Graham's sentiment. I have watched many of my loved ones pass away due to extended disease or other infirmities.

My father's death was horrific and untimely, but my mother-in-law's slow passage to her heavenly reward seemed almost cruel and beyond my imagination. Still others slipped away rather peacefully. My mother passed quietly, but alone, which is certainly tragic. Her solitary death was ironic, because as a private-duty, end-of-life nurse, she had held the hands of many who passed.

My mother struggled with the fact that she was not present when either my father or stepfather passed. She had kept vigil by both their sides but left for short periods, only to learn of their passing while she had been away. I recall consoling my mother that, in light of the dozens she had been with at the end of their earthly journeys, maybe God had wanted her to be spared from seeing the last breaths of two so close to her.

While I do not know what lies ahead for me as I close out my journey, I see my life to this point as incredibly blessed. I have lived a life of abundance, and I believe I have lived the life that God intended for me. Certainly, I have fallen short on many occasions, but I have always gotten back into the game and thrived as a result.

Many have long lists of regrets. If I was offered the opportunity to receive a do-over, there are several paths I might not have followed, and still others I would have explored with much more zest. Certainly, some events I would opt not to have endured – such as falling down the steps twice, tearing both of my quadriceps.

I have but one regret – I never served the country I have loved for my entire life. I see that as a lost opportunity.

I have loved my God and I have served Him, but not without acts of omission and commission. I have also loved my family and I have served them, but also not without acts of omission and commission. I believe that both God and my family have forgiven me. I have loved my country and have strived throughout my life to champion her in every action, but I failed to serve in her military. For that, I have regret.

When we die, our earthly tent decays, but our spirit lives on eternally in heaven. As the apostle Paul reminds us, it is grace through faith that leads to eternal life. From a historic perspective, our lives are but an instant. When loved ones pass into their eternal reward, we mourn their loss because we will miss them; but in a historical moment we are reunited in heaven.

What follows are a few select writings that are tributes to loved ones, both living and dead, whose spirits will shine brightly for eternity.

He will wipe every tear from their eyes.
There will be no more death or mourning or crying or pain,
for the old order of things has passed away.

– REVELATION 21:4

For Dotty and Dewey

Two lights shine as One
Illuminate the darkness
Warm Glow Beckons
Shows us the Way
Life Eternal

Written in 1999 as part of a celebration for two friends.
My only attempt ever at poetry.

Aunt Barbara

Written upon the occasion of her 90th birthday.

Four score and a decade ago, this very special lady commenced her journey here on earth. Thirty-seven years later, my mother, Barbara's younger sister Margaret, sought my Aunt Barbara to be my godmother. My great uncle, John Howitt, was selected as my godfather.

Throughout my early years, my mother regularly reminded me that these two unique people had been specifically selected to be my godparents for three reasons:

- Their love of God
- Their love of family
- Their love of country

Through my 50 plus years, I have learned much from my aunt. We have laughed together and we have cried together. We celebrated victories, debated politics (I have been compared on more than one occasion to Genghis Khan), enjoyed sunsets on a lake, and mourned the passing of loved ones, but through it all, three things have remained constant:

- Love of God
- Love of family
- Love of country

Barbara has made the Curwen, Howitt, Mickle and Stewart families proud.

And in closing, today, we celebrate the turning of a page, as the self-proclaimed Outspoken Octogenarian has traveled the road to become the New World Nonagenarian.

I have brought a special dessert fork with me today. It comes from the sterling silver collection of one Margaret Lydia Mickle Howitt. The dessert fork reminds us that even late in the evening after a luscious repast, the best is yet to come.

Good health and the greatest of happiness.

The best is yet to come.

Margaret Stewart Haverlack Wood

Eulogy for Mom, 2004

Margaret Stewart Haverlack Wood (Mom, or Mother, as she preferred) was born on July 19, 1922 in Hamilton, Ontario, Canada, to the Reverend Thomas Hudson Stewart and Elsie Jane (Howitt) Stewart.

Her father was a priest in the Anglican Church and the family moved periodically.

Her sister Barbara (my aunt) remembers summer trips to Atlantic City, and a trip to a farm where – after seeing a cow being milked – Margaret claimed she would never drink milk again. My brother and I recall that but for some cream in her beloved tea, she was not seen to ever partake of milk.

Margaret went to boarding school at Havergal College and went on to the Toronto General School of Nursing, where she earned a nursing degree in 1944. Nursing became her calling and she "nursed" all she met.

Margaret moved to the United States and worked in public health in Virginia. She met her husband, my father, Frank Haverlack, in 1951 and they were married on September 4 of that year.

They lived in Omaha, Nebraska, for a short while. There, she always claimed it was so hot in the summer that the young couple decided to go to the movie theater every night just to enjoy the air conditioning, despite having to watch the same movies over and over again. In those days, cinemas only had one screen.

There were a few other moves until Margaret and Frank bought a home in Monroeville, Pennsylvania, where my brother and I were born.

Her first son, my brother, Frank Stewart, was born on May 10, 1956. Later that year, Margaret became a United States citizen, but never forgot her beloved Canada.

I was born on June 5, 1958.

Mom was a devoted wife and mother, and maintained a Christian household. Every meal began with a blessing and every evening ended with bedtime prayers.

Mom was extremely involved in all activities with my brother and me. She was active in church, school, and Cub Scouts, and always found time to help us with school projects and homework.

In 1965, our family purchased a set of New Standard Encyclopedias. Mom read them from cover to cover, and wrote to the editors and advised them of their errors. One response from the company included, "Mrs. Haverlack, thank you for your most recent letter, of course you are correct......."

Mom was always very proud of the accomplishments of both my brother and me, taking particular pride in the fact that both of us earned the rank of Eagle Scout. Stewart accomplished it at age 12, and also earned the God and Country Award, an achievement in which she took particular pride.

Dad became quite ill in the early 1960s and Mom returned to nursing, working night shift, to help make ends meet. Despite the challenges of nursing my dad, being a mom, and working full-time, she still found time for her only vice, the game of bridge. She taught both of us boys to play, and in later years I would be called on to sub at bridge parties – Stewart had moved to California – a wise move indeed.

In 1973, Mom and Dad purchased a small and struggling store in Slippery Rock. Under their management, the business grew from $30,000 in annual sales to over $250,000 in less than three years. At age 15, I opened a small fishing and hunting equipment store, and she would often reflect that it gave her much pleasure that I had successfully accomplished that feat. She became quite ill in 1974 and spent 12 weeks in the hospital. A year later, Dad was diagnosed with cancer, and died a short while later in 1976.

Dad's death was a devastating blow to the family, but she found inner strength and kept the family together and the business running. The business was sold in 1978, and shortly afterward she returned to nursing.

In 1980, she moved to Grove City and met her closest and dearest friend, Esther Plouse. She and Esther found strength in each other's company, and they remained friends until Margaret was called "home" in January.

Another of her proudest memories was my brother's military service and the fact that he excelled in the Strategic Air Command. Among her cherished possessions was a handwritten note from his commander, which called him "one of the military's brightest and best."

On August 1, 1985, her two grandchildren, Frank Zane and Ashley Margaret, were born. The children quickly became her pride and joy, and she looked for excuses to babysit. In fact, upon her death, over 30 framed pictures of them adorned the walls of her apartment and countless others, unframed, were displayed on every ledge.

When the twins were 6 months old, she and Esther volunteered to babysit over a weekend, as my wife and I had a business trip. Mary, my wife, had just gotten over the chickenpox and the trip was almost canceled, but the dynamic duo insisted. We likely had not made it to the airport when the first pox appeared on both infants. Mom never informed us of the crisis. She and Esther endured until we returned to speckled children. In fact, calls to check on the children were answered with, "Everything is great and enjoy your trip."

In 1988, Mom moved to Southern California and met and married Thomas Crosswell Wood. Tom was a wonderful match for Mom and they were inseparable. Tom quickly became a surrogate father and grandfather.

When Tom passed away in 2001, Mom was devastated. She never gave up hope and her faith in God.

Mom was extremely active in her community, Leisure World, and touched many lives and had many very close friends. My family was overwhelmed with the outpouring of sympathy at the memorial service held for her at her local church in California.

While this may sound more like a story about her family and friends than of Margaret herself, it is simply the most remarkable thing about her. Family and friends were her life, and the reality is that she accepted and excelled in her calling to be a nurse.

She was a nurse to the body and a nurse to the soul, and loved every minute.

Just Like Me

Eulogy for Don, 2019

Five or six years ago, my phone rang. It was my old friend Don. We had not spoken in two or three months. There really was not any greeting; he said, "I need a favor; I need you to speak at my funeral." I asked if he was trying to tell me something, and his answer was, "No, just making plans." I agreed, so here I am with you today.

Don told me I would have 10 minutes and instructed me not to go over. As a good old Methodist, I cannot even get warmed up in 10 minutes, so I am a bit anxious and pensive this morning. Not only that, but also I flew in from Kansas to Buffalo yesterday to pick up my car and then drove directly here – so I am a bit road-weary as well.

Today is a celebration of life for Don – Christian, patriot, father, grandfather, and friend – another one of God's amazing creations.

Just like you, just like me.

My name is Elliott Haverlack, and Don and I have been friends for just under 30 years. In fact, my first encounter with Don was in January 1990, in Terminal Island, California – in an ominous place, with an ominous name, at an ominous time.

Talk about baptism by fire – Don's previous boss had been, shall we say, a man of questionable resolve. Our job was to undo just about everything and start over – No small task. Not only that, but the place smelled really bad, as the combination of fish being processed and hundreds – if not thousands – of seagulls feeding on their remains left an indelible mark on my olfactory nerve.

Shortly after joining, within a week or two, I recall having my Miranda rights recited to me on four occasions, all within a one-hour period. I recall lamenting to the officer that I had not even been employed at that location when the alleged crimes had been committed. "Bad timing on your part," Don commented afterward. In retrospect, the timing could have been better – and of course, Don's signature humor just added to the memory now seared into my cerebral cortex. He always seemed to know what to say, and when to say it. He certainly had a unique ability to break the ice.

And so it was – a friendship commenced – a friendship based on common values, an unwavering moral compass, and a truly twisted sense of humor. Who was this man? This co-worker? This friend?

He was as unique a character as you will ever find – and yes, full of flaws.

Just like you, just like me.

I struggled a bit when Don asked me to speak at this event, as I wondered what I would say – or more candidly, what should I say? Don retorted, "Say something funny." So, in keeping with that request, I offer the following:

A horse walks into the bar, and the bartender says, "Why the long face?" The horse says, "I don't know, I've had it all my life."

Seriously, most of my funny stories about Don have to do with food, and his lifelong battle with his weight. I have seen Don from sub-200 pounds to close to 400 pounds. In case you have not noticed – just like me. Of course, you are going to have to trust me on my 200-pound phase, but I promise you it happened.

Don and I were a potent duo. We could strike fear into restaurateurs who had foolishly offered an "all you can eat" buffet. I know we set the bar high on a regular basis, as the attendants feverishly attempted to keep up with our ravenous appetites. An honor and moniker in which I do take great pride.

We ate ten wiener schnitzels on the hill in San Pedro. That is, ten each.

We ate four Dodger Dogs before the seventh-inning stretch,
And something that was known as Donutgate.

A couple other Don fun facts: Don had the most comprehensive working vocabulary of any individual I have ever met. Words I had never heard rolled off his tongue with great regularity, ease, and acumen. After making a mistake one day, he retorted to me that he was chagrined. I actually kind of knew what that one was, but had never heard anyone in the pet food or tuna business use it. I recall demanding that he take his chagrined self somewhere and fix the problem.

For those who are not familiar with the definition of chagrin, it is defined as: disquietude or distress of mind caused by humiliation, disappointment, or failure. In many ways, I think Don might well have written the definition for Mr. Webster.

Don was fluent in Spanish, and I used to watch with amazement as he would console or correct a Spanish-speaking employee with great passion. I recall commenting, "Dude, you talk with your hands when you are speaking Spanish." He responded, "Dude, I sometimes think and even dream in Spanish." I had to think about that one for a while – of course, only in English. Side note: we called each other "Dude" a lot.

He had a heart of gold, and his genuine love of his fellow man shone brightly. Mighty or meek, strong or weak, rich or poor, Don had a unique capability of treating everyone equally.

I recall him calling me one day, proud as he could be that he had given $100 to a man in need at the airport. "I think you were scammed," I told him, and he immediately responded, "Yeah, maybe so, but that is his problem, not mine. The money was given with good intent."

When I learned of Don's diagnosis, I immediately wanted to visit. Is that not what we always seem to do, or are expected to do? Go do the right thing, say goodbye, and then move on.

Don refused to see me, and provided an exquisite rationale for refusing my offer. So, I made a commitment to myself that I would call him weekly, and I did so for just under a year – up to and including last Tuesday. Sometimes, he was too sick to visit for more than a second or two. Other times, we prattled on for hours. We laughed, we cried, and we shared war stories. We talked about kids and grandkids, struggles and triumphs, politics, and faith. It is okay – we were aligned on just about everything.

In April, I called him and said, "I am coming to visit, whether you want me or not." On May 6, we enjoyed a time of true fellowship and we said our goodbyes. I spoke with him about another 10 times after that, but that time this past May with him was priceless.

Through the year, as Old Man Winter extinguished the vibrancy of autumn and then finally ceded his grip on the area to springtime (trumpeting the rejuvenation that always reminds me of our renewal through Christ), I got to know my friend better than I ever imagined. I had known Don to be a Christian – I had known Don to be a patriot – I knew Don to be a father – I knew Don to be a grandfather – and I knew Don to be a friend – but there was so much more.

I learned about the depth of his faith, his unconditional love for his family, and his concern for his country and mankind in general. In his preparation for death, Don demonstrated to me a mettle and grace that I have rarely seen in most I have encountered in life. We talked at length about death and dying. He was not afraid, but rather more sad; and his sadness seemed to be for those left behind and for the things he would miss. Throughout the nearly one year before his death, he demonstrated a total and complete aura of selflessness. Not once did he lament his fate.

Just like you? Just like me? Boy, I sure hope so.

You know, we all must face our own mortality. Last I checked, the mortality rate of the human race is 100 percent. I stole that line from my preacher, so it must be true. So, it is coming, my friends. What will it be? "Well done," or "I'm so disappointed"?

I believe Don got a resounding "well done" on Tuesday morning, with trumpets blaring.

I will leave you with a final thought.

When you leave this place today, I want you to strongly consider doing something. I think this is really why Don wanted me to be here today. Find someone and connect with them.

Who, you might ask?

I am not sure I know that answer; but God will lead you to that person.

We need to do this; we are called to pay it forward. I tell you, it is your responsibility. You know the funny thing about responsibility is that it is really two words in one. It is made up of response and ability. We all have the ability, so what is your response? What is your response?

If not you, then who?

If not now, then when?

When you answer this call, you will be blessed beyond your wildest imagination. Trust me – blessings abound, and we are richly rewarded when we do the work that God has for all of us. Each in our own way.

Do not do it for me.

Do not do it for Don.

Do it for you.

Don – Just like you. Just like me. I would like to think so.

The Fighting Tater

Eulogy for my nephew, 2019

I should not be here. In fact, none of us should be. Not in this place, not at this time. Yet we all are. Each one of us is here for a reason; it is a time of mourning, yet a time of great celebration. A tragedy of epic proportions has befallen us.

I am angry, I am sad, and I am heartbroken. In fact, my emotions have run the gamut since I heard the news on Monday. A bright light had been extinguished. It would be far too trite and far too hypocritical for me to use this metaphor in the traditional sense. He was not a traditionalist.

Those who knew him best would be quick to point out – and rightfully so – that in the latter years, he and I had little direct contact. We did, however, communicate from time to time on instant messenger and I got to know him better through his writings. He was committed to his country with a singular mettle and passion so unique in our time and age. In many ways, he reminded me of those from the Greatest Generation – the men and women who pulled the world from the grip of Nazi domination. Those people made the world safer and better for future generations.

Three years ago, he bought me a book titled *Rules for Radicals*, and requested that I read it. It was a horrific tome, in the view of this aging conservative. I asked him why he had me read such nonsense. He simply said, "It's a war, Uncle; and if you want to win it, you need to know how your enemy thinks." Sage advice. I do not believe we could have been more aligned philosophically on the things that mattered.

James David was a warrior, and he volunteered for a lifetime of sacrifice, "defending the Constitution of the United States from all foes, foreign and domestic." He chose a lifetime of service to the country over any of the many paths he could have trod. Selfless love of country; a bright light for sure.

Jimmy, as we knew him, came to the world on a warm September day. I recall, because I chose to go to the family farm that afternoon instead of visiting the new addition to the family. Who could blame me? I was a 20-something outdoorsy type. Why would I subject myself to a hospital room?

At the farm, the corn was planted differently that year. Planted perpendicular, exposing part of the field that was normally shrouded from view. Then it happened – one, two, three, four bucks emerged and walked toward me, with one being the biggest I had ever seen. I thought about the epic battles that these warriors would have over the next several weeks for supremacy and survival. Had they emerged on this day, at this time, to announce to me the warrior who had been born in Sharon earlier that day?

When the hunting season arrived, all four bucks were still together. While at least five of us had the opportunity to shoot at them, the biggest survived an onslaught of lead. Maybe it was not his day to die. I recall thinking that he was safely in the swamp, laughing at our fallibility.

Jimmy was an amazingly brilliant child. From my earliest memories, I think we all knew Jimmy was going to be special. At age 6 or 7, he came to visit us in Philadelphia and we went to the museum. Jimmy was enthralled with dinosaurs. I recall walking toward what I thought was a Brontosaurus skeleton; he calmly said, "I believe you will find that that is a Brachiosaurus." As we neared the bones, of course he was proven correct. I do not think I ever admitted to him that prior to that moment I had never heard of a Brachio. . . whatever it was.

A few years later, his Aunt Mary and I sent him some money for his twelfth birthday. It was a nominal amount, but he drafted an amazing thank-you note – one I will never forget. It read in part, "Thank you for the money. I intend to use it to help me with my plan to take over the world, and when I am successful, you will be handsomely rewarded."

Other fond memories of Jimmy would be: sharing a drink before one of his countless deployments; seeing him "own" the dance floor at his sister Amanda's wedding; and him goading his younger cousin Zane to perform some act of mischievousness at family functions.

So, I am angry, sad and heartbroken. I never dreamed I would be here in this place at this time, but I am. I think I am angriest at myself, sad for my family, and heartbroken for our great country. I struggle to make sense of all of this; and simply stated, I cannot. I am sure that over time these emotions will subside. God has us, and he will wipe every tear away in His time.

A bright light of service to country and countrymen is no longer here. The warrior has gone home, and I am sure that heaven is a bit safer today. Rest well, Jimmy. The fight is over, and you have won. A grateful uncle wishes you Godspeed, until we meet again.

With love and admiration,
Your Uncle

Intertwined and Inseparable

When I think about my journey *From Fear to Fulfillment,* I reflect upon the elements of faith, family, and freedom that have become so ingrained in my psyche. Each element is interspersed within the others, rendering them inseparable.

I am unable to contemplate God's grace without immediately considering the blessing of having been born in the United States, as well as the gifts of those souls living and dead who have helped make my journey so abundant. Knitted into each star and stripe of our great flag are the stories of the men and women who have championed her and defended her. God has poured everything into each element, creating an omnipresent symbol of hope to inspire the future.

I often reflect on how different my journey might have been if even one of those souls had not been part of it; or, if I had not been fortunate enough to live in the freest country ever known. God's artistry knows no bounds, and my life has been yet another one of His masterpieces. I have been abundantly blessed.

When you reflect upon your life journey, do you consider how your life has been enriched by the others who have been a part of it? How has God blessed you? What role has being born in your homeland played? As your life journey progresses, what changes can you make that will lead to fulfillment – for both you and for others?

THE COMMENTARY

Introduction to

Book III

★ ★ ★ ★ ★ ★

FTER MY RETIREMENT IN 2012, I drafted commentaries that I felt were worthy of consideration by my friends. Book III is a collection of some of those essays, and they challenge you to open your mind and consider new paths that may lead to fresh thinking on important societal issues. To present these essays, I took to social media, as it appeared to be the most expedient avenue to reach the largest audience.

As an educator, my motivation was to provide insights on important issues for people who did not have the time or the interest to evaluate them on their own. I addressed topics spanning the gamut, from current social unrest through environmental issues. Many of my writings have been lost, but those that remain may provide the reader a window into the public discourse of the day.

After rereading them as part of the collaboration for the book, I am shocked that they appear rather benign in today's environment.

Sadly, the public acrimony has risen to a level that is unprecedented. I find it almost incomprehensible that the citizens of a nation as amazing as the United States of America can be as apparently hate-filled as they have become.

As the reader will see, some essays are worded a bit more tersely than others. The differences stem from a purposeful decision to attempt to persuade, rather than to inflame. When writing or speaking, we must first decide what our goal is and what outcomes we desire from the effort. Restating for the sake of reinforcement is a common and effective tool to gain understanding. As such, insulting or condemning others is mostly an ineffective and often overutilized method to try to change hearts and minds.

My transition *From Fear to Fulfillment* has fueled my passion for these topics, and has equipped me with the courage to commit them to print. I want to share them with the world for the betterment of all. We may not agree on all topics, but hopefully in the pages that follow, we can learn to disagree – without being disagreeable. These commentaries are included herein largely unedited (but cleaned for obvious errors), as they appeared at the time of their publication.

Chapter 18

When Hypocrisy Reigns

Written and posted on January 23, 2017, after the Steelers' loss to the Patriots in the AFC Championship game.

NEEDED A DAY TO mourn the embarrassing loss last night. I am recovered, and ready to commence doing my part to help Make America Great Again.

As I see it, my role is to support our new president and his team through prayer and deeds. I am also praying that those citizens of these United States who seek to do our country harm will find it within their hearts to stop the hate.

Madonna threatening to blow up the White House is bad but understandable, as she is an amoral individual. The hundreds of thousands who cheered her as she said it scared me to death. Can they truly support such hate?

Ashley Judd cursing with the use of the vilest of language is bad, but understandable. She made her living for decades in amoral conduct on the big screen. The hundreds of thousands who cheered her profanity while our daughters watched appear to be misguided.

Are these the same people who asked, "What should we tell our daughters?" I am not sure what to think. Incongruity and hypocrisy at the core?

Chapter 19

A Life Paradigm Shift

**A series of opinion pieces I wrote after
I decided to stop supporting the NFL.**

M Y LIFE CAN BE segmented by several phases: Single, Married,
No Children, Two Children, Working, Retired – to name a
few. On September 24, 2017, a significant change occurred
in my life. That was the day when the Pittsburgh Steelers elected to
disgrace themselves and disrespect our great country by remaining
in the locker room during the national anthem at Soldier Field in
Chicago.

The players turned their backs on the men and women who put
their lives on the line; people whose sacrifices enable them to earn tens
of millions of dollars playing a game. Their cowardice disgusted me.
To make matters worse, the one extremely brave Steeler, Alejandro
Villanueva, made the courageous decision to break from the weaselly
pronouncement and take the field to honor his country – only to be
ridiculed by the team and its management.

That day was a secular epiphany for me. After 40-plus years of
passion, tens of thousands of dollars, countless late-night drives

home from games, and attendance at 10 Super Bowls, it was over. I had watched my last Steeler game.

Looking back on that decision, it was likely one of the best I have ever made in my life. Football had become almost an addiction. A win brought euphoria, and a loss brought despair. I planned my weeks around when Steeler games were being played. I even changed travel schedules to watch games. Every trip's planning started with where I would watch the game.

My Sundays are quieter now, but I am far more content. As I have watched the league spiral into disgusting displays, I am ever heartened that I made the correct decision. The 2020 season opened with the names of rapists and murderers written on the helmets of the players, and with the league apparently adopting an extraordinarily divisive practice of playing two national anthems before the games.

"A House Divided Cannot Stand," appropriately stated by Abraham Lincoln. It is my sincere hope that a mere game played mostly in controlled environments will not seed a division in this country and lead to its demise.

What follows are a series of messages I penned during that time.

Part I

I stand for the national anthem, and provided God gives me the strength to do so, I will until the day God takes me home. The national debate is so disgusting that I am sickened. Never in my wildest imagination did I ever expect that this would be a conversation.

Folks, every once in a while one has to forget what they have the "right" to do and stand up and do what is right. Politicizing this issue is an outrage. This is not politics. It is patriotism. It is about respect for the men and women of all creeds and colors who have signed up to defend this country. It is about those who paid the ultimate sacrifice; despite their gender, race, or creed, all came home in red, white, and blue. We can disagree on politics, but in my view, billionaire owners enabling millionaire players to disrespect the men and women who have defended this great country is unacceptable under any circumstance. No excuses ever.

Part II

I have officially ended my affiliation with the NFL and the Pittsburgh Steelers. Steeler Nation has one less member.

I have written to the president this morning, requesting that the flags be lowered to half-staff in honor of our military – past, present, and future. I have also requested that this be combined with a national day of prayer.

As part of that missive, I requested that our military never again participate in any NFL-related activities.

I hope you will join me.

Part III

I am taking a break from Facebook for a while. I am keeping my account so I can connect with old friends. I will have my IM open if anyone wants to connect.

The debate over the blatant disrespect for our flag and thus our military has made me sick. A dark day for America. We should fly the flag at half-staff.

1440 minutes in a day. America standing united for three minutes to honor our military, and putting our differences aside for love of country is too much to ask? Sad times.

Politicizing this issue is a national disgrace. I have had two people cite Rosa Parks in the past hour. She was a civil rights icon; yet to my knowledge, she never knelt during the national anthem on a national stage.

Protesting during such a sacrosanct period is unacceptable.

Chapter 20

Christians Beware

Written on September 20, 2020, after witnessing some of my Christian friends trash each other for their political views.

A S MANY OF YOU know, I have been quite concerned over the growing division in our country. As the rhetoric becomes more poisoned and debilitating, I am further saddened as I see many of my fellow Christian friends being duped into commingling their Christian faith with a certain social agenda. I recognize that there are plenty of notable Christian leaders who appear to feast on these messages. Their motivation is unknown to me, but fostering this kind of thing until it permeates our daily lives feels far away from goodness.

I am no theologian, and I suppose it is fair to say that my life is wrought with shortcomings and vast areas for development. In fact, it is fair to say that I have no business preaching to others, so I will not.

My education on biblical teaching continues and I am not in a position to have all the answers. In fact, I think if we are fair-minded as Christians, we would admit that there continues to be areas for enrichment in all our understandings. However, through my business career I have studied at length the psychological implications of being unproductive, as well as productive interactions between groups of people and individuals.

There are two theorems that appear to me to be irrefutable. The first is simple – when emotion drives our decision-making, there is a great risk for unintended consequences. The prisons are full of good folks who had one bad emotional afternoon.

The second is even more basic, but often much harder to comprehend. There is no way for me to know the motivations of others. Even when they share their motives, there remains the risk that their explanation is wrought with deception or that they have a lack of understanding. To build on that notion, it is impossible for me to completely assess what is in another's heart. My default position is to assume positive intent unless proven otherwise.

At one business I led, our rallying cry was, "Every day you get our best." I always added that "Only you and God know if this is true."

One tool I have employed while working with teams is the Ladder of Inference. In an over-simplified explanation, we climb up the rungs of our emotional ladders until we reach the top, where the most unproductive exchanges are cultivated.

We are divided as a nation, and we start to hear unproductive accusations shouted from the tops of our emotional ladders such as, "You Can Not Be a Christian and _____." (You fill in the blank.) Next, many cherry-pick scriptures to support their assertions, seemingly forgetting that the recipient is likely left deeply offended and probably reeling from the sting of the statement. Of course, many are much more subtle in their criticism of others who cannot see what is obvious to them.

Interestingly, I have seen individuals use the exact same scriptures to support opposing views. In my opinion, this is very dangerous territory and creates an environment for divisiveness that is counter-productive. It appears to me that the Christ I know is reaching out to all of us, and seeks to bring us together rather than tear us apart. Friend against friend, family member against family member does not represent my understanding of God's wishes for us, His children.

I do not presuppose that I know the motivations of those who have chosen to walk this path, but I urge you to consider the possibility that you might be treading on sinking sand and that you risk slipping into a chasm of discontent while fueling the acrimony. Sadly, many have been deceived into believing their position must be right, because it appears so obvious to them. Deception results in havoc, dissension, and long-term chaos.

At times like these, I am reminded of the following scripture, Mark 12:31: "The second is equally important – 'Love your neighbor as yourself.' No other commandment is greater than these." I urge us all to view our positions through that lens prior to casting the net of opinion.

Chapter 21

Leap Year

Written on February 19, 2020 to encourage others.

I N 1999, WHEN I was assigned the role as Y2K czar for Star Kist Foods, I became enthralled with the rules surrounding calendars. I learned that at the end of a century, there is no leap year; however, at the end of a millennium, there is a leap year. I reflected that most people only see one turn of the century in their lifetimes, and those of us fortunate enough to see this one had been bestowed with a bonus day that only occurs once in a thousand years.

Further contemplation had me think about February 29 as a bonus day that we get to enjoy every four years. I commenced a self-disciplined campaign to make February 29 a day of purposeful transformation in my life. In 2012, and again in 2016, I gave speeches on the topic of encouraging attendees to consider contemplating and committing to engaging in meaningful change in their lives on February 29.

Leap year is upon us again in 2020. Considering the divisive environment in our country, I think making February 29 "Act of Random Kindness Day" is worthy of our consideration. How powerful would it be if we could start a movement to promote this notion, and ultimately make it part of our daily routine.

An act of random kindness can be as simple as a warm reassuring smile. Such acts might include buying the coffee for the person behind you in line at your coffee shop. When you clear your mind, the ideas will flow.

Chapter 22

The Tipping Point

**Written on August 5, 2020, when I learned that athletes were
being challenged for standing during our national anthem.**

THERE IS A BOOK by Malcolm Gladwell entitled *The Tipping
Point.* He opines on the concept that timing, place, and people
can align to create a significant change; good or bad. Relevant
in today's environment, the book compares social viruses, as Gladwell
names them, with medical epidemics.

Professional sports are back, and we see an increase of disrespect
for our flag and our country as entire teams kneel during our national
anthem. This is an extraordinarily complex topic, and not as easily
distinguishable or defendable, as many would lead you to believe.

Let us examine the concept of players having the right to kneel
for the national anthem. While that is technically true, it is not quite
so simple. Case in point: most do not realize it, but the NFL has some
of the most draconian rules in professional sports. A player was fined
$75,000 for wearing a pink scarf to recognize his mother's battle with
breast cancer because it was not October, and another was fined for
putting a Bible verse descriptor on his eye glare sticker. There was

zero tolerance. While I was – and remain – very sympathetic with those players, I also understand that rules are created to ensure that behaviors remain within a certain framework.

As most know, at the time that the kneeling commenced, there was a rule in place that required all players to stand for the national anthem. Interestingly, the commissioner decided not to enforce the rule – a rather unprecedented event. He seemingly forgot his vehement defense of the need to enforce all rules as they pertain to other violations. A double standard?

I spent most of my life working in the food industry. We had a rule that everyone would wear a hair covering, and you could not work or enter our factories without one. As individuals, each of these people had the right not to wear a hair covering; but as a work requirement, all were so adorned or they could not work in our facilities. This rule extended to our distribution centers, where all products were packaged. We had multiple employees challenge the rule, including one who shaved his head bald. He too was required to wear a hair covering. Zero tolerance is zero tolerance.

When the kneeling commenced, with it came intense scrutiny and public outcry. In fact, over 70 percent of Americans decried the actions as disgraceful. Many wrongly assumed that since our Constitution gives us the right to engage in such activities, it should be allowed (while distasteful). Unfortunately, the blatant disregard for the rules was generally ignored.

I do not blame the players. Many are in their early 20s, and frankly, they likely have not been educated as to the reasons for showing respect for the country and the society that has afforded them the opportunity to earn great wealth and the admiration of millions.

I blame the commissioner for his cowardice, and the owners for their combined greed and cowardice. It is their league, and it is up to them to make and enforce the rules. Their failure to do so is a portrait in spinelessness. The fear of being tarnished with the moniker "bigot" or "racist" appears to be the motivation. As reasonable-minded folk, we recognize that love of one's country should not come with unrelated "scarlet letters." Conflating the two is a tactic that grips most of us with intense fear.

Fast forward four years – it looks like we have reached a tipping point. The other morning, I listened as an American athlete – who happens to be black – was required to defend his brave decision not to kneel for the national anthem.

If you honestly believe that kneeling is acceptable, I acknowledge and respect your opinion. I would urge you to be reminded of the multitudes who have paid the ultimate price to protect your freedom. They came from all races, creeds, colors, sexual orientations, and genders to protect you and your rights. They all had two things in common: their love of country was great, and their blood all ran red.

If you are like me and find the kneeling reprehensible, you must act. Our country is on the precipice of irreversible decline, as has happened with all the previous great powers in history. We are at our tipping point, and one only needs to understand history to recognize the danger.

Professional sport is fueled by greed, and if you vote by electing to turn off the television and not buying the merchandise, we can and will return to a better place. It takes patriotism, courage, and resiliency to hold the line.

I am not asking that anyone change their view. Rather, I am urging those who feel as I do to understand that their inaction and lust for the sport is tacit approval of the activities you claim to detest.

Childhood heroes like Roberto Clemente, Willie Stargell, Joe Greene, and Jack Lambert inspired and entertained me. I do not recall politics in the sports of my youth, and while I suspect players may well have been politically active, they did so off the field.

Chapter 23

Today in History

**Written on July 20, 2019, on the
anniversary of the moon landing.**

FIFTY-ONE YEARS AGO TODAY, my family and I were nestled along the banks of the Slippery Rock Creek. We huddled around our 19-inch TV as we watched Neil Armstrong emerge from the lunar module Eagle and place the first human foot on the moon. Shortly afterward, Buzz Aldrin joined him. Prior to completing his descent, Armstrong uncovered a plaque to be left behind as part of the landing apparatus. It read:

> *Here men from the planet Earth*
> *first set foot upon the Moon*
> *July 1969, A.D.*
> *We came in peace for all mankind.*

Amongst the duties the two completed was to plant the American flag on the lunar surface. Both saw this task as a singular honor.

Arguably the most famous phone call to ever be transmitted from the White House was President Nixon's to Armstrong and Aldrin.

In part, the president said: "For every American, this has to be the proudest day of our lives." And so it was for most Americans.

For me, it was one of the most amazing accomplishments I would ever witness. As I recall, the entire country was "space crazy."

This event, like no other, brought together a divided country. The assassinations of Martin Luther King Jr. and Robert F. Kennedy had rocked the country and those two outrages, along with the war, created an extremely volatile environment for the public. Admittedly, it is hard for me to compare and contrast that day with today, as I was too young to fully grasp the dissent and its scope.

Today's discord seems far more divisive, abundantly more toxic, and certainly extraordinarily more troublesome.

Chapter 24

The Humble Hero

**Written on August 13, 2020, after
a chance meeting that left me inspired.**

RECENTLY I HAD THE chance meeting to be invited into the home of a person who I did not know; a rather rare experience in the age of COVID. I spied in the corner of the room a crisply folded American flag and it was surrounded by over 20 medals, ribbons, and other notable items earned from a lifetime defending our country.

I immediately requested the opportunity to take a closer look, and was absolutely overwhelmed with emotion as I perused the display. I queried the individual regarding the story behind the soldier. She was quick to regale me with what she knew about the service of this man, her father.

My opportunity for questions was limited, but I learned he had been a mechanic on bombers, including the B-52. His career spanned 35 years and he participated in three armed conflicts. "What can you tell me about the Bronze Star?" I asked.

Her answer shook me to the core. "I really do not know much about my father's service, as he rarely spoke of it. In fact, I had no idea that he had earned any of these medals until after he died," she said. She added that she was cleaning out his house and discovered the medals and ribbons in a box.

Since she discovered the awards, she has inquired of the U.S. Air Force a bit more about her father's service. In addition to verifying that each was earned by him during many acts of valor, she learned that her father had chosen to keep his combat-damaged BUFF (the nickname of the B-52) in the air after others on the crew had determined that the group should eject. The air crew skillfully guided the plane to a safe landing. His courage, skill, and confidence was worthy of the Bronze Star.

I suspect that there are a significant number of these stories left untold – stories of men and women who have dedicated their lives in defense of this great land. They sought no glory, they sought no fame, they only sought to defend the greatest land the world's ever known.

When I am asked why respecting our flag is so vitally important to me, stories like this fuel my passion. Patriotism is not racism. Conflating the two is a vile tactic employed by individuals who are either too self-absorbed or too uneducated to understand why we stand for our flag and for our anthem. Men like this hero dedicated their life to freedom so that protesters can have their voices heard and suffer no consequences of their actions.

We can erase and besmirch our history and our heroes, but without both we devolve into just another country – a 244-year experiment that may fade into antiquity.

Chapter 25

Rights vs. Doing Right

**Written on July 31, 2020, after months
of rioting had been justified by the media.**

T HE NEWS IS FULL of talk regarding rights. "I have the RIGHT
to ___" is a common refrain echoing throughout the land. As the
dissent creates a massive chasm dividing the country and threatening to cause irreparable damage, I find myself wondering if anyone
has considered the vast difference between **rights** and **doing right.**

In my life, I have always tried to do right, versus worrying too
much about my rights. In business and in life, I had the right to
several remedies that I opted out of, as I felt it was not right to
exercise them. For example, in business one of my skills was to
execute contracts that were very favorable to me. In all cases the
other party executed the contract of their own free will. On many
occasions, and despite their best efforts, those parties failed to
meet their obligations. I almost never held those parties to account
because doing so felt away from goodness. In almost all cases, my
decision not to demand restitution led to a stronger and more
productive relationship. However, if the other party had chosen not
to be cooperative, I had the law on my side.

I deeply support the rights that are bestowed upon us as part of the blessing of being a citizen of this great land. Case in point: the protests that are ongoing across our country are certainly within the rights of the participants. Frankly, they should be championed for their passion and willingness to express their views. When these protests get hijacked by anarchists and property is destroyed, and people are injured and even killed, then it becomes illegal activity and should be disavowed by all decent people.

As I struggle to reconcile the disparity between productive activity and illegality, I see a very clear choice. If I am compelled to have my voice heard and I am truly interested in making things more equitable, but know that in doing so, I will enable evildoers to inject their poison into our society, I must travel a different path. When I realize that the tactics I am employing come with unacceptable consequences, I must stop. Simply stated, it is not doing right.

I see it as akin to the generation of energy in the 1960s and 1970s. The energy was productive and essential, but the emissions that were a byproduct of the generation threatened our environment. Acid rain plagued our forests, and many of our streams were literally killed by acid mine waste. I grew up on the banks of the Slippery Rock Creek, and massive fish kills were not uncommon after a torrent of rain flooded the mines and the polluted water made its way into the ecosystem. We found a better way, and our air and water is much cleaner today than it was 40 years ago.

I implore all who seek a more perfect Union to stand up and be heard. It does not make you either a bigot or a racist to want to see this violence end. Let us all take a time out, and reflect on **doing right** versus worrying about **our rights**. It is not too late, but I see us on a very dangerous pathway.

Chapter 26

The Fourth of July, 2020

Written on this day in an attempt to remind others of our history.

THIS MORNING I POST with a rather heavy heart. On the 244th anniversary of the signing of one of the most historic documents that the world has ever known, the reputation of many signatories are being blemished. They lived in an era when participating in certain activities, now known to be unacceptable, were commonplace and generally considered acceptable. Over 25,000 died to create this great nation and another 20,000 died in the War of 1812.

My thoughts turned to the great Civil War where another nearly 400,000 died in the war generally viewed as the conflict to end slavery. Certainly, historians know that slavery was one of the major factors that precipitated the bloodiest confrontation in our history, but states' rights in general would be an overarching factor.

Today our cities are burning, and my thoughts turned to Abraham Lincoln and his amazing Gettysburg Address. Reflecting upon him and his legacy, I learn that his statues are being removed from the

public square. What follows is an edited Gettysburg Address. I have
changed three words to reflect my feelings this morning.

*Twelve score and four years ago our fathers brought forth on
this continent, a new nation, conceived in Liberty, and dedicated to the proposition that all men are created equal.*

*Now we are engaged in a great social war, testing whether
that nation, or any nation so conceived and so dedicated, can
long endure.*

*We are met on a great battlefield of that war. We have come
to dedicate a portion of that field, as a final resting place for
those who here gave their lives that that nation might live. It
is altogether fitting and proper that we should do this.*

*But, in a larger sense, we can not dedicate – we can not
consecrate – we can not hallow – this ground. The brave men,
living and dead, who struggled here, have consecrated it, far
above our poor power to add or detract. The world will little
note, nor long remember what we say here, but it can never
forget what they did here. It is for us the living, rather, to be
dedicated here to the unfinished work which they who fought
here have thus far so nobly advanced. It is rather for us to be
here dedicated to the great task remaining before us – that
from these honored dead we take increased devotion to that
cause for which they gave the last full measure of devotion
– that we here highly resolve that these dead shall not have
died in vain – that this nation, under God, shall have a new
birth of freedom – and that government of the people, by the
people, for the people, shall not perish from the earth.*

My fellow Americans, the ball is in our court. How will future generations judge us? To be sure, as social mores evolve, many of us might be vilified for participating in certain activities that become known to be unacceptable, but which are commonplace and generally considered acceptable today.

History is a cruel arbiter, and it is true that it is written by the victors. However, we cannot allow it to be rewritten by evildoers of future generations who are led to despise this nation and our citizenry. I turn to God – and in times like these, many ask, where is he? He is here, but sadly we kicked him out of the public square decades ago.

Chapter 27

How Many More of Our Children Need to Die?

Written on February 18, 2018, after the senseless shooting at the Marjory Stoneman Douglas High School.

O NCE AGAIN WE EXPERIENCE – amid political division that is tearing our country's very fabric apart – another mass shooting at a high school. This tragedy, like most, was completely avoidable.

In this case, the egregious nature of the neglect is so outrageous that it is mind numbing. The FBI received a tip six weeks prior that named the monster who would make the top news by executing 17 innocent souls on Valentine's Day. The informant described the perpetrator's behavior and even alerted the FBI that he was planning a shooting at the school. Nothing was done.

Was the leadership at the FBI too distracted with sexting each other? Were they too distracted with chasing Russian internet trolls?

Were they too distracted by trying to bring down a presidency? Who knows?

What we do know is that we have 17 dead Americans. We also know that the Broward County Sheriff's Office responded to thirty-eight 911 calls on the perpetrator. How does this fall through the cracks? Is it political correctness run amok? Is there a fear of addressing mental illness?

Now we face a dishonest media, who irresponsibly looks to color the matter and manufacture facts to move an agenda. They report that 18 shootings in schools have occurred just in 2018. This is inherently dishonest, as well over half of the cited shootings were fabricated. The most outrageous mention is a case involving a 31-year-old man who committed suicide in a parking lot of a school that had been shut down for seven months. Frankly, one shooting is one too many.

Your media lies to you, folks. Plain and simple. They lie about shootings. They lie about the president. They lie about just about everything. Research for yourselves.

So now, the debate rages over which gun laws could have prevented the tragedy. The answer is simple: This matter has nothing to do with guns, and everything to do with a divided and distracted country.

The real implication of the Russian meddling is that we have wasted millions of dollars on a wild goose chase. Our country is divided like I have never experienced. We are so intent on fighting each other that we forget who the enemy is. Meanwhile, they are raising iced vodkas in the Kremlin.

When a man becomes intoxicated and gets in a car and kills some innocent children, we blame the man. He broke the law. When a man somehow walks into a school with a gun and kills some innocent children, we blame the gun. The gun did not break the law – the man did. In this case, so many things went wrong: everyone in the country should be outraged.

In closing, I find it tragic and ironic that the first thing we do after one of these tragedies is that we invite God into the school to help. Maybe, just maybe, we never should have thrown him out. Maybe we need much more God and much less hatred.

Chapter 28

Checkers or Chess

Written on June 3, 2020, after learning of the death of David Dorn.

THE WORLD IS ON fire, and many of my friends and family have seemingly gone mad. It appears like there is unbridled anger everywhere. Over the past 36 hours, that anger has manifested itself into the most outrageous statements by many of my friends and family members.

The four most outrageous are as follows and in no order:

1. Trump is directing the military to shoot citizens in the streets.
2. Pelosi is intentionally funding and directing the actions that are resulting in the burning of our cities.
3. At least 20 percent of the people who join the police force do so because they want to be able to shoot people legally.
4. Looting is completely justifiable, because peaceful protests just do not work.

These comments are not attributed to crazed ideologues. These were either stated or written by people who I know and love. Since I know these people so well, I believe that their rage has completely sullied their objectivity. Most are engaging in a very dangerous game of checkers, but the contest is chess, and our enemy is a master.

I think everyone needs to take a time out and do a bit of reflection, followed by an education on the topics at issue. Throwing literary or verbal firebombs is almost as dangerous as throwing the actual ones. Please be reminded that when we make statements, even in the face of intense anger, they cannot be unspoken. The same is true for writings and actions. My brother-in-law, a retired corrections superintendent, regularly states that the prisons house many inmates who are great people, yet they had "one bad afternoon." Crimes of passion are more regular than one might believe.

We must ask ourselves: What do we want from our actions, our speech, and our writings? Frankly, in a quixotical sense, it comes down to the notion that the end justifies the means. When the ends justify the means, we enable despots akin to Hitler, Stalin, and Osama bin Laden. For those who know me well, I absolutely despise it when people invoke Hitler in the conversation – but in this case, I see distinct parallels. Simply stated, when the ends justify the means, we can rationalize the most abhorrent behavior.

Let us examine two of the statements that were the impetus for this missive through a factual and objective lens. There are 668,000 police officers in the United States. Twenty percent of the police force would be almost 140,000 people. If one's primary motivation is to be able to kill legally, one could reasonably expect that each of these officers might kill at least one person per year. The concept of this is as ridiculous as it is outrageous. A quick check of the facts reveals that annually, less than 1,000 people are killed by officers in the line of duty. All incidents are thoroughly investigated and the vast major-ity are without dispute. This noted, certainly there are bad cops; and it is very evident that evil appears to be at the root of this current tragedy.

If one can stomach the notion that looting and the burning of buildings is somehow justifiable, how does that individual then defend the unintended consequences of those actions? Many of the businesses looted and burned have residences above and behind them. In those residences live people. They are someone's aunt, father, daughter, grandson. What do we say to the single mother who is afraid for her 5-year-old's safety as the flames drive them from their home?

Do we really believe that the husband and wife who were nearly beaten to death by looters will be more sympathetic to the cause for having been battered? Will the cause be advanced? Certainly not.

The sad truth is that in most cases, the looters and rioters are not there for the protest. They are using the protests as a cudgel to inject chaos and move forward their agenda to reshape our country. These activities are right out of Alinsky's playbook. I believe that the vast majority of police officers are good and decent people. I also believe the same about the vast majority of the protesters.

Frankly, I have never been a fan of protests. Even when I believe in the cause, I see protests as extraordinarily risky and fraught with unintended consequences. This noted, I accept that people have a right to protest. Each and every legitimate protester should be outraged when forces, intent on evil, hijack their protest to advance their agenda. It is quite evident that this is being played out on our city streets each night. Simply stated: It is not okay.

I would like to introduce you to David Dorn. Possibly you have not heard his name. He was the 77-year-old retired police captain who was murdered by rioters and looters yesterday. He was executed for the crime of trying to protect a friend's store. In an equally heinous action, the perpetrators posted the slaying on Facebook live. Mr. Dorn was described as a good man, just as many have described George Floyd. Mr. Dorn happened to be a person of color, just like Mr. Floyd. In my view, the two have one more important thing in common – they both should be alive tonight. They are not; they were both murdered, and I see this as a tragedy of epic proportions.

We are now fighting two wars with multiple fronts in the same theater. This new battle, the conflict for anarchy, is a generational one. Make no mistake, the burning of our cities has little to do with the killing of George Floyd. Puppet masters are exploiting the understandable fear and anger over Mr. Floyd's tragic murder to advance their chaos.

I recommend that you read Saul Alinsky's Rules for Radicals. You will become educated into the mindset intent on destroying America. The contradiction for me is that I know not where the royalties go if you decide to purchase the book. I fear that in buying it, we might unwittingly fund the anarchist agenda.

We should all notch down the rhetoric a bit, educate ourselves on the issues from an unbiased source (no easy task), think critically about the America that we want to leave for our grandchildren, and cast informed votes in all our elections. As it stands today, we are tearing our country apart both literally and figuratively. We are causing much more damage than any foreign terrorist or government ever imagined. Our enemies are on the verge of declaring checkmate. We can, and must, muster the courage and discipline to move beyond our current discourse. This is worthy of your strong consideration.

Since the pandemic began, my wife and I have been engaging in nightly prayer at 9 p.m. This evening felt a bit more desperate.

Chapter 29

'Beam Me Up, Scotty'

Written August 30, 2020, after the
Abbie Johnson speech at the RNC.

L IKE NO WORDS EVER uttered previously in my life, I have been haunted by the title's four words for the past 72 hours. On Tuesday evening, Abbie Johnson delivered an impassioned plea for the most vulnerable of us all, the unborn. I am a bit unclear as to why these words have so severely triggered my emotions.

I recognize that this is a hotly-debated topic, and it is one that I try to avoid. It is too raw and way too emotional for most to address rationally. In my own poorly-scripted words, I am going to try to address the topic without emotion – although I am cognizant that it will be a struggle.

To my friends who are pro-life, calling abortion "murder" is not helpful – and it is technically not accurate. Since the federal laws allow abortions to be performed, they cannot fit into the definition of murder. The more appropriate words should be "termination of life," or more aptly, "execution." I see it much like capital punishment – a legal ending of life.

To my friends who are pro-choice, celebrating the termination of a human life in the womb feels far away from goodness. If you can stomach the action, it should be a somber and sober event.

We hear many of our leaders who support abortions rave about following the science in unrelated subjects, such as the current plague debilitating our world and the climate change debate. Of course, one of the issues is that scientists do not always agree. Scientists come from many genres, and examine complex subjects through multiple lenses. This seems rather appropriate. These are not easily-solved issues.

Interestingly, we do not hear a peep about following the science when we discuss abortion. I think all fair-minded people can agree that the science would clearly state that abortion is the termination of viability of a being – also known as death.

I suspect that if you are not a person of faith, we can argue about the viability of life and when it commences. This noted, when a viable heartbeat exists, by definition, it connotes life; and when that heartbeat is unnaturally ended by humankind, death ensues. Therefore, the use of the descriptors "termination" or "execution" appears most appropriate.

Addressing the laws currently in the books, I think we can agree to disagree as to the appropriateness of them. I would remind many that in our country's history, there have been numerous unjust laws in place from time to time. Slavery, segregation, and the prohibition on a woman's right to vote, are three that – examined through a 21st-century lens – are universally considered reprehensible.

I ask myself regularly what current laws in place today will become known as reprehensible to future generations. Will legalized abortion become one of these?

Over the past few years there has been a movement to adopt laws legalizing third-term abortion. In my view, late-term abortions are among the most heinous acts that one person can inflict upon another being. The thought of it sickens me.

Have we as a people become so callous that we put so little value on life? According to Ms. Johnson, she was present while an unborn baby was fighting for its life. A doctor simply sucked it out of the womb while stating the four words I have now come to despise.

It is true that I was not present, and Ms. Johnson may well have sensationalized the phrasing, but I believe there is enough empirical evidence that it is indeed plausible and probable. I have spent enough time around medical professionals to know that many tend to joke about patients when they are under anesthesia.

I am in no way indicting medical professionals, but I find it repellant that anyone would make light of such a somber and sober procedure as the execution of a baby.

It is also true that I am a joke teller, and I am certainly guilty of telling jokes that might well be considered in poor form. In my view, joking about an idea is far different than creating a jocular mockery of an actual life-altering circumstance when it is being conducted.

I urge you all to spend a bit of time reflecting on the sanctity of the life of the unborn. It is far too easy to ignore the realities of the revolting nature of abortion procedures. More incredible, the very people who support the execution of innocent babies are the very souls who will rant from the rafters over the state-sponsored execution of a murderer. That is a thought process that is rendered incomprehensible when viewed through even the most lenient lens of objectivity.

Chapter 30

The Cruel Arbiter

Written April 29, 2020, after watching history being rewritten.

M ANY HAVE HEARD THE mantra that "history is a cruel arbiter," or have heard people ask how history will judge an event or a person. I think it is more apt to say, "The future is a cruel arbiter."

As society evolves, two salient realities come to the forefront. First, history is written by the victors. I would add, at least for the near future. Case in point: Curtis LeMay, who led Operation Meetinghouse – also known as the firebombing of Tokyo – most assuredly would have been executed if Japan had been victorious in World War II. LeMay was dubbed a hero at the time in America and even was a candidate for vice president in 1968.

Fast forward 75 years – the besmirching of LeMay has already begun. My point is not to presuppose the legitimacy of LeMay's legacy. FDR gave the go-ahead for the operation, so it is not a stretch to imagine that Roosevelt's legacy will be the next to be tarnished, not unlike the aging dime I found on the street the other day.

The other reality is linked, and would affirm that as social mores evolve, what was once considered altruistic, admirable, or at least acceptable can be later considered evil and even vicious. Case in point: the history of mental health treatment.

The starkest example from my life experience was a trip to Prague Castle. It has been 10 years since I visited, and I am still haunted by the torture chamber. The implements employed to punish dissidents are unimaginable. This tabernacle of horrors resided within the very house of the seat of the Holy Roman Empire and the Kingdom of Bohemia. In my view, learning about it or reading around its use does not compare to seeing the implements of torture and envisioning how any right-minded human could have inflicted such harsh treatment onto another. It was done under the guise of the social justice of the day.

Turning to more recent history, we see atrocities like slavery, inequality of women, compulsory sterilization, and segregation all deemed perfectly acceptable by most of their era. In fact, there are many countries today where such activities remain in place. Most folks prefer not to discuss them, as they are uncomfortable topics. It is far easier to go to our cocktail parties and see our wallets fattened from investments that we have in countries that employ some of the most horrendous human rights abuses.

In my view, two significant sets of questions percolate out of the evolving discourse. The first is: Is it fair to judge people through a lens that has had the benefit of hundreds of years of refining and refocusing? Or is it more appropriate to allow them to stand on the merits of their day? If a person was born, lived, and died during a time period where a practice – now deemed barbaric – was viewed as completely acceptable, should they now be vilified? If they conducted themselves at the pinnacle of altruism in all their dealings, but fell victim to the social norms of their era, is it acceptable now to sully their memory?

An equal and even more important question is: How will the future evolution of societal acceptability judge our generation? What is our slavery?

Recently, I was asked to opine on my views on American exceptionalism and Manifest Destiny. Looking through historic events, there is plenty of evidence that Manifest Destiny created an environment of tacit permission that enabled many unjust practices in the 19th century. However, looking through the lens of that time, it all seems more understandable. During that period, imperialism was a very accepted and expected practice.

The phrase "The Sun Never Sets on the British Empire" comes to mind. In fact, there is an 1898 Canadian stamp with the inscription, "We Hold a Vaster Empire Than Has Ever Been."

In many ways, I see American exceptionalism as an evolutionary step that sprang from the activities that came before. It is true that its seeds were sown in our founding documents, which helped enable the phenomenon, but in my view, the most shining examples bloomed in the 20th century. The Marshall Plan seems to be one of its poster children.

After WWII, the Marshall Plan poured billions of dollars in grants and loans into Western Europe. In fact, the plan, along with other programs administered across the globe in the decade after WWII, contributed over $40 billion. That would be equivalent to over $400 billion in today's dollars.

There are plenty of other examples where America led the way. That noted, the most exceptional thing about America is her people. The American experiment has created a base for arguably the most pioneering entity in history. Our innovations in medicine and technology are as vast as they are revolutionary.

Furthermore, Americans are the most generous people in the world. According to Forbes magazine, the United States ranks 12th globally in per capita wealth. Two notable examples of countries who eclipse the US in per capita wealth are Singapore and Norway.

Examining charitable giving as a percentage of the GDP, the United States ranks first, at just under 1.5 percent of the GDP. It is followed distantly by Canada and New Zealand at just under .8 percent. Where do Singapore and Norway rank? Their giving as a percent of GDP stands at .39 and .11 percent, respectively.

Admittedly, American history is fraught with flaws and errors in judgement, but when one examines the full body of work, it shines like no other. It continues today – annually, the United States as a nation gives $50 billion in aid to more than 100 countries. I suppose it may be fair to say, "The Sun Never Sets on American Generosity."

Chapter 31

A Portrait in Courage

**Written on August 11, 2020, after
reflecting on many of my heroes.**

URING THE SUMMER OLYMPICS in 1968, and during a time
of great racial unrest, something amazing happened. With
a backdrop of protest on the medal stand by other athletes
who had won the gold medal, George Foreman raised a small
American flag in the boxing ring and waved it proudly. His opponent,
Ionas Chepuli, 10 years Foreman's senior, was widely considered
unstoppable. The fight was seen by many as "The Cold War Clash."

At 10 years of age, I did not quite grasp the significance of the
gesture, but I recall my father explaining the courage it took for Mr.
Foreman to engage so. My father said, "There is a good boxer and
even a better man. Watch him, son; that man will do great things.
Courage like that is very rare."

During that time I did not understand the implications of the
action, but George Foreman became a hero to me that day, and
remains so today. I recall Howard Cosell's famous call, "Down goes
Frazier, down goes Frazier," as Foreman again stunned the world less
than two minutes into the fight. A round later, he would earn the
heavyweight boxing title.

Foreman went on to be one of the most iconic men of our time. While boxing paved the way, he is more likely known for his famous grills. He is a minister, an entrepreneur, a motivator, a husband, and a father. A man of great wealth, but with even a greater character. I was honored to meet him as he trained for the Michael Moorer fight that earned him the title again at age 45.

Upon his return to Texas in 1968, George indeed faced a significant backlash for his patriotic gesture. Some even questioned his motivation. He has maintained that he simply wanted people to know where he was from. There was no politics and no agenda.

He has been asked many times if he regrets his actions on that day. In 2018 he was again asked what he would do differently. He simply responded, "If I had to do it all over again, I would have had two flags."

Chapter 32

A Tale of Two Cities

**Written on May 12, 2020, after our
annual trek north and witnessing fear run amok.**

*It was the best of times, it was the worst of times, it was the
age of wisdom, it was the age of foolishness, it was the epoch
of belief, it was the epoch of incredulity, it was the season of
light, it was the season of darkness, it was the spring of hope,
it was the winter of despair, we had everything before us, we
had nothing before us, we were all going direct to Heaven, we
were all going direct the other way – in short, the period was
so far like the present period that some of its noisiest authorities insisted on its being received for good, for evil, in the
superlative degree of comparison only.*

– **CHARLES DICKENS**

So goes the first passage of my favorite novel that I read as a teen. I
absolutely love Dickens's writing and how he brings characters to life.

The past week has felt a bit like the sentiment in that tome.
Written nearly nine score years ago, I can feel Charles Darney

reinventing himself and Madame DeFarge knitting furiously in our current environment.

We spent the last week preparing for, and executing, our annual move from Lee County, Florida, to Chautauqua County, New York. It is a trek we have made for a decade now. This year it seems so dissimilar; so conflicted.

I suppose the weather might be contributing to the aura of uneasiness. We left 85 and sunny; this morning, I awoke to 34 and the high is predicted to be 45. Snow is forecasted again today, and it is actually sticking in the flower beds.

In the age of COVID-19, one tends to reflect a bit more than normal, and during our 20-hour journey there was plenty of time for contemplation. Amongst my observations is: while this disease clearly knows no boundary, the artificial boundaries created by our forefathers have resulted in a chasm of disparity in the response to it.

Personally observing the differences between the states – and cities, if you will – breathes a stark breath of life into this apparent reality. Compare a simple trip to Costco. In Florida, many begrudgingly don their masks almost in defiance as they enter, yet most seem to be in rather good spirits, removing them almost immediately as they return to the fresh air and out of range of others. In Pennsylvania, everyone dutifully adorned masks with what felt like Gestapo-like rigor. Not being able to see faces makes it difficult to discern body language, but people's demeanors appeared guarded – almost as one might expect from a prison community. Certainly, it added to my general sense of uneasiness. In fact, as I removed my mask after exiting the store, I felt much like a pariah.

Not more than an hour and a half south of that location in northern West Virginia, my wife and I affixed masks when entering a gas station for a biologically-necessary break. Interestingly, there we were the recipients of crazed looks and jeering from the 15 or so unmasked customers. No social distancing in that establishment. In fact, we were the only masked travelers that we encountered at any of our respites during our migration. In fairness, at one convenience store, an attendant was so adorned.

Questions have been swirling since then. Most perplexing is: why does the incident rate appear to be so inconsistent with the responses? I can find almost no correlation between results and the disparate tactics employed to combat the virus.

Based on what one learns from the news and from discussions with others, opinions run the gamut. It is certainly above my pay grade to know, but I expect the future will be chock-full of so-called experts dissecting the varying responses.

The past week has truly opened my eyes to a concern – many of our leaders are engaging in an odd sort of mind control. In general, I am not a fearful person, but in this prospective reality, I am becoming filled with apprehension.

For me, I am going to become much more concerned with my vote for governor. Before this pandemic, I had no idea the intense power each governor wielded. They have a supremacy that appears to be unchecked, other than by a public who appear terrified – but who each hold that sacred vote. I will avoid sharing my opinion, but I ask each of you to search your hearts for the governance you desire, evaluate the candidates, and cast your votes accordingly.

Is it the best of times, is it the worst of times, is it an age of wisdom, is it an age of foolishness, is it an epoch of belief, is it an epoch of incredulity, is it a season of light, is it a season of darkness, is it a spring of hope, is it a winter of despair? What about the noisiest authorities, and where is Sydney Carton when you need him?

I pray for wisdom, belief, light, and hope. It truly can be the best of times. Will it be so? I will keep us all in my prayers. I ask each of you to do the same, if you are so inclined.

Reader note: During our trip home, on I-75 in Florida, I piloted the car from Estero to Ocala and neither touched the gas or the brakes in the 230 miles. That is a feat that I would have considered impossible in normal times.

Chapter 33

When Enough Is Enough

Written on May 5, 2020, after California released dangerous sexual predators from prison due to COVID -19 concerns.

A S WE HAVE BEEN traversing this pandemic, I have watched intently as our leaders make decisions. I would say it is accurate to suggest that many of the decisions have been gut-wrenching; and, in many cases, not in line with a leader's personal beliefs, but rather as part of a group decision made using the best information available at the time.

The problem is that our leaders are working with less-than-accurate information, and in many cases, using data later learned to be certifiably false. None dare admit that they erred, as a seemingly vindictive media is ready to pounce. I do not see the media's tendency as altruistic as it has been framed in the past; but rather as bombastic, self-absorbed, and intent on being destructive – or, minimally opposed to any form of constructiveness.

I promised myself that I would stay out of politics in my Facebook life this time around, so I am trying not to take any sides. Rather, I want to point out what I see as the obvious facts that are plaguing our ability to align as a people and win this war. Unless and until we can find common ground, the fight feels fruitless.

Fact 1: During this episode, ALL our experts and leaders have been very wrong at some point. Without getting into tiresome details, Trump has been very wrong, Cuomo has been very wrong, Fauci has been very wrong, and the list goes on. Errors know no position or party. At the same time, I believe they have all been doing their best, and I laud their ability to stand in the face of disaster and try to calm fears. I wish they would all be a bit less supercilious and admit that they are making the best decisions possible considering the information available.

In my view, much of the media has conducted itself with unprecedented contempt, and I find it abhorrent and certainly not productive. I suspect that this reality has much to do with the motivations of our leaders to conduct themselves in less than pristine fashion. There will be plenty of time to criticize and second-guess our leaders and scientists after this pandemic has concluded. Now is not that time.

Examine, if you dare, the 1941 attack on Pearl Harbor. It appears evident that while the attack is generally regarded as a surprise, there was plenty of intelligence that suggested something of its ilk was in the offing. One only need to research the political climate of the time, and recognize that the mounting tensions between Japan and the United States created the environment where war was all but unavoidable. Can you imagine how destructive it would have been for a rabid media to have challenged our leaders and to have made them account for every action and decision at that time?

Fact 2: The pandemic has impacted all of us differently. My immediate family has generally weathered this crisis relatively unscathed.

I suppose we are one ill-advised inhale from an impending disaster; but so far, we have been spared. For this, we are quite grateful. Many others have not been so fortunate. Beyond the obvious implication of death and serious illness, the toll on jobs, poverty, and mental health has been severe. It will likely take years – if not decades – for much of the mental illness implications to run their course. For some, their lives will be cut short by consequences from those maladies. Drug addiction, alcoholism, and suicide will most assuredly take many. The implications to the survivors are no less stark.

People are angry and scared. I wish our leaders would act more empathetically, versus engaging in snarky accusations that are both vindictive and sanctimonious. A young man in prison – and one who I have come to respect – once shared this with me: "When you cannot feed your kids, you will do just about anything." It feels like many are at that point of desperation. To me, it seems quite cruel to treat these folks with such contempt.

Fact 3: Fear is a strong motivator, and can easily – if left unchecked – lead to horrendous decisions. In fact, the news item that drove me to draft this missive appears, in my mind, to be one of the most misguided and potentially destructive decisions ever perpetrated. The release of violent sex offenders back into the community was carried out as a panacea for COVID-19 fears in prisons. I suspect that some might debate me, but I cannot see a more vile crime that that of child abuse. Other crimes can certainly be deemed as equally dreadful, but none more vile.

We also know that chronic abusers most likely are themselves suffering from some form of mental illness, and they do not miraculously heal themselves. I think most fair-minded folks will agree that the risk of repeat offense is highly likely; and children, the most vulnerable among us, deserve better.

When is enough, enough? I think we have found the answer. I pray that our leaders can find it within themselves to recognize the peripheral consequences of their decision-making.

Chapter 34

Loaves, Fishes and Heartwarming Blessings

Written May 1, 2020, after working at the food bank at our church and watching people in desperate need demonstrate an outpouring of love.

M OST OF YOU HAVE heard the biblical story of the loaves and fishes. The Old and New Testaments are packed with stories of miracles. Many wrongfully ask questions like: Where are the miracles today?

Miracles abound, but many fail to see them. It is far too easy to try to explain miraculous events away as luck or happenstance.

Rhonda and I have been working at our church's food bank, which was created to help families through the pandemic. Each week, we have seen demand swell, and today we fed over 150 families. The need is great, and growing.

We started with $3,000. After four weeks, we have fed over 500 families, and our coffers stand at around $20,000. This week, we had over 200 whole chickens donated. All have been prepped and frozen for next week. Recently, we learned that 200 pizzas will be donated next week as well. Loaves and fishes? It certainly appears evident.

Then the blessings that fill your heart pour in. Today, a lady who I have come to know as a regular visitor handed me a bag. In it were a half-dozen homemade masks. She did not speak much English, but what I understood was that while she felt she had little, she thought she could make us some masks. How could she have known that masks were the perfect gift?

Shortly afterward, a mom and her daughter arrived with signs that read, "Thank You Lunch Heroes." Has your heart been melted today? Mine has.

If you are looking for a blessing during these difficult times – and like us, have a bit of free time – I urge you to put yourself out there and do some volunteer work. You probably will receive abundant blessings like we have experienced.

Miracles abound. Go find yours.

Chapter 35

Learning from History

Written April 20, 2020, after watching the media defend China's actions with regard to COVID-19.

A COUPLE OF WEEKS AGO, my daughter recommended that I start to write, and I have done so each day since. Yesterday, I felt led to draft this essay – probably not what she had in mind. LOL.

There is an adage that states, "You either learn from history or you are doomed to repeat it." I have been thinking a great deal about what we could have learned from history that could have helped in this crisis. Equally important, what should the key lesson of this current crisis be for future generations?

As many are aware, history is being rewritten, and it is an ongoing metamorphosis. For example, when I was a child, we were taught that Christopher Columbus was an explorer who set out to prove the world was round – and in doing so, discovered America. Today, many scholars claim that is a myth. Frankly, I do not know the truth, as I was not there, but it seems like a bit of an incongruity

that society could have gotten it so wrong for so long. It is one thing
to theorize and have those theories challenged, but historical events
seem a rather odd repository for such strident alteration. (For those
who take great pride in engaging in the art of spin doctoring, please
note that I made no reference to Columbus's landing being a positive
or negative event.)

How will future generations rewrite this history, our history? An
interesting point to ponder, for sure.

Let us review a bit of relevant history occurring in my lifetime.
First, let us examine the Great Leap Forward. It was an economic
and social campaign that was implemented in the PRC – the People's
Republic of China – from 1958 to 1962. I invite you to learn more
about it; the results were a calamity of catastrophic proportion.
Estimates of deaths of up to 45 million people have been referenced.
Much of the death was the result of mass starvation, and the PRC
government blamed the weather.

The crisis also impacted the birth rate by similar metrics. The
Communist Party of China (CPC) laid blame on the weather and
counter-government forces. Neither claim tends to hold much
credence. It appears that the fear of retribution resulted in very poor
decision-making.

The Banqiao Reservoir Dam failure in 1975 is another example of
a significant cover-up. In that case, 11 million people were displaced
and almost 200,000 died. As in previous crises, the CPC cast blame
on external forces or weather phenomena. Sloppy workmanship and
poor maintenance practices appear to be the likely culprits.

One could cite a litany of examples of human rights abuses that
fall squarely on the CPC, including the 1989 Tiananmen Square massacre, known in China as the June 4th Incident. All have been either
shrouded by or completely expunged by the CPC.

In this country, with the exception of the Tiananmen Square massacre, our historians barely even address them in our schools. I suspect it is likely that the massacre will fall into the same abyss as its predecessors.

So now we are in the midst of a worldwide pandemic. Death counts are staggering, and the economic impact and associated health issues emanating from it will be most likely felt for years to come. Purportedly – if you believe much of the media and the CPC – the virus originated from Italians visiting China, or the American military, or a wet market in Wuhan. Take your pick. None of those explanations appear credible

As will likely be further exposed in days to come, it appears that the virus originated in a laboratory when an infected worker shared it with others in Wuhan province. It further appears that sloppy procedures in the lab are the root cause, although many believe intentional skullduggery is afoot.

With the track record of the PRC and the CPC, I think it is fair to propose that we do not take their word at face value. A government that has racked up such an impressive resume of human rights abuses appears to be capable of heinous atrocities that are hard to fathom. When and what is the next Great Leap Forward, Banqiao Reservoir Dam Failure, or Coronavirus?

In my view, one of the most significant errors that many make is applying the assumption that others share our moral compass. History teaches us the harsh reality that all cultures do not apply their values equally. Even within our own orbit, we find regular incidences of moral compass discrepancies.

I am a fervent believer that all people are created equally, and in kind should be treated as such. All governments are not guided by the same compass, and a failure to understand the differences is extraordinarily dangerous. The United States has plenty of flaws; but in my view, it is the least imperfect entity in human history.

We can learn from this disaster, or we can be doomed to repeat it. Much of the answer lies in the courage and resilience of the world's leaders. I am saddened and worried that they will fail us, that identity politics will win the day, and that our grandchildren will suffer the consequences.

Chapter 36

Jesus's Armor

**Written August 18, 2017, after an exchange
with a youngster in a convenience store.**

HAD AN INTERESTING EXCHANGE yesterday afternoon in the Sheetz convenience store in North Warren, Pennsylvania. A little boy behind me in line appeared to be having a great day.

Me: How are you?

Boy: I'm great. Do you believe in Jesus?

Me: As a matter of fact, I do.

Boy: I pray every day that Jesus's armor will protect me.

Me: Keep praying Jesus will protect you forever, and that's
       a long time.

Boy: Yep.

He was 5.

I have been sickened by the division in our country.

We need a lot more Jesus and a whole lot fewer dishonest people fanning the fire of dissent.

A 5-year-old gets it. Made my day.

Chapter 37

The Paris Climate Myth

**Written June 3, 2017, after the US withdrew
from the Paris Climate Agreement.**

SUPPOSE I AM WASTING my time, but I am deeply troubled by the effect that recent events may have on long-term pollution. It is truly tragic, and my biggest concerns are the long-term implications to our children and grandchildren.

This pollution is a true poison and it is poisoning the minds of our youth. I urge all – and particularly our impressionable youth – to become educated.

Please get your education from unbiased sources. They are almost impossible to find. I have spent a lifetime as a champion of the environment, and have learned that the policy of deceitful fear mongering is regularly employed as a tool of ideologues who care more about power and elitism than the environment. It is much more about the ideologue than the idea.

There are dozens of examples. What does the decision to leave the Paris climate deal mean for the environment? Most assuredly, almost nothing. The Paris accord is form-over-substance elitist glad-handing, and candidly, it probably does more to hurt the environment than help.

That noted, CO2 emissions are of concern, but there are plenty of tangible things we can do, and none of them start with or include Paris.

The risks of withdrawal from Paris are mostly geopolitical in nature, and they are real. If you believe in globalism, then the action this week is a step that should be of great concern. I see globalism as inherently risky, so I am happy about the decision.

If you care about the environment and want to make a real impact, there are many things we can do that will make a huge impact. As I see it, one of the easiest is to eliminate our addiction to paper.

The average American uses 700 pounds of paper every year. Most of that is wasted. An average tree produces less than 200 pounds of paper. So, each American on average consumes four trees every year.

An average tree absorbs 50 pounds of CO2 annually. So our paper addiction is 200 pounds of CO2 negative impact, per person, per year. Your lifetime implication of your paper addiction is 8 tons of CO2.

This does not include the CO2 created to produce and transport the paper. Make no mistake, those quantities are significant. Please do not forget the hyper-eutrophication of our waterways, which results from the manufacturing of paper products. Don't care? You should. Trust me, the fish care. On warm summer days, oxygen levels in water are reduced; it becomes toxic and death results. This occurs, and it is not some hypothetical calculation twisted to incite fear.

Our paper addiction rarely gets discussed. Why? It is not cool or hip. It is far more exciting to create a globalist summit.

Care about the environment? Start screaming about paper. Start screaming about serious recycling programs. Start screaming about water conservation. Start screaming about deforestation.

The list is long, and can generate meaningful change. How about smoking? You thought it was just about the health of the smoker, but how about the additional CO_2 created by the burning of a cigarette? In the United States, cigarettes are estimated to emit more CO_2 than diesel cars. To be fair, the CO_2 absorbed by the tobacco plants during their growth is significant, so there is an offset. I am not stating that cigarettes are a major contributor to CO_2, but there is a case to be made for the implications.

Take the energy and airtime that is being expended on whining about a do-nothing globalist scheme and repurpose it toward a campaign of environmental education, and we would be much further ahead.

Let the criticism begin.

Chapter 38

The Long Journey Home

Written May 3, 2020, after realizing that fear was gripping many of my friends and family.

E ACH OF US IS on a journey, and depending on your beliefs, it begins with conception, when you are born, or at some point in between. Each journey ends as we draw our final breath. In a biological sense, it has been referred to as the circle of life.

As we endure the current crisis, there has been much talk about death, and often I wonder if our leaders would have us believe that we can indeed somehow avoid it. "People will die," they scream; and indeed, people do die, and each of us will join those that have gone before us. It might be deemed a bit trite, but the mortality rate of the human race is 100 percent – and absent a desperate act of hopelessness, we have little control over how and when we will draw our last breath. The purpose of this missive is not to speak of morbidity, but rather to issue an invitation for hope.

Since I am a fervent believer in not dwelling on what cannot be controlled, I prefer to focus on how each of us can plan our life journey in order to achieve the fulfillment that is available to all. Fulfillment is extremely subjective; mine will not be yours, and vice versa. In fact, it seems as if fulfillment is as individual as each snowflake that might fall on a winter day.

While most would not leave their home without knowing why they are departing, where they are going, and how they will get there, many traverse their life journey without a compass, a purpose, or a plan. This represents a stark and salient incongruity; but more importantly, a vital and enabling opportunity.

During this crisis, many are looking for purpose, find themselves bored, and might even slip into despondency. Truly the only things that limit us are time and our self-inflicted inability to push ourselves. Consider this a challenge to write your future.

Regardless of your age, your health condition, or your circumstances, if you are reading this, it is an invitation worthy of your strong consideration. As has been stated by someone far wiser than me, "If you ain't dead, you ain't done."

I have been studying fulfillment and life journey planning for over a decade. If you are a person of faith, you will recognize that God has a plan for all of us. He blesses us with talents, and to me, it feels "away from goodness" to allow all our abilities to go unexplored. If we fail to explore our abilities, we fail to enhance the world around us.

So where does the power come from to see the race to the end?
From within. I believe God made me for a purpose, but he
also made me fast, and when I run I feel his pleasure.

– Chariots of Fire

Chapter 39

Please Do Not Fuel the Fire

Written Feb 14, 2017, after watching the dismantling of our unity.

I am saddened by the divisiveness in our country. There is so much grossly misleading reporting coming from both sides that it is mind-numbing.

I suppose it is a result of an unprecedented election cycle, exacerbated by the fact that the losing side is in total shock because they were blindsided. I do not say that to be political, but rather see it as a rather evident reality.

Throughout the tumult filled with lies and unhealthy intentional disruptive activity, you may have missed that there have been trillions of dollars made in the stock market since the election.

Imagine what could be created and accomplished if we all came together. Many of you have been misled that when Wall Street wins, Main Street loses. That is a folly. They are not mutually exclusive. That said, unhealthy greed is a hurdle we need to leap.

Almost anyone who has a 401k has a vested interest in Wall Street. The money earned will get taxed, either now or in the future, and the remainder will either be reinvested or spent. Regardless, a healthy Wall Street is a positive for our economic outlook.

We are experiencing the beginning of what can be achieved when we expand the economy. It is difficult to achieve, and even more difficult to sustain. At the same time, it can come crashing down in a whisper.

This rally is in its infancy and as such is extraordinarily vulnerable. Those who wish us ill will would delight in an economic downturn.

I am asking friends from all sides of the political spectrum to do three things:

- Pray for wisdom and patience for our leaders, our citizenry, and those in our country and across the globe who want to see us advance.

- Stop passing on fake or misleading news. It only furthers the divisiveness. It is your responsibility to vet the story before you share it. I see it as unpatriotic to share such spurious information, regardless of the source or the aspect of the political spectrum that it attacks or supports.

- Start looking for areas where we can come together in alignment. In my lifetime, I have only seen this country truly come together once. That was after 9-11. It is a very sad testimony that it took the worst domestic attack for that to occur.

I can still recall seeing our leaders together on the steps of the Capitol, singing in unison.

I am keeping you all in my prayers and ask that you keep me in yours. I, as much as anyone, can use a good dose of wisdom and patience; maybe not in that order.

Chapter 40

Following the Science

Written on September 15, 2020, after
listening to commentary on COVID-19.

W<small>E REPEATEDLY HEAR THE</small> three-word refrain, "Follow the science," like some sort of cultish chant. As a person who studied science, I believe there is much credence in using scientific methods as we analyze serious issues and explore solutions.

Unfortunately, the phrase has been hijacked by our political elites and the media, rendering the suggestion rather impotent. The typical exchange sounds a bit like a broken record. We never seem to quite learn what the science says; and when we do, it tends to be more subjective and wrought with opinion, forcing a predetermined set of outcomes.

We have seen this kind of talk on display for decades as we have heard about climate change, and more recently as it pertains to the COVID-19 virus. On both topics, it is quite clear that two important realities are omnipresent.

First, scientists are often wrong. The COVID virus is the personification of this reality. "Do not wear masks" becomes "Wear a mask," and morphs into "Wear three." "We need two weeks to slow the spread" becomes an 18-month shutdown. Differing governmental entities adopt starkly divergent approaches, and the net of the results have us wondering if any of the solution sets made the slightest bit of impact. In true red-herring fashion, the root causes and corresponding answers seem not to align.

The second reality is that the scientists do not agree. In fact, the scientific solutions are as varied as the images on a deck of playing cards. Hydroxychloroquine as a treatment for COVID is the poster child for such disagreement, and it became hijacked as a political football.

Next, we transition into what I refer to as "Chicken Little predictions." "If we do not resolve climate change, the earth will be uninhabitable in 10 years," and other such nonsense, become regular talking points. Those statements were quite popular two years ago, so we likely only have eight years remaining. What will these fire bombers of misinformation say when the calendar flips to 2029?

When I was a college student earning my degree in environmental science, we had passionate and bright professors who I admired greatly – and my admiration for them remains through to today. On multiple occasions, at least three of my professors warned that there would be no fossil fuels remaining in 20 years. The statements were not couched with the words "unless" or "until," but rather they were very simple primary sentences, and I believed every word (as I believed they did). Simply stated, they were wrong, and we are 20 years past the mythical cliff that loomed so precipitously at the time.

During that period, the continent was grappling with the sulfur dioxide fallout from burning fossil fuels, and its impact on air and water. Acid rain was a significant issue that was literally killing thousands of acres of foliage and polluting thousands of miles of waterways. During that period, we did not hear a peep about carbon emissions.

When one understands the biological and chemical intricacies of the carbon cycle, we can create sustainable solutions to minimize the impact of the burning of fossil fuels. We can lessen the associated implications in the animal world, along with decay and other carbon-impacting realities.

As we seek meaningful real-world solutions to this important environmental issue, we can continue to explore other energy solutions. There are alternatives that are more environmentally-friendly and more economical than the ones currently on the radar. Tragically, the world leaders tend to opt for esoteric solutions that sound great on paper, but fail the slightest credibility test when we examine their impact.

One of the most tragic limiters to much of our thinking is that we do not tend to put much faith in our ability as humanity to seek solutions to currently unsolvable problems. For example, I have thought for over 40 years that a solution to harnessing hydrogen in a safe and controllable fashion could lead to a truly sustainable answer to the energy crisis. When hydrogen and oxygen combine under the correct conditions, water is created and massive amounts of energy are released. Hydrogen can be made from methane or through the electrolysis of water.

It is well beyond my scope or expertise to weigh in on the commercialization of such a notion, but sound scientific principles would render it worthy of consideration. Alas, it does not serve a political purpose – and as such, gets very little attention.

Further, as it pertains to our purportedly fatal carbon imbalance, I think some stewardship and reasonable conservational approaches would go much further to resolving the crisis than the current elitist-sponsored solution du jour. A three-pronged approach could deliver tangible and lasting results.

Prong one would be to limit the usage of products that consume significant energy in their manufacture. For example, we should be able to truly migrate to a paperless society. The manufacture of paper worldwide consumes massive amounts of trees, and significant carbon is emitted through the manufacturing process. It is a double whammy of epic proportions. Applying this limiting principle to other similarly wasteful product lines would deliver material results.

Prong two mandates a robust and required recycling program. Our landfills are full of paper, food, and other compostable materials. Moving forward, we need to remove all compostable materials from our landfills. Data suggests that this step alone would cut landfill requirements in half. Plastic, glass, and metal recycling programs, if executed properly, would conservatively remove another quarter of the landfill needs – and that is just scratching the surface.

Prong three involves implementation of a stewardship program that would result in millions of trees being planted per year on an ongoing basis. An average tree consumes 48 pounds of carbon dioxide in a year while emitting oxygen in its place. Do the math – it is material.

This relatively simplistic approach likely will not solve the entirety of the crisis. But if it is done properly, it will go a long way to dramatically slowing the evolving issue. It will do so without crushing the economy or providing dramatic advantage to countries who are intent on usurping the United States' leadership in the world – countries that implement draconian and devastating human rights atrocities.

As is the case with most serious matters, the esoteric solutions come with significant and complex unintended consequences. Feel-good solutions do not work, and create a much more dangerous world.

Returning to the global attack on the COVID-19 virus – we are just now learning the devastating implications of the government-mandated shutdowns. The mental health crisis has exploded. In the age group from 13 to 18, in particular, we are seeing an almost doubling of serious mental health issues as a result of the government-enforced isolation.

We will likely see further erosion in mental health statistics across all age groups. It is also likely that we will see that the death count or significant life-altering disabilities within most age groups will be far more severe from the consequences from the shutdowns than from the actual virus.

I believe it is reasonable to believe that our leaders and scientists should have known that these would be likely outcomes, and that the action that they demanded would come with horrific side implications. I see this as borderline criminal behavior.

Concluding this notion of "following the science," we see stark examples of science being ignored by the experts if it is inconvenient and does not support their political agenda. The two most outrageous examples are abortion and transgender sports. Males are biologically equipped to be stronger, faster and more aggressive. Allowing biological males to compete in female athletics is a classic example of not following the science. It is incredulous to believe that any reasonable science-based approach would allow for this type of atrocity to remain unchecked. The purpose of female athletics is to allow biological women to compete on an equal level with others of their gender.

When you hear the phrase "follow the science," prepare yourself for a political hijacking, as it likely has little to do with anything connected to science.

Conclusion

The Journey Continues

WRITING THIS BOOK HAS been mentally exhausting, yet extraordinarily therapeutic. When I imagined the final book, I dreamed of creating a volume that would guide others along their life journey while also reaffirming my love of God, country and family. My intent was to provide a road map on how to live a life of abundance. As the words migrated from my mind to paper, I realized that it would be away from goodness not to address the issues of our day. While I have left many important issues unaddressed, I attempted to cover those that are the most dangerous and destructive to our lives and our great country. To steal a much-overused phrase, "they pose an existential threat" to the future of our way of life.

In my 64th year, I believe I am healthier than I ever thought conceivable – I have a full tank of gas and am ready to roar. I am extraordinarily excited to experience what is next, and to learn what God has in store for me. My wife and I engage in deep discussions, and we are aligned in the desire to bless others as we have been so blessed, in the time we have left. In doing so, we seek to glorify God, reassure others that the United States of America is without question the greatest entity of humans in all of world history, and to celebrate family.

Sadly, destructive and divisive identity politics have transmuted into a scourge that has weakened our land on the world stage. Our political leaders engage in such rhetoric to gain power and advantage, but either fail to realize how they gnaw at the very fabric of our great land or simply do not care. Motivations aside, this behavior is extremely destructive and must end.

Hope Rises Amid The Tumult

There is great evil in the world, and it exists in lands that are led by despots who seek to usurp the leadership of the United States. Please do not be hoodwinked. The standard of living in the United States far exceeds the standard in any of these countries who seek to supplant us, and their unchecked advancement would lead to great hardship for the global community. The true tragedy is that the toxic and dangerous environment in which we are immersed is largely of our own doing.

The great news is that God remains in control, and He has provided this great land and her citizens with everything we need to emerge victorious. We only need to act. My wife and I are eagerly waiting to experience what God will provide, and to find out what role He sees us taking in this vital mission. We intend to invest what is given to us in helping others live lives of abundance, like we have. In doing so, we can strengthen others' resolve to champion our great land. The scale of our effort is indeed in question. Are we called to touch thousands, or only a few? We will answer either call with equal vigor. We will do so with joy in our hearts, and we absolutely intend to relish each step of the journey that lies ahead.

There is a story about a man walking down a beach. Thousands of starfish were dying in the sand. The high tide had deposited them in a vulnerable place, and when it retreated, they were left unprotected. With the sun rising brightly, the incoming tide would be too late to rescue them. The man picked up one starfish and gently placed it in the cool water. A passerby asked him if saving a single starfish would really matter. The man answered, "It matters to that one."

Despite all the tumult, the United States stands as the beacon of light, shining God's love around the globe. She is far from perfect, but she is the best that has ever existed. It is our charge from the Lord to protect her, nourish her, and mold her. In doing so, we answer a vital call and enrich future generations of families throughout the world.

It is a call worthy of all our consideration. We live in disquieting times that require brave souls to rise up and take the mantle of leadership with the courage of our convictions. We can shepherd our countrymen through the fervor and acrimony. With God's armor protecting us, we will be victorious and we will witness the return to that **shining city on a hill** that illuminates the path for all to follow.

Fear appears to be running rampant in our great land, and I ask each of you to consider lifting us – our fellow citizens and our country – up in prayer, for a release from fear and division.

Last year, I discovered a letter that my grandmother wrote to my mother around the time of my father's death. Written almost a half-century ago, its content inspires me – especially this part:

I continually remember you in prayer, but the most important thing of all is for you to ask for yourself. Sometimes, fear prevents us from doing so, for fear can interfere with our communication with God and we have to ask to be delivered from it.

It is my earnest desire that you have found inspiration within the pages of this tome. While each person's life is unique and precious, each life expedition will be fraught with twists and turns, victories and defeats, and placidity and tumult. Missteps will likely occur with regularity. In fact, they may become commonplace; but if you stay true to your moral compass, you will move beyond those elapses and find fulfillment.

Quips for Consideration

I will leave you with a few gentle reminders in the form of quotes that I absolutely love. One is a phrase rather than a quote, and it can be found within the content of this book. "Away from goodness" is a phrase I picked up during my life journey. I have never heard another person use it as part of their lexicon, but it is hard-coded within me. In my view, all of us should strive for goodness in everything we do, and while many activities might not technically be bad or wrong, they may be **away from goodness. Away from goodness** could even include a failure to act, and strong consideration should be given before following a path that leads there.

As for the quotes, I have been repeating them for so long and so fervently that I am unclear on which ones are mine and which ones I borrowed from others. Regardless of their origin, the advice is worth repeating.

Never take yourself too seriously.

God wants you to win. He told me.

Assume positive intent, until proven otherwise.

Winning is important; how you win is vital.

Learn from your losses; they make excellent teachers.

You cannot do anything about what happened in the past, other than learn from it.

Calibrate your moral compass through intense reflection, and once standardized, do not allow yourself to stray from its course.

Life is the most important journey we take; planning it is essential.

Treat all you meet with dignity and respect.

Things are normally neither as good or as bad as we lead ourselves to believe.

A day you do not learn something is a lost day.

Always give your best; only you and God know if you truly did.

Work on you first; only then are you best equipped to help others.

When faced with a challenge, ask yourself: will this matter in 100 years?

Stand up straight; look people in the eye; adopt a warm, yet firm, handshake.

Fear debilitates; with God, fear is eradicated.

Never let the stuff you own, own you.

A smile changes everything.

While many of my idiosyncrasies will fade into obscurity and soon be forgotten, I pray that the future generations of Dinosaurs –

yet to be born – will hold dear the cause of faith, family and freedom, for it is a noble triad.

Be just, fear not, have fun.

My metamorphosis *From Fear to Fulfillment* has not only enabled me to live a life of abundance, but has prepared me for my next chapter. I plod forward unapologetically and without fear. After I have breathed my last breath, I will be excited to learn what God has next for me. For those who are left behind, I hope they will celebrate my passing by knowing that I have lived an incredible life – the one God had planned for me all along. I will not have a tombstone, nor will I have a tomb; but if I did, I would want eight words on it:

He Loved Children
for They Are the Future

Epilogue

Inches and Seconds

I T HAS BEEN 10 months since this book migrated from mind to paper to print. Much of the news of the day has been chronicled within the pages of this text, but a one-week trip to Northern Manitoba in late August 2021 crystallized for me just how fragile the balance is in the world, and in my life. With limited ability to connect with the outside world, seven days proved to be transformative.

Chasing my lifelong passion for fishing, my wife and I found ourselves on the edge of civilization, but enjoying the amenities of a world-class lodge. One morning, we were fishing a remote lake with our guide. It had been a short 10-minute flight on a De Havilland Beaver to our watery oasis. We boarded our 14-foot Alumacraft, equipped with a 15-horsepower motor. In the only boat on that majestic lake, my wife and I, along with our guide, were taking in the beauty. A fire had ravaged the area several years before, but fireweed had filled the hillsides with its alluring pink flowers.

It was an awe-inspiring sight as the blackened, branchless trunks of the once-vibrant conifers appeared like tombstones amid a blanket of pink winsomeness. God's promise of renewal was on full display.

As the morning gave way to the afternoon, the sun pushed its way through a heavy layer of clouds, warming our windburned hands and faces. That morning, we had endured temperatures in the low 30s, with spitting rain and a steady breeze. Now, with the temperature in the mid 50s and a subsiding wind, we were enjoying a respite from the morning's inclement weather.

Having been aboard that same type of boat hundreds of times in my life, I am unsure why I decided to ask the guide, "Has anyone ever fallen out of your boat?"

The guide was a skilled boatsman and had honed his craft for 32 years. His answer: "No."

Within an hour, I slipped off the seat of the boat, causing the small vessel to surge quickly to the right. That resulted in the guide stumbling and careening to the same side of the boat, along with all the tackle and our fuel tank. In an instant, I saw the waters from the lake within an inch of the side of the boat and I was certain we were destined to capsize. Miraculously, my wife leapt to the opposite side of the boat. Her 115-pound frame was just enough to stop the momentum – and almost as quickly as the disturbance had occurred, we were stabilized.

Never before had I ever contemplated capsizing. Never before had I asked a guide if anyone had ever fallen from a boat. The entire episode was surreal. When our pilot returned to transport us to our lodge, I could not contain my mirth.

"You must have had a great day," he mused, hearing my laughter and seeing my broad smile.

"The fishing was good, but the story is better." I answered. "We were one inch from tragedy, but also an inch from yet another great tale."

That night, I awoke at 2 in the morning and reflected on that instant the day before. We were attired in five thick layers, along with heavy insulated boots; the prospect of us surviving a tumble into the cold waters seemed unlikely. Just over 100 pounds of quick human force had offset nearly 700 pounds of flesh, clothing and tackle.

The pilot had returned to three happy souls, but he could have just as easily found three lifeless bodies, bobbing in the water, miles from the pickup site. Without a doubt, inches and seconds had made the difference. A miracle? I saw God at work throughout the entire episode, and I offered a prayer of thanksgiving.

The day we returned to the United States turned out to be one of the darkest in our country's recent history. On that day, 13 of our brave military members would be assassinated by two suicide bombers in Afghanistan. It happened just 16 days short of the 20-year anniversary of the worst attack on American soil in my lifetime.

The war that had commenced as a result of that 2001 attack was ending in defeat. It represented a tragedy of epic proportions. In one second, 13 Blue Star Families had become part of an unenviable club, as their blue stars had been extinguished and replaced by gold ones. Gold stars are a status that all of the families of the men and women who volunteer to serve our country dread.

Twenty years of blood, treasure and intense bravery was wasted on a mission that, in retrospect, was doomed to fail from the onset. Historically, a phrase uttered by many of the despots of the Middle East is, "You have all the watches, but we have all the time." They simply waited us out, and we lost our resolve to win, while allowing the objective of the original mission to be softened and modified to its ultimate conclusion.

In many ways, it feels like a complete collapse of everything we hold dear. Since I began writing this book, deeply-troubling events – both domestic and worldwide – have abounded. We are experiencing a disaster at our now out-of-control southern border, while our northern border remains closed to the citizens of one of our closest allies. It appears we are heading into another wave of draconian and ineffective lockdowns, while crime sprees are raging throughout most of our major cities at an unprecedented rate. We are experiencing a disaster in the Middle East, and we hear nothing about what is happening in North Korea.

It is disquieting at the very least. Simply stated, the world is less safe today than it was a few months ago. Our country's status on the world stage feels less dominant, as our leaders scramble to cast blame and shirk responsibility for their actions.

Our leaders have pitted our citizens against one another. Race, wealth, religion and status have been used as tools of division for decades. Now, the vaccinated are compelled to loathe the unvaccinated. It feels like just another way to slice up the population. Just another division of **the house** that has been so divided.

In spite of these struggles, there remains great news. Could it be that these events can offer an opportunity to strengthen our resolve and further enrich our fulfillment? When I reflect upon the earthly challenges faced by Jesus, I am reminded that it was all part of God's plan, and that the triumph over challenges makes the journey even sweeter. Rising above the challenges facing our great land enriches our faith and can be our reality. God never promised that it would be easy. It was not easy for His early followers, and each generation that has followed has faced their own share of tumult. The question is, **Where do we go from here?**

Despite all the questions, God remains in control, and He loves us. He has us all in the palm of His hand, but we must take action to protect the blessings of faith, family and freedom. God's door is always open; we simply need to step through its threshold.

Inches and seconds, will you take that step?

Acknowledgments

Special thanks to God, the brave men and women who have defended this great country, and my family and friends – aka my Dinosaurs – who have nurtured me. Without you, none of this would be possible. Because of you, my life has been forever enriched.

Gratitude to both my wife and daughter for their tireless efforts to support the creation of this book and the marketing activities for it – past, present and future. Your outpouring of love is humbling and deeply appreciated. My love for you knows no bounds.

Thanks to my son for being so grounded. Your inner goodness is on full display every day. I am proud to be your father.

To my friends, family and colleagues – thank you for being a part of my story. It's been illuminating and entertaining. I cannot imagine my life without you having been part of it. We are indeed better together.

Appreciation also goes out to everyone at O'Leary Publishing. I have learned a great deal through your counsel. This *tome* has not been *besmirched*, and *abundancy* has been my reward.

About the Author

Elliott Haverlack is an ordinary man who follows a higher calling – led by God, he willingly embarks on new journeys. This has led to an extraordinary life. He worked his way from the factory floor to a Fortune 500 company boardroom, then walked away. He led a struggling family-owned business to global recognition, then walked away. His first book, *Unbundle It,* supported the mission of his consulting business dedicated to helping people and companies thrive. A lifelong storyteller, his passion for life is contagious. Elliott knows that the impossible can be your reality. Start on your path to fulfillment today at www.cehaverlack.com.

CPSIA information can be obtained
at www.ICGtesting.com
Printed in the USA
BVHW040852111121
621362BV00015B/546

9 781952 491320